MODERN HERITAGE

REUSE
RENOVATION
RESTORATION

ANA TOSTÕES (ed.)

MODERN HERITAGE

REUSE
RENOVATION
RESTORATION

BIRKHÄUSER | BASEL
DOCOMOMO INTERNATIONAL | LISBON

INTRODUCTION

HOW TO KEEP MODERN HERITAGE ALIVE?

APPROACHES AND STRATEGIES FOR INTERVENTION

Juan O'Gorman, Casa O'Gorman, Mexico City, Mexico, 1929–1930.

WAKE UP, SLEEPING BEAUTY!

INTRODUCTION

Entitled *Modern Heritage. Reuse, Renovation, Restoration*, this book offers a unique and unparalleled view of the different ways that the preservation of Modern Movement architecture is addressed. Its aim is to discuss approaches to intervening in Modern heritage and revealing exemplary processes ranging from restoration and renovation to deeper transformations for reuse. Architects and art historians discuss the challenges faced in preserving Modernist buildings, and 24 examples of best practice are highlighted, illustrating various approaches to rehabilitation. Encompassing an astonishing constellation of buildings, it reveals the amazing global diversity of circumstances, solutions, geographies, and budgets, and the impact made by their reutilization.

Modernism was the defining architectural expression of the 20th century – a movement that transformed built environments around the world in an unprecedented way. Today, the original function of many of these buildings is no longer required, or they are in urgent need of repair. This publication, produced in cooperation with Docomomo, explores strategies of rehabilitating work from this era.

The moment that the first pioneering architects started to explore the symbiosis between a new way of living and new constructive possibilities, they laid a path for the architecture of contemporary man, guided by visionary concepts of form, space, technique, and social responsibility.[1] Modern Movement architecture meant contemporary technology, form, expression, and above all, a belief in the architect's social mission to create a new and better world. Today, more than 100 years have passed since the first built manifestations of the Modern Movement. In the meantime, some values have been reassessed, adapted, or even rejected. Nevertheless, its founding spirit, intrinsically associated with the foundation of contemporary society, continues to be valid today and, one might say, is still in progress. After a period of great unpopularity, the values of the Modern Movement have been rediscovered and put into practice by a new generation of architects who are reexploring the path of a reawakened modern architecture, to learn and create something new from it, in a continuation of the modern tradition evoked by Otavio Paz.[2]

At the end of the 1980s, when Docomomo – a non-profit organization dedicated to the Documentation and Conservation of buildings, sites and neighborhoods of the Modern Movement – was founded,[3] many modern masterpieces had already been demolished or changed beyond recognition. This was mainly because they were not considered built heritage, their original functions had been substantially changed, or they had been unable to weather the unrelenting pressures of technological innovation. The Modern Movement was often "mistakenly related to a style, perceived in a skin-deep point of view and superficially adopted as simple form, as a modern shape."[4] It was thus not seen as an architecture that sought to respond to issues such as economic and energy efficiency, social equality and inclusion through the precise use of materials and forms, stressing the social mission and responsibility of architects toward the future, an intelligent approach to design that saved resources and helped create a better world. The premises of the Bauhaus continue to be relevant today, with "the great issues of sustainability and democracy needing to be addressed through art and technology."[5]

By combining the research of architectural historians with architectural practice, the conservation of modern heritage has revealed its potential and vitality, and

1. Ana Tostões, "Modern and Sustainable," *Docomomo Journal*, No. 44 – "Modern and Sustainable," Lisbon, Docomomo International, 2011, 2–3.

2. Octavio Paz, *El Laberinto de la Soledad*, México, Cuadernos Americanos, 1950; *Los Hijos del Limo*, Barcelona, Seix Barral, 1974. Translated into English as: *Labyrinth of Solitude. Life and Thought in Mexico*, New York, Grove Press, 1961; *Children of the Mire. Modern Poetry from Romanticism to the Avant-Garde*, Cambridge, Mass., Harvard University Press, 1974.

3. Docomomo was founded in 1988 by architects Hubert-Jan Henket and Wessel de Jonge at the School of Architecture at the Technical University in Eindhoven, The Netherlands, compelled by the risk of the imminent demolition of several Modernist buildings. In 2002, its headquarters relocated to Paris, where it was hosted by the Cité de l'Architecture et du Patrimoine in the Palais de Chaillot. Subsequently, in January 2010, after my election as Docomomo International's chair, its secretariat moved first to Barcelona, hosted by the Fundacion Mies van der Rohe, and then to Lisbon, at Instituto Superior Técnico – Lisbon University, and remained here until the end of 2021. From 2022 on, a new team takes over the secretariat and it will move back to The Netherlands, to the Technical University of Delft.

4. Ana Tostões, *op. cit.*, 3.

5. Ana Tostões, "100 years back, 100 years forward," *Docomomo Journal*, No. 61 – "Education and Reuse," Lisbon, Docomomo International, 2019, 2–3.

ANA TOSTÕES

refreshed the way architectural culture is addressed. As Docomomo International's Chair for 12 years (2010–2021), I am proud to have been involved in this continuing effort. During this mandate, not only has Docomomo enlarged its visibility in the debate on the values of the Modern Movement, there has been, collaterally, a growing, and very welcome, awareness by the general public of the importance of its built and ideological legacy.

Having been committed, for over 30 years now, to shed light on and to improve the understanding of the importance and innovative role of the modern project, Docomomo has established itself as a major player not only in the realm of conservation, but also in the broader field of architectural culture. Thus, its pluralist, interdisciplinary nature, due to its ability to bring together historians, architects, town-planners, landscape architects, conservationists, teachers, students, and public officials, has been a strong asset. Breaking the initial Eurocentric and westernized globalization of knowledge, 30 new working parties have been created since 2010, with particular emphasis on Latin American, Asian, and African countries. They now represent more than a third of the 77 actual working parties located all over the five continents, moving beyond Eurocentrism and reaching out to create a more balanced global representation.

Moving from an initial mission focused more on documentation and conservation, it has progressed to pursue a program of expansion of territories, times and points of view, which led to the update of the Eindhoven-Statement (1990) with the Eindhoven-Seoul Statement in 2014, marking a shift in Docomomo's mission, scope, and work, to more fully address the topics of reuse and sustainability.[6] Furthermore, the development of the Docomomo virtual exhibition (MoMoVe), along with the *Docomomo Journal*,[7] the 12 biannual International Docomomo Conferences, the Docomomo workshops, and its participation in research projects worldwide,[8] has broadened Docomomo's role in education and open source knowledge. Thus, we can now state that discussion on the longevity of built heritage, today, far exceeds the scope established at the start of the 20th century. The Modern Movement, and the environments built in its spirit, are now starting to be cherished and recognized by the general public, for the milestones they truly represent in the overall history of mankind.

During this time, Modernity has come to be seen as world heritage, and is now perceived "as a sustainable design tool, a project method, and finally, as being crucial to the future of architectural production and cultural debates."[9] Matters such as the reuse of materials and technology, spatial and functional transformations, as well as updating legislation, are becoming more and more a part of the contemporary agenda. Knowing that many modern architects sought to attain new levels of functionality and changeability, the challenge, nowadays, is how to deal with the heritage in a context that is continuously changing in physical, economic, and functional terms, as well as socio-cultural, political, and scientific. Along with restoration and conservation, renovation and adaptative reuse are starting to "make history," by pursuing the idea that "heritage transforms itself with us."[10]

With this in mind, the Docomomo Rehabilitation Award was created in 2021 precisely to recognize and disseminate the best efforts to preserve modern architecture while adapting it to contemporary standards, to raise awareness of the

6. An important role in the spread of Docomomo's mission is played by its six International Specialist Committees (ISCs): ISC/Registers, ISC/Technology, ISC/Education+Training, ISC/Urbanism+Landscape, ISC/Interior Design, and ISC/Publications.

7. *Docomomo Journal* is Docomomo International's open-access, international, peer-reviewed journal, that, since 1990, has provided a twice-yearly summary of recent and original research on the documentation and conservation of Modern Movement buildings, sites, and neighborhoods. It has affirmed itself, in recent years, as a significantly influential publication in the field of conservation and intervention in Modern Movement architecture, providing a link between theory and practice. Recently, in addition to the printed version, it has been made available as open access at: https://www.docomomo.com/journal

8. Among them is the Reuse of Modernist Buildings (RMB) research project, which aims to initiate an educational framework of common definitions, approaches, and methodologies on a European level, based on existing research, educational practice and reference projects found in the countries associated with the RMB project. It is also intended to lead to the creation of a joint master's program that bridges and enriches the growing field of rehabilitation and reuse.

9. Ana Tostões, "High Density and the Investigations in Collective Form," *Docomomo Journal*, No. 50 – "High Density," Lisbon, Docomomo International, 2014, 2–4.

10. Ana Tostões, "Reuse, Renovation and Restoration (the 3 R's)," *Docomomo Journal*, No. 52 – "Reuse, Renovation and Restoration," Lisbon, Docomomo International, 2015, 2–3.

works' value, to inspire a conscious reflection on Modernity as living heritage, and to appeal for a global approach to modern architecture buildings. For its inaugural 2021 edition, different categories were considered to recognize outstanding projects of adaptive reuse, renovation, restoration, and maintenance involving Modern Movement work anywhere in the World, completed between 1 January 2010 and 30 April 2021. Fortunately, the last 12 years have been fruitful, and produced a number of outstanding interventions on modern architecture.[11] This has given us the opportunity to extend the mandate's motto[12] into the realm of the award's structure. Instead of just recognizing a handful of projects in much the same spirit, we had an unprecedented opportunity to bring to public attention a wide variety of projects from all over the world. Conscious of the Modern Movement's *status quo* as a work still in progress, Docomomo International wished to identify not only interventions that simply reinstated a building's original appearance, but also those that satisfied demanding contemporary technical upgrades, or which successfully responded to profound changes in form and/or use. Furthermore, it was also important to bring to light not just the work of safeguarding the heritage itself, but also the many and varied efforts that lay behind some of these projects, so that they could be used as examples and inspire future projects.

11. Therefore, an initial call for entries was opened to all Docomomo working parties, resulting in a total of 53 submissions. Along with these, the 27 good practice fiches developed by the ISC/Registers were considered, as well as projects included in the 24 *Docomomo Journals* published between 2010 and 2021. This resulted in a total of 84 entries for the award.

12. The mandate's motto was moved by the ideas of "other territories," "other times," and "other viewpoints."

For the accomplishment of such an ambitious goal, Docomomo International is forever indebted to the jury of the Docomomo Rehabilitation Award – Barry Bergdoll (USA), Horacio Torrent (Chile), Scott Robertson (Australia), Uta Pottgiesser (Germany), and Yoshiyuki Yamana (Japan) – that joined me in this difficult but exciting task. Without them, it would not have been possible to arrive at such an outstanding selection of projects, or to establish such an extensive and varied group of categories.

Taking as its premises the importance of considering the extended chronology of the Modern Movement, of pursuing a global vision, not only worldwide, but also from the monumental heritage to the more current architecture, and of reflecting the diverse types of intervention on Modern Movement architecture and their importance – from restoration and preservation, to renovation and reuse – the award is intended to reflect outstanding practices of intervention on Modern Movement heritage to extend its life. Thus, ten categories, nine of them comprising two awarded projects each, and one honoring a person deeply committed to the preservation of Modern heritage, define the first edition of the Docomomo Rehabilitation Award:

- Enhanced Masterpieces: outstanding in-depth interventions in renovating Modern Movement masterpieces, while keeping the principles and character of these jewels.
- Lasting Heritage: practices that consider conservation and maintenance plans as key tools for defying the effects of time.
- Engaged Societies: innovative research applied to current architecture, such as housing complexes, involving institutional and community engagement.
- Metamorphosed Functions: exemplary works that safeguard the distinctive identities of modern buildings, while allowing them to be adapted, in use and form, to contemporary needs.

- Educating Practices: pioneering studies and low-budget interventions that contribute to raising awareness of the importance of preserving the Modernist legacy in adverse locations and conditions.
- Preserved Vanguards: restorations able to bring back the lost innovative features of fragile and experimental vanguard creations, while improving them to resist the wear and tear of time.
- Sustained Uses: renovations that introduce contemporary standards of safety and sustainability, and improved technologies while keeping the buildings' function and identity.
- Conservation through Activism: interventions that result from individual or group action promoting the awareness of modern heritage, while spreading the concept of renovation for the public good.
- Open House: practices in the restoration of remarkable modern houses that are now open to the public.
- Exemplary lifetime achievement for the promotion of the Modern Movement's legacy.

Nevertheless, if this book, based on the Docomomo Rehabilitation Award, was merely a catalog of the winning projects and the person honored, we would have failed in the retrospective and critical role we wish the award to convey. If Docomomo's initials stand for the documentation and conservation of buildings, sites and neighborhoods of the Modern Movement, then we need to go beyond the practical cases of conservation and delve into the documentational and theoretical side of Docomomo. Hence, the present book intends to not only be a description of the awarded interventions and personality, but much more function as a dissemination tool of the best efforts to preserve and extend the lifespan of Modern Movement architecture, undertaken worldwide and based on different pre-conditions. Thus, for a full understanding of the role that these selected interventions play, the detailed descriptions of the awarded projects, as well as some of the most emblematic projects undertaken by the award-winning person are preceded by ten reflective essays that can be, in turn, subdivided in two categories: the first seven, more general, are focused on different approaches to Modern Movement architecture aiming at its preservation and the dissemination of its values; the three latter texts, each focused on a specific case, introduce different modes of activism envisaging the preservation of the modern buildings they relate to.

History and life – two intertwining concepts engrained in our contemporary understanding of modern architecture that, to some extent, are mirrored in the present book. On the one hand, modern architecture has already earned its place in history, but on the other, it is not a frozen relic. It provides the shelter for our daily life and the inspiration for shelters yet to come. The sleeping beauty has awoken, and it is the architecture for the 21st century.

WHY PRESERVING MEMORY MATTERS FOR BUILDING A WONDERFUL WORLD

The intervention in the Glaspaleis (Herleen, The Netherlands) conducted by Wiel Arets (1955–) was the happy end of a beautiful story that began many years earlier when, as a child, the building and the adventurous experience of its space stirred strong emotions within him. Later, as a young architecture student, he rediscovered the building as modern heritage. For Arets, despite its evident decay and obsolescence, the Glaspaleis remained inspiring and exciting. Moved by curiosity and a desire to learn more, he tracked down the family of the architect Frits Peutz (1896–1974) who, in 1935, had designed the Schunck fashion house and department store – the Glaspaleis – one of the first glass-curtain-wall buildings in Europe. Looking through Peutz's archives proved a fascinating experience and allowed Arets to analyze the project's drawings and construction process, while access to Peutz's library provided a compelling contextual framework of influences. Peutz's son was surprised, as no one had particularly valued, or even looked at those drawings before. Therefore, he entrusted Arets with what could be called the Peutz archive. Arets then organized an exhibition on Peutz in 1981, and subsequently wrote a book about the architect and the Glaspaleis: *F.P.J Peutz Architekt 1916–1966*.[1] Later, between 1998 and 2004, now a prestigious and internationally recognized architect himself, Arets personally designed a rehabilitation project for the building, to restore the splendor of its spaces, their transparency, their light, and the optimistic spirit of adventure the building inspired and then embodied, by becoming a unique and precious landmark of the city: "I felt that I had to restore the Glaspaleis, because the building is so important for the city of Herleen."[2] The department store became an office space with added new features, such as a museum, a music school, a library, and a small theater. This all revitalized the cultural life in the city, and more importantly, its citizens considered it "the best thing the city has recently done."[3]

This story of the project reveals the steps taken in a process that began by recognizing the valuable heritage represented by one of the city's most innovative and influential buildings that, at the time, had been abandoned and condemned to disappear. It first recounts the moment when Arets realized that this object in the urban landscape held important memories that needed to be preserved, and he saw the beauty and creative power that this old, abandoned building contained. Then came the survey-based documentation phase, and the essential search to determine the conceptual process, the design decisions, and the history of its construction, using the archive as an invaluable key to understanding the conceptual and constructional aspects of the work. Finally came the phase of disclosing the findings: "Peutz's archives provided the materials to make a major exhibition that traveled to four places. It was also the first time I made an over 300-page book myself."[4] This newfound acknowledgment of the Glaspaleis and Peutz, its architect, is an example of how a local icon[5] can be duly recognized while addressing the design of a building for people's daily life.

One might say that a book can change the world. In this case, it led to the recognition of the need to maintain the building and its legacy. Architectural preservation is a discursive practice that seeks legitimacy, not only by drawing on history, but also, and perhaps more importantly, on (collective) memory.[6] Here, the collective memory and action of the local inhabitants were crucial in keeping this modern heritage alive.

1. Wiel Arets, Wim van den Berg, and William Graatsma, *F.P.J Peutz Architekt 1916–1966*, Eindhoven, F.P.J. Peutz Foundation, 1981.

2. Robert MCarter (ed.), *Wiel Arets, Autobiographical References*, Basel, Birkhäuser, 2012, 29–30.

3. *Idem.*, 29–30.

4. *Ibidem.*, 31.

5. Hubert-Jan Henket, "The Icon and the Ordinary," in Allen Cunningham (ed.), *Modern Movement Heritage*, London, 1998, 13–17.

6. John Lagae, "Ambivalent Positions on Modern Heritage. A Dialogue Between Wessel de Jonge and Réjean Legault," *OASE*, No. 69, 2006, 46.

ANA TOSTÕES

Collective memory has been studied since Maurice Halbwachs (1877–1945),[7] and the crucial importance of spatial and temporal references has long been known. If memory is a reconstruction of the past, then space is considered to be a stable, memory-forming element, and objects within space serve as lasting testimonies of social reality: all we can say is that objects are part of society, and the world is recognizable through them. This does not mean mere harmony and physical congruence between place and person,[8] but that each object appropriately placed within the whole recalls a way of life common to people.

7. Namely Frederic Bartlett, Michel Foucault, or even Pierre Nora, who formulated the concept of "realm of memory" in his *Lieux de mémoire.*

8. Maurice Halbwachs, *La mémoire collective*, Paris, Presses Universitaires de France, 1950.

In recent decades, an active connection between architectural historiography and architectural design practice has led to significant shifts. These new perspectives and methodologies have not merely brought about internal changes, but also called into discussion the boundaries and relationships between the two disciplines, exploring themes such as the everyday, and the role of heritage in the transformation of landscape and visual culture. There is a need to include anthropological and sociological discourses within our understanding of Modernity, so that heritage can encompass new dimensions, deal with the dichotomy between the icon and the ordinary, and consider both spiritual and environmental aspects, as well as more specific and objective questions, the importance of a deeper understanding of the history of construction and domestic architecture in documenting everyday life.

Frits Peutz, Glaspaleis, Heerlen, The Netherlands, 1935; restoration by Wiel Arets Architects and Jo Coenen, 1998–2004. Exterior view.

Oral history has also given innovative clues about the value of Modern Movement architecture. This was evident in the recent *Growing up Modern* investigation. In it, questions such as "What was it like to grow up in a Modernist home?" and "Did these radical environments shape the way that children looked at architecture later in life?" focused on testimonies of how the world was seen by children who had grown up in homes that are now icons of Modernity, featuring, "at the time, these were incredible amenities for what was considered 'cheap lodging for poor people.'"[9] Revealing how these modern environments encouraged the act of play, penetrating and thus fascinating the adventure of the childhood age, from the Villa Tugendhat to the Unité d'Habitation, the Weissenhof Siedlung and the Schminke House, first-person accounts convey the intimate scale of these modern spaces, their transparency, light, indoor-outdoor relationships, and engagement with nature. Their everyday domestic spaces became extraordinary containers of playful potential to explore and made growing up modern "a lot of fun."[10] These childhood recollections highlighted and praised the generous functionality of their architectural design, recalling "we played very intensively there" or "play everywhere."[11]

9. Julia Jamrozik and Coryn Kempster, *Growing up Modern. Childhoods in Iconic Homes*, Basel, Birkhäuser, 2021, 255.

10. *Idem.*, 34.

11. *Ibidem.*, 174

The role that memory plays and the importance of remembering, not just the monuments of modern architecture, but also oral histories of everyday life, the experience of children happily exploring and playing in it, with its promise of adventure and innocence, as it was identified by Ernesto Nathan Rogers (1909–1969) in the moment of the critical Modern Movement architecture shift as *"l'esperienza dell'architettura."*[12] The expansion process of information sources allows, in Juhani Pallasmaa's (1936–) words, to admit that buildings not only provide shelter and sensory pleasure, they "are also mental extensions and projections, they are externalizations of our imagination, memory and conceptual capacities."[13]

Harry F. Mallgrave (1947–) states that, more often than not, we regard buildings as extravagant objects rather than palpable environments into which our neurological systems and bodies are inextricably connected or woven.[14] In contrast, modern dwellings are designed to create environmental comfort for daily life through sustainable design, even within the realm of social housing, aspirations that recall the concerns raised by Friedrich Engels (1820–1895) in *The Housing Question* (1872).

12. See *Docomomo Journal,* No. 65 – "Housing for All," Lisbon, Docomomo International, 2021; and Ernesto Nathan Rogers, *Esperienza dell'architettura,* Milano, Skira, 2002.

13. Juhani Pallasmaa, *The Embodied Image: Imagination and Imagery in Architecture,* New York, Wiley, 2011, 19, cited by Harry F. Mallgrave, *Architecture and Embodiment. The Implications of the New Sciences and Humanities for Design,* London/New York, Routledge, 2013, 87.

14. Harry F. Mallgrave, *op. cit.*, 88.

THE ARCHITECTS' SOCIAL MISSION AND OPTIMISM

The ideals of human freedom and prosperity, which stem from the Age of Enlightenment, have been implicit in the programs of the Modern Movement. Changes in social values have transformed inherited conditions and created new ideals of freedom and material expectation. Architects have striven to transpose the paradigms of freedom and prosperity into architectural and urban forms designed for future generations. The emphasis on universally held ideals has favored internationalized practices although, in most places and countries, Modern Movement architecture has developed its own specific characteristics related to geographical, cultural, and social circumstances.

The Modern Movement is considered to encompass social, aesthetic, and technological innovation, and a search to meet the demands of the new world emerging from the contemporary age of industrial transformations. It represents an innovative approach to community life, public space, and the organization of the built environment. Currently, its most urgent mission is to search for a sustainable future.[15]

Despite the urgent and unprecedented environmental and climate challenges facing mankind, and a global pandemic that has shaken faith in a peaceful future guaranteed by science, architecture remains optimistic about the future and about architects' creative capacities to solve the world's forthcoming demands.[16] As stated by Rem Koolhaas (1944–), "I think of optimism as a fundamental position, in the sense that it is almost an implicit obligation of an architect. I cannot imagine an architect who conceives out of anything but optimism."[17] What the Modern Movement was, what it intended to be, what it gave us, and what we can now do with this living legacy is an unparalleled and exciting theme to explore.

While addressing the concept of reuse as a key factor in the construction of sustainable life, one must recall the Modern Movement's social commitment, which, for the first time, addressed the issue of housing for the greatest number of people, and the concept of an architecture that could provide not only a decent home for all,[18] but also the promise of a healthy life, based on comfort and well-being.[19] In other words, it envisaged architecture as a decisive factor in the search for happiness.[20] Thus, architecture as a key for a new and egalitarian society was one of the Modern Movement's most important themes. In this context, Walter Gropius' (1883–1969) vision of architecture responding to the "chaos of the world," revealed his conviction

15. See Ana Tostões and Zara Ferreira (eds.), *Adaptive Reuse. The Modern Movement Towards the Future, Proceedings of the 14th International Docomomo Conference,* Lisbon, Docomomo International/Casa da Arquitectura, 2016.

16. See *Docomomo Journal,* No. 64 – "Modern Houses," Lisbon, Docomomo International, 2021.

17. Rem Koolhaas, *Conversations with Students,* edited by Sanford Kwinter, Rice University School of Architecture, Houston/Texas/New York, Princeton Architectural Press, 1996, 53.

18. See *Docomomo Journal,* No. 51 – "Modern Housing – Patrimonio Vivo," Lisbon, Docomomo International 2014; *Docomomo Journal,* No. 54 – "Housing Reloaded," Lisbon, Docomomo International 2016; *Docomomo Journal,* No. 65 – "Housing for All," Lisbon, Docomomo International, 2021; Ana Tostões and Zara Ferreira, "Social Endurance at the Barbican Estate (1968–2020)," *The Journal of Architecture,* Vol. 26, No. 7, 2021, 1082–1106.

19. See *Docomomo Journal,* No. 62 – "Cure and Care," Lisbon, Docomomo International, 2020.

20. See *Docomomo Journal,* No. 60 – "Architectures of the Sun," Lisbon, Docomomo International, 2019.

that the architect could transform the world,[21] and he envisioned architecture as an agent of civilization that could help "suppress the chasm between reality and ideology,"[22] rendering hereby the architect, a professional who makes choices and seeks solutions, an instrument for a better society.[23] The architect is not a mere object of progress, but an agent who can influence the collective conscience and, thereby, influence the process of progress. Richard Neutra's (1892–1970) *Survival Through Design* (1954) realized the importance of the intersection of the body and brain, establishing the implications of design as a guarantee for the maintenance of human life. In fact, in the 1920s, several architects and historians published on the topic of achieving a better living environment, condemning the traditional house while espousing the liberated dwelling that was then emerging. Le Corbusier (1887–1965) published *Vers une Architecture* (1923), Bruno Taut (1880–1938) *Ein Wohnhaus* (1927), and Sigfried Giedion (1888–1968) *Befreites Wohnen: licht, luft, öffnung* (1929), all announcing a modern daily life, based on hygiene and satisfaction, consisting of sports, air, sun, terraces – and an insistence on the color white. Today, at the beginning of the 2020s, questions regarding the survival of humanity are once again at the top of the agenda, inevitably headed by climate change and its implications for future design.

21. Giulio Carlo Argan, *Gropius e la Bauhaus*, Torino, Einaudi, 1951.

22. Lionello Venturi, *História de la crítica de arte*, Barcelona, Gustavo Gili, 1980, 321 [Original Italian edition, 1948].

23. Giulio Carlo Argan, *op. cit.*.

Lucio Costa, Superquadra, Brasilia, Brazil, 1957–1960. Exterior view.

João Garizo do Carmo, Palace of Public Offices, Quelimane, Mozambique, 1959–1960. Exterior view.

In fact, Modern Movement architecture has always been a vehicle for social change and for promoting collective aspirations and ambitions. As a vast global process, modern architecture has had to adapt to each specificity, so that the identity of different places and cultures, geographies and people can be seen in their nuanced variety. Nowadays, efforts to preserve this architecture must take into account these differences, and pursue diverse approaches to reuse, based on case-specific social, cultural, climatic, geographic, and financial requirements. Thus, Modern Movement architecture has been rescued in recent decades on a global scale, from Brazil to Singapore, from Portugal to Mozambique or South Africa, and from Australia to Canada, bearing in mind local circumstances and design characteristics.

REUSE WHILE KEEPING THE MEMORY

Combining technology, spatial form, and social commitment, through an optimistic faith in progress, modern architects sought to attain new heights of beauty, functionality, and flexibility of use. The challenge nowadays is how to deal with this modern legacy in relation to a context that is continuously changing over time, in physical, economic, and functional terms, and against an ever-changing backdrop of sociocultural, political, and scientific values.

Preserving the architectural heritage of the 20th century requires considering both the opportunity and the obligation to reuse buildings which have lost their original function, are physically and/or technically obsolete, or are no longer up to today's increasingly demanding standards. Matters, such as the need for physical restoration,

Koji Fuji, Chochikukyo, Kyoto, Japan, 1928. Interior.

for spatial or functional transformation, and meeting contemporary requirements for comfort and safety within the scope of responsible environmental sustainability are all part of the contemporary agenda. This inevitably highlights the question of the value of the existing built fabric, which can be a rich resource, but requires attention in terms of social, economic, and environmental sustainability.[24] Accordingly, intervention strategies are an artistic judgment that requires a detailed knowledge of the history of a building's design, a keen awareness of the materials and techniques used in its construction, and an understanding of its life and uses.[25]

Research into the history of construction and theory of Modern Movement architecture is vital for a more informed and conscious restoration practice. There are three main qualities for which evaluation criteria are fundamental:[26] firstly, innovation, in technical, aesthetic, or social terms; secondly, the status of the building, whether iconic or commonplace in character, including any characteristics that are shared or repeated as part of a series;[27] and lastly, the building's importance as an international, national, or local reference. The conservation strategy should consider a range of options, from a "back to the original" restoration, to a pragmatic rehabilitation that incorporates economic adaptation and reuse. Wessel de Jonge (1957–) acknowledges that Adolf Behne's (1885–1948) critical analysis of the fundamental concepts of Modern Movement,[28] combining transitoriness and transitory construction with permanency, have been instrumental in his approach to restoration practice.[29] Behne distinguished between Functionalist and Rationalist approaches in his contemporary architecture of the early 1920s.[30] Wessel adapted this theory to two major case studies: the Zonnestraal Sanatorium and the Van Nelle Factory.[31] For the former, he deduced from historical research that Johannes Duicker (1890–1935) had opted for a "transitory" architecture, designing the building for its defined function, making it impossible to adapt it to any alternative use after restoration. He justified restoring the building to its original condition, because, having acquired the undeniable status of an international icon in architectural history and a landmark in social history, its "philological" restoration was consensual. In contrast, the intervention strategy for the Van Nelle Factory was one of reuse. Although also iconic, the rational and open character of the Johannes Brinkman (1902–1949) and Leendert van der Vlugt (1894–1936) building, enabled an intervention that involved substantial changes and its conversion into contemporary offices, studios, and production facilities for the creative industry. In this approach, historic meaning was daringly balanced with new functions and sustainable solutions to reduce energy consumption. Maintaining the transparency of the buildings was the guiding principle for keeping the essence of the original project. Along with restoration and renovation, the reuse project has started to "make history," as heritage transforms itself within society. As Hubert-Jan Henket (1940–) remarks, "for those who are dedicated to the ideas of the Modern Movement, this attitude shouldn't come as a surprise. Isn't one of the driving forces of Modernity, ever since the Enlightenment, the dedication to dynamism and the constant new?"[32]

This question hints at the essence of any sensitive modern-heritage reuse project. Any transformation should respect the intentions of the original architect, it should be in balance with the cultural value of these intentions and should add to

24. See *Docomomo Journal*, No. 44 – "Modern and Sustainable," Barcelona, Docomomo International, 2011.
25. John Lagae, *op. cit.*, 46.
26. See Hubert-Jan Henket, *op. cit.*, 13–17.

27. George Kubler, *The Shape of Time. Remarks on the History of Things*, New Haven/London, Yale University Press, 1962.

28. Adolf Behne, *Der moderne Zweckbau*, Munich, Drei Masken Verlag, 1923.

29. Wessel de Jonge, "The Technology of Change: The Van Nelle Factories in Transition," in Hubert-Jan Henket and Hilde Heynen (eds.), *Back from Utopia. The Challenge of the Modern Movement*, Rotterdam, 010 Publishers, 2002, 44–59.
30. "Functional planning departs from the brief and involves the careful design of each individual space for each particular function, with specific dimensions and performance characteristics, organically producing an architect 'tailor made' suit. This approach is ruled by a sense of short-term economy (...) Rational planning, instead, strives for objectivity and *sachlichkeit* involving a neutral multifunctional layout which can be partitioned and adapted according to changing functional requirements." – Wessel de Jonge, in John Lagae, *op. cit.*, 54.
31. Wessel de Jonge, 2002, *op. cit.*, 44–59; Joris Molenaar et al., *Van Nelle: Monument in Progress*, Rotterdam, Uitgeverij De Hef Publishers, 2005; Paul Meurs and Marie-Thérèse van Thoor (eds.), *Sanatorium Zonnestraal. History and Restoration of a Modern Monument*, Rotterdam, NAi Publishers, 2010.

32. Hubert-Jan Henket, "Reuse, Transformation and Restoration," *Docomomo Journal*, No. 52 – "Reuse, Renovation and Restoration," Lisbon, Docomomo International, 2015, 12.

the architectural quality of the new whole. Furthermore, reuse, renovation, and restoration raise not only constructional questions regarding materiality and physical obsolescence, but also conceptual matters that relate to the essence of buildings. According to António Damásio (1944–),[33] joy or sorrow can emerge only after the brain registers physical changes in the body: feelings are what arise as the brain interprets emotions, which are themselves purely physical signals of the body reacting to external stimuli. He argues that our internal, emotional regulatory processes not only preserve our lives but actually shape our greatest cultural accomplishments. The question is how to maintain the intensity and emotion that architecture causes when it is necessary to intervene in its materiality to renew and adapt it to the current situation. Wessel notes here "that our practice is informed by a historical consciousness and sensibility that goes beyond purely formal or technical dimensions."[34] Beyond purely economic arguments, the benefits of the adaptive reuse of modern buildings are starting to be recognized for enhancing vital issues of identity, as well as the sustainable life of buildings. As Pallasmaa stresses "Cultural identity, a sense of rootedness and belonging is an irreplaceable ground of our very humanity."[35] Franz Graf considers that the "safeguarding of architecture is the practice of intervention in the existing which combines, with rigor and competence, technical and cultural knowledge,"[36] and he assumes that architects have always been passionate about it. Thus, as a contemporary and complex type of design, the practice of intervention has become particularly exploratory when applied to modern heritage. In fact, these new shifts in the approach to heritage have emerged as an operative relationship between the practice of preservation, the act of valuing the building's materiality, and deciding on a suitable preservation strategy.

Hence, the decision implies an artistic judgment. Following Cesare Brandi (1906–1988), "restoration is the methodological moment in which the work of art is recognized as a physical object with both aesthetic and historical value with a view to its transmission to the future."[37] When one approaches the built heritage, the limited function of an artwork is enlarged by the social realm of architecture, its purpose and use. Thus, the dichotomy of "art and technique," which embodies reason and sensibility, is enhanced in the discipline of architectural design. If restoring the built heritage implies using appropriate restoration techniques and maintaining

Nuno Teotónio Pereira and Bartolomeu Costa Cabral, Águas Livres Housing Block, Lisbon, Portugal, 1953–1955. Entrance hall.

Álvaro Siza Vieira, Portugal Pavilion, Lisbon, Portugal, 1995–1998. View toward the waterfront.

the artistic value of the work, then reuse suggests bringing the building back to its rational roots while retaining the authenticity of the building fabric.

Modern architecture is now part of the world's memory – authentic, real, and imagined. With its unitary proposal, the only one capable of responding to the challenges of contemporary life and reacting to the aggression of the industrial world, the Modern Movement set out believing in the emergence of a new age, of summoning "a wonderful world"[38] as Louis Armstrong sang so beautifully in 1967, the sentiment invoked here is, in homage to the joy, enthusiasm, and optimism brought by modern architecture.

33. António Damásio, *Looking for Spinoza. Joy, Sorrow and the Feeling Brain*, London, William Heinemann, 2003; Manuel Castells, *Communication Power*, Oxford, Oxford University Press, 2009.

34. Wessel de Jonge, in John Lagae, *op. cit.*, 58.
35. Keynote lecture held at the 12th International Docomomo Conference, Espoo, 2012, cf. Juhani Pallasmaa "Newness, Tradition and Identity – Existential Meaning in Architecture," *Docomomo Journal*, No. 49 – "For an Architect's Training," Barcelona, Docomomo International, 4–9.

36. Franz Graf, *Histoire Matérielle du bâti et projet de sauvegarde*, Lausanne, Presses Polytechniques et Universitaires Romandes, 2014, 401.
37. Cesare Brandi, *Theory of Restoration*, Florence, Ed. Nardini, 2005 [1963].

38. Wiel Arets and Robert McCarter also entitled their joint research "A Wonderful World," in Robert MCarter (ed.), *op. cit.*, 497.

WHAT TO DO WITH MODERN TRADITION?

What we call modern architecture was configured in a short period. It is rooted in the emergence of conceptual, formal, and spatial instruments put into action in an initial set of buildings that gave material form to new programs and demands that Modernity imposed as a necessity. These new instruments of modern architectural thought were displayed in a series of revealing cases that appeared in that short time – "the heroic period" – as Alison (1928–1993) and Peter Smithson (1923–2003) called it, in a sharp and intelligent interpretation.[1]

1. Alison Smithson and Peter Smithson, "The Heroic Period of Modern Architecture," *Architectural Design*, Vol. 35, No. 12, London, The Standard Catalogue Co., Ltd, December 1965, special issue.

CANONICAL INTERPRETATIONS, CANONICAL STRUCTURES

A range of tools for conceiving architecture quickly dominated the scene: abstraction as a source; pure shapes and the idea of volume instead of mass; the openness of the architectural box; freedom in the correlation between the load-bearing structure and the arrangement of the program; the promenade and the physical dimension of time; the interior-exterior relationship; material objectivity and the tectonics of construction, among many others. Some architects designed so superbly that these instruments of architectural thought came to be characteristic of their works. Some even managed to conceive buildings in which these concepts interacted in an exemplary way. Such buildings autonomously represented these concepts, that is, without significant contamination from the social, economic, or political tensions imposed by the moment. Others made advances by confronting these relationships and stood out for the way they did so. Masters and their masterpieces became part of the collection that is now known as modern architecture. They were considered masterpieces for their didactic capacity to demonstrate the conceptual, formal, and spatial instruments of emerging Modernity.

These buildings deftly represented these new ways of thinking about architecture and, thus, acquired incredible notoriety. That was why they attained great prominence in the publishing world, mainly in magazines that achieved such preponderance in the diffusion of knowledge that they supplanted the manuals of architectural theory.[2] The engagement between mass media and modern architecture was vital.[3] All forms of representation contributed to the impact of these works, but photography was the main ally in the rise of the new buildings to their canonical status. The best examples of modern architecture were published extensively and repeated *ad nauseam*, obsessively showing them over and over again, as if the repetition of images would consolidate the "instrumental meaning"[4] they embodied. In terms of the anatomy of the process of interpretation in architecture,[5] these repetitions broke out their initial unseen condition, taking a step forward toward their canonical interpretation.

The architects themselves commented on the novelty of their projects in the *avant-garde* magazines of that time. At the same time, a number of critics established the first pre-canonical interpretations of modern architecture. The essays by Adolf Behne[6] and Walter Curt Behrendt[7] (1884–1945) were perhaps the earliest, with Ludwig Hilberseimer[8] (1885–1967) and Bruno Taut corroborating the international claim very early on.[9] This critical writing started a collective and more systematic reflection on interpreting the city and the possible ways to influence reality through the instruments of the new architecture. By 1928, these ideas were given concrete

2. Hélene Janniere and France Vanlaethem, "Architectural Magazines as Historical Source or Object?," in Alexis Sornin, Helene Janniere, and France Vanlaethem, *Revues d'architecture dans les années 1960 et 1970*, Québec, IRHA – ABC Art Books, 2008, 41–68.
3. Beatriz Colomina, *Privacy and Publicity: Modern Architecture as Mass Media*, Cambridge, Mass./London, The MIT Press, 1996.
4. Expression used in Dalibor Vesely, *Architecture in the Age of Divided Representation. The Question of Creativity in the Shadow of Production*, Cambridge, Mass./London, The MIT Press, 2004.
5. Juan Pablo Bonta, *Architecture and Its Interpretation: A Study of Expressive Systems in Architecture*, New York, Rizzoli, 1979.
6. Adolf Behne, *Der moderne Zweckbau*, Munich, Vienna, and Berlin, Drei Masken, 1926.
7. Walter Curt Behrendt, *Der Sieg des neuen Baustils*, Stuttgart, Akademischer Verlag, 1927.
8. Ludwig Hilberseimer, *Internationale neue Baukunst*, Stuttgart, Julius Hoffmann Verlag, 1927.
9. Bruno Taut, *Die neue Baukunst in Europa und America*, Stuttgart, Julius Hoffmann Verlag, 1929.

HORACIO TORRENT

form through the collective action of the CIAMs.[10] A short time later, the architectural exhibitions received wide diffusion throughout the western world.[11] The dissemination of modern ideas even evoked a comparison with the Vitruvian trilogy to establish the modern experience as a definitive theory of architecture.[12]

10. Sigfried Giedion (ed.), *CIAM. Les Congrès d'Architecture Moderne, A Decade of New Architecture. Dix Ans D'Architecture Contemporaine*, Zurich, Editions Girsberger, 1951.

11. *Modern Architecture: International Exhibition*, New York, Museum of Modern Art, 9 February–23 March 1932.

12. John McAndrew and Elizabeth Mock, *What is Modern Architecture?*, New York, Museum of Modern Art, 1942.

Historians and critics did the rest of the work. By the end of the "heroic period," a catalog of paradigmatic buildings had consolidated the Modern Movement as a historical subject and had begun its definitive canonical interpretation. They bequeathed us a canon and a collection of exemplary cases whose singular dimension could only grow and mystify. Efforts to broaden and integrate the new social concerns of architecture and the tensions of overcoming Rationalism and abstraction rapidly forged another set of instruments for dealing with the changes of the middle of the century. Ideas about the new monumentality, the interaction between art and architecture, a greater emphasis on popular manifestations, nature, and the reconsideration of urban aspects, consolidated what Giedion called "the new tradition."[13] Historiography has reviewed and confirmed this selection and its qualities on countless occasions. The exaltation of its values, or even its shattering critique, has established a concept comparable to the classical tradition: the modern tradition.

13. Sigfried Giedion, *Space, Time and Architecture: The Growth of a New Tradition*, Cambridge, Mass., The Harvard University Press, 1941.

FROM TRADITIONAL RESTORATION TO MODERN ARCHITECTURE

Docomomo has frequently worked within this canon, documenting and preserving it. The actions taken to conserve the canonical cases have also been exemplary, aiming both to maintain these masterpieces and to renew their didactic influence. The preservation actions bring the buildings' values back to the forefront, displaying their authenticity while also showing the paradigmatic conservation procedures.

People at the central square of the Huemul 2 Housing Complex, by Julio Cordero, in Santiago, Chile, 1943.

Modern architecture seemed to be a field in which the orthodox theories of monumental restoration were put in place. However, during the last decades Docomomo has warned about the impossibility of applying the theories and practices of traditional restoration to modern heritage. The characteristics of modern architecture that prevent a treatment in this way are already evident. The experimentation with materials, undertaken at the time of construction, poses technical difficulties today and makes handcrafted restoration impossible. Moreover, certain industrial modes of production can no longer be used because they are completely unavailable. It would be inappropriate to replace the elements produced this way at the time because of their cost, their energy expenditure, or simply because they are reminiscent of the unbridled development caused by non-renewable energies. Today it seems feasible to situate the conservation of modern architecture within the framework of the circular economy as part of a global effort to reduce energy consumption, and to broaden the ways of operating within modern heritage.

During the 20th century, modern architecture took on countless new programs to meet the population's needs. It was disseminated throughout the entire planet, on a par with the aspirations for improvement and the well-being of its inhabitants. Out of necessity and with great creativity, it built a new world. New places, new homes, and new facilities housed many people who, then and now, used and enjoyed this legacy.

Despite modern architecture's proclaimed internationalism, its architects accepted the conditions imposed upon them in each place in different ways, altering the canon, and enhancing their buildings by incorporating the differences imposed by the diversity of climates and local cultures. This was something which the proponents of the canon were unaware of or failed to acknowledge, and they maintained the idea of universality, even though it only represented a partial view of the world. Today, the vastly increased possibilities offered by modern architecture in different areas of the planet should be recognized, and these differences should be celebrated. Furthermore, it hardly needs saying that, because of the diversity of programs encompassed by modern architecture, most buildings have been, and still are in use. Consequently, because of the ever-changing demands of the people who use them, they are subject to frequent interventions.

People at the swimming pool of Centro Urbano Miguel Alemán, by Mario Pani, in México City, Mexico, 1946–1948.

Children playing in front of the Pedregulho Housing Complex, by Affonso Eduardo Reidy, in Rio de Janeiro, Brazil, 1946–1951.

Paradoxically, the mode of production that gave birth and continuity to modern architecture has often led to the deterioration of its qualities. To conserve means to keep alive the main components of modern architecture, not only in its materiality, but also in its sense and meaning. Those of us who are concerned with preserving modern heritage know the restrictions entailed in it. In a short period, we have managed to build up a field of debate on the conservation of modern heritage, and we have accumulated a significant amount of solutions and experiences. Only a few canonical structures can escape the dynamics of time and the daily life they have housed since they were built. Few modern architectural works are suited to conservation by orthodox criteria, and thus are treated on a case-by-case basis. Could it be then, that our work is situated in the restricted field configured by a few exemplary cases?

THE EXPANSION FROM CANONICAL STRUCTURES TO AVERAGE EXAMPLES OF MODERN ARCHITECTURE

The need for a substantive expansion of sustainability and new ethical treatment of societies imposes a somewhat different working perspective. Both make it necessary to review the enormous number of modern heritage buildings scattered over the earth and incorporate the vast diversity of architectures built during the 20th century in so many parts of the world. This means that the basic problem of preservation becomes more complex through the addition of territorial dispersion and cultural differences that need to be addressed. In addition, most of these architectures are in full use as living heritage, and it is impossible to extract them from the dynamics of everyday life. On the contrary, remaining in full use, and continuing to provide a service, is their most outstanding quality. There are buildings that though modern, are not part of the canon. Contrary to Alois Riegl's (1858–1905) interpretation,[14] they do not acquire their value through a current attribution of meaning, but rather their value lies in the ongoing use they allow for, as well as the service they have provided since their construction, as a place of daily life. The size of the challenge is such that the evidence provided by a limited number of paradigmatic restoration cases is not enough and seems far removed from the issues that technicians and architects face with different policies in different places.

14. Alois Riegl, *Der moderne Denkmalkultus, sein Wesen und seine Entstehung*, Vienna and Leipzig, W. Braumüller, 1903.

Children in the public spaces of Unidad Vecinal Portales, by Bresciani, Valdés, and Castillo y Huidobro, in Santiago, Chile, 1958–1968.

We have systematically expanded efforts to document interventions on modern buildings. In many places, conservation practices encounter multiple obstacles, facing localized difficulties, technological and design challenges, as well as management and financing problems. Paying attention to practices, above all, good practices, may constitute that monumental conceptual effort needed to significantly expand our coverage of a greater number of cases and localized responses in dimensions previously unaddressed. Today, it is not a question of ousting or dismissing the buildings that make up the canon, or of replacing it with a new, more inclusive one. They are, and will continue to be, magnificent examples that require an exceptional effort to maintain them as a testimony of the past. Even when ongoing conservation freeze canonical buildings in their original time, they remain evidences of a transformative capacity of thinking, and of architectural instruments that were put into action to change the world. Their greatest achievement nowadays may be that they make us reflect on the limitations of the actions undertaken for their preservation, in order to expand the experience of restoration and make it valid for those buildings that escape the canon. While the paradigmatic cases maintain an incredible demonstrative capacity, the constrained application of restoration techniques to their canonical condition result in the loss of accuracy and didactic sense when applied to more complex cases and buildings that are considered average examples of modern architecture.

It is not possible to comprehensively preserve the countless buildings arising from the experience of Modern Movement architecture with the demands presented by a few of its masterpieces. At Docomomo we need to stimulate the necessary reflection to face the world of living heritage. We cannot make an effort to only preserve buildings but much more tackle the problem of maintaining their use and public appreciation. What we need is to preserve also the social and community life that the experience of modern architecture brought to the world.

The impetus for change today may be at least as great as it was a century ago. The evidence of the preservation of some paradigmatic cases is enough to alert; but not enough to produce a significative transformation. The ability to transform reality was, and remains, one of the striking characteristics of modern architecture. The conservation of an enormous number of modern buildings, still in use today as living heritage, with very different characteristics depending on their place in the world, is still a task largely untackled. It needs that ability to confront problems and propose daring solutions, it needs that imperative solution provided by the transformative impulse that still resides in modern architecture. That is what we can do with the modern tradition.

THE IMPORTANCE OF RESEARCH IN THE RESTORATION OF 20TH CENTURY ARCHITECTURE

FRANZ GRAF

TWO TYPES OF RESEARCH, TWO OBJECTIVES

Restoration and its implementation are nurtured by different ways of researching history. Deliberately stretching the point, to make the issue perfectly clear, we could say that it appeals to two types of history: the historian's history and the architect's history, each with its specific objective.

The former lies in the field of the history of architecture, where the aesthetic, social, and technical aspects of the object of study are explored using critical analysis and the genealogy of the project, combining the use of the building and its reception, with close scrutiny of the construction and techniques that place it within the material culture of its time. This research work establishes rationally – rather than subjectively – the heritage value of a work of architecture, a fundamental phase in its protection, and in defining the intervention strategy to be chosen from among the principal possible approaches (conservation, restoration, renovation, reconstruction, conversion, etc.).

The architect's history, or the material history of the built environment,[1] explores the knowledge accumulated while incorporating the history of the object into the long-term future and determining the working methods to intervene in it. The detailed analysis of the elements and components of the building, and their configuration, ranging from the completed project to its possible future variations, identifies its consolidated parts and its possible future. This closer gaze is not a question of scale, but of the approach to the project. The analysis of its materials and their application and construction systems is extended by that of their biological cycles, their changes, amputations, and accumulated strata, and of their behavior and potential for development as supports for new material or devices. The material history contains the specific objects of its development, the materials of the self-reflexive relationship between the building and the restoration project, which makes it possible to pass from a knowledge that records, to one that informs the project.

1. Franz Graf, *Histoire matérielle du bâti et projet de sauvegarde – Devenir de l'architecture moderne et contemporaine*, Lausanne, PPUR, 2014.

RELYING ON SCIENTISTS AS EXPERTS: TECHNICAL ANALYSES RATHER THAN FORMAL SPECULATIONS

Inseparable from historical research, restoration calls for and builds on the scientific and technical research conducted by the experts required for the diagnosis of deterioration and loss. Depending on each project, which is unique in nature, a team of specialists from various scientific disciplines should be formed at the start of a study, to extend material knowledge of the buildings and help refine the restoration process. These will be civil engineers for structural issues, construction physicists for hygrothermal ones, art restorers for furniture and polychromy, botanists for landscape matters, etc. Close collaboration with laboratories is essential. Examples are the *Laboratoire de Recherche des Monuments Historiques* in Paris, the *Istituto per la Valorizzazione dei Beni Culturali* in Rome, the *Instituto Torroja* in Madrid and the *Laboratoire de la Maintenance, Construction et Sécurité des Ouvrages* in Lausanne. The restoration of modern creations sometimes poses difficult questions for them: Can the polyester in Heinz Isler's (1926–2009) domes be restored? When it is part of a building of monumental value, the answer is, of course, yes, just as it was for César Baldaccini's (1921–1998) expanded polyurethane foam lacquered in white acrylic. We need technical research that analyzes deterioration, and conservation expertise, not hasty speculations that turn those involved in monumental heritage into enthusiastic forgers.

"MONUMENTAL": THE HERITAGE OF THE INTERWAR PERIOD

The monumental heritage of the interwar period has been identified as a whole, its condition documented, and its heritage value has been recognized and reinforced by its level of protection.[2] Historical research has played a fundamental part, as demonstrated by the mobilization of more sentimental opinion around movements to safeguard "iconic" objects of "heroic" Modernity, such as the Zonnestraal Sanatorium, the Villa Savoye, or the Penguin Pool in London. Nevertheless, there have been many demolitions and significant alterations, as well as clumsy restoration work. "Recent" monuments are clearly not treated with the same consideration as "ancient" ones, and the deontological and ethical rules are not always respected.

2. John Allan, "From Sentiment to Science," *Proceedings of the 12th International Docomomo Conference*, Espoo, Docomomo International, 2013, 175–184.

Le Corbusier and Pierre Jeanneret, Apartment-studio at Porte Molitor, Paris, France, 1931–1934.

MATERIAL HISTORY OF A BUILDING PUT TO THE TEST

The research method required to understand the material history of a building has been put to the test during recently conducted studies of built heritage, such as the one regarding Le Corbusier's apartment-studio at 24 rue Nungesser et Coli.[3] Far from the stripped-down image conveyed by the images published in the 1930s, the apartment-studio is the result of a complex stratification with multiple meanings, a true "permanent building site," and a place of incessant experimentation – architectural, sculptural, and constructional – in which the paradigms of the work intersected with a very personal idea of domesticity. This research produced an exhaustive understanding of the constructed object, focusing, in particular, on the meticulous definition of its material substance – the nature of its materials, their

3. Franz Graf and Giulia Marino, *Les multiples vies de l'appartement-atelier de Le Corbusier*, Cahiers du TSAM 2, Lausanne, EPFL Press, 2017.

Maurice Novarina, Jean Prouvé, and Serge Ketoff, Buvette d'Evian, France, 1954

implementation and their finishes, as well as the transformations they may have undergone from their original state. On the basis of this analysis, a series of recommendations was put forward for the intervention, on the one hand, identifying the "sensitive" parts and their difficulties, enabling the most judicious decisions to be made by experts in their respective specialist areas, and assisting them in the diagnostic phase, and on the other hand, by defining a series of guidelines for the conservation and restoration of the apartment-studio. The study of the design, site, and life of the Buvette d'Evian provides another illustration of the power of the method in action.[4]

4. Franz Graf and Giulia Marino, *La Buvette d'Evian, Maurice Novarina, Jean Prouvé, Serge Ketoff*, Gollion, Infolio éditions, 2018.

THE WORK SITE AS RESEARCH: SURVEYING THE WORK

While the material history is an integral part of the project, the work of restoration is not just execution, but an extension of research. It is a close encounter with the original and only document; it is a verification of the hypotheses formulated and the decisions taken. It requires careful observation of the degree to which the building can tolerate the repairs, the treatment or even the additions made to it. But it also involves the inevitable, troublesome, yet often stimulating "discoveries" that are revealed only when one embraces the totality of the object, with the essential probing and sampling being, by definition, just part of the work. When forced to face the facts, the architects and specialists involved may question their initial certainties, and revise and reassess their preliminary research, which they may then expand, potentially sending the project in a different direction. Restoration of the exterior of Le Corbusier's Petite Maison at Corseaux was completed in 2015, alternating periods of building work with its function as a museum. To ensure the best possible result, the client, the *Fondation Le Corbusier* (FLC), supported by federal and cantonal authorities for the Conservation of Historic Monuments, brought together experts in modern restoration and specialists in the fields of polychromy, mineral and metallic facade materials, an art restorer, and a landscape architect.

Le Corbusier and Pierre Jeanneret, Petite Maison on the shores of Lake Geneva, Corseaux, Switzerland, 1923.

The work was as close as possible to sustained maintenance – in fact, the most desirable form of conservation – and was concentrated mainly on the exteriors, the envelope of the house, the garden, and the fence. The reference period for the restoration and the question of authenticity were also central to the project for the garden of the Petite Maison; a wooded outdoor room. It bears saying that research on the restoration of modern gardens and landscaped complexes, lying between nature and architecture, is only in its infancy. Each major project on an "iconic" object is the subject of seminars and field trips, and sets new benchmarks for research and practice, which thereby develop.

The worksite as a place of research can undoubtedly involve some friction because, while time, testing, and reflection enrich research and those who are involved in it, they are also considered an impediment to the work by the main contractor and builders. The last point – which should be a fundamental element of continuous research but, unfortunately is often omitted – is the documentation of the building site, which provides invaluable cumulative knowledge and informs the material history of the restoration or preservation project.

ACADEMIC AND INSTITUTIONAL RESEARCH: LIMITED RESOURCES FOR KNOWLEDGE IN EDUCATION

Research and teaching about restoration in general, and that of the 20th century in particular, are rather rare in architecture schools, universities, polytechnics, and the academic world in general – except in Italy, though recent reforms have drastically reduced them. Somewhat obsessed with the training of the generalist architect, the designer of the "smart cities" of the future, restoration is seen as a specialization, cutting-edge knowledge certainly, but rather peripheral. However, if we consider that its methods are essential for designing in the existing, and that the existing built in the past century is the very place where architects exercise their profession in the 21st century, it is all the more surprising that this discipline, covering theory, history, construction, statics, and the project, is not a part of every architecture school's program, if only for its educational potential. Spanning technology and the humanities, it attracts little attention from institutional funders of research, with projects that lack the symbolic power or visibility of issues such as energy or transport. However, research[5] is being undertaken, primarily at a European level, albeit somewhat fragmentarily, and is often entrusted to schools with recognized technical expertise, such as the *Istituto Superiore per la Conservazione e il Restauro* in Rome, founded by Giulio Carlo Argan (1909–1992) and Cesare Brandi, or the *Hochschule für angewandte Wissenschaft und Kunst* at Hildesheim. From the latter, Professor Ivo Hammer (1944–) launched several studies that led to the restoration of Villa Tugendhat and, in particular, its plasterwork.[6] Every care was taken to preserve the "old" mural paintings in this restoration, which respected the original material. In restoration, the worksite is the only testbench, and the technical gesture is not neutral, but imbued with culture and theory.

5. See, for example, "Critical Encyclopaedia of Restoration and Re-Use of Twentieth-Century Architecture," 2008–2012, EPFL-EPFZ-USI in Switzerland and "Architecture du XXe siècle, matière à projet pour la ville durable du XXIe siècle," 2016–2020, Ministère de la culture in France.

6. Ivo Hammer, "Materiality. History of the Tugendhat House 1997–2012," in Daniela Hammer-Tugendhat, Ivo Hammer, and Wolf Tegethoff, *Tugendhat House: Ludwig Mies van der Rohe*, Basel, Birkhäuser, 2015, 162–223.

INTERNATIONAL NETWORK OF EXPERTS: KNOWLEDGE FROM OTHER HORIZONS FOR THE BENEFIT OF RESTORATION

Each restoration project dealing with an iconic building is the subject of work meetings with the architects and those in charge, drawing on an international network of experts, sometimes formally constituted, as was the case with the restoration of Villa Tugendhat, and other times more informally, as it was during the restoration of the Vyborg Library.[7] The International Specialist Committee on Technology of the Docomomo International organization met there on numerous occasions, to exchange information about strategies, techniques and management of projects of this complexity, in a pooling of knowledge resulting from research based on professional experiences (such as the restoration of the Zonnestraal Sanatorium, the Villa Tugendhat, the Maison de la Culture, and Aalto's own house) and the skills of academic researchers from European universities or the Getty Research Institute.

7. Eric Adlercreutz, Maija Kairamo, and Tapani Mustonen (eds.), *Alvar Aalto in Vyborg – Saving a Modern Masterpiece*, Helsinki, Rakennustieto publishing, 2016.

The operation of faithfully reproducing the original performed in the Vyborg Library, which no one would dare to question, nevertheless raises a fundamental question on the theoretical level: if it is generally proscribed for earlier heritage, why is it widely practiced when it comes to 20th century architecture? When we rebuild the Pavillon de l'Esprit Nouveau or the German Pavilion in Barcelona, it may be seen as an original idea, a testament to our affection for their architects, or a kind of educational tribute. But in the reconstruction of a housing complex like the Weissenhof Siedlung, which happened now more than 30 years ago, what critical assessment can we draw from it today, at a time when certain buildings have been "restored" for the second time? Can we reconcile the expectations of tenants, homeowners, and conservation authorities? Obviously, to the detriment of architecture, in what has been a return to a largely vanished original state, a cleansing of additions viewed as damaging, and destructive technical improvements.[8]

8. Alberto Grimoldi, "Un sintetico quadro internazionale," *Parametro*, No. 266, *Il restauro del moderno*, Faenza, 2006, 36–41.

HERITAGE AFTER 1945: CHRONOLOGICAL, TYPOLOGICAL, AND QUANTITATIVE EXPANSION

In the 1960s, at the same time as the "L'inventaire général" was being introduced in 1964 under the guidance of André Chastel (1912–1990) and André Malraux (1901–1976) in France, and Oreste Ferrari (1927–2005) was creating "L'ufficio centrale per il Catalogo del Ministero della Pubblica Istruzione" (1969) in Italy, European cities were being built very rapidly. After this initial haste, 50 years later, when the scope of such inventories has considerably broadened their fields of intervention[9] – first taking in stained glass, then the industrial, scientific, and technical heritage,[10] and 19th century and modern architecture and gardens – in an irony of history, it is now the most recent built heritage, that of the post-war period, for which new inventories must be drafted. This is because the more or less heavy-handed transformation of this heritage is a daily occurrence, due to essential maintenance work, upgrades to meet draconian energy requirements and the inescapable demands of profitability. The heritage value of the work built since 1945 is becoming clearer, the idea of a monument is gradually expanding, and research is urgently engaging in this field to a sometimes surprising degree.

9. André Chastel, "L'invention de l'inventaire," *Revue de l'Art*, No. 87, Paris, 1990, 5–11.

10. This is probably the most difficult heritage to preserve, insofar as the loss of its productive function makes it particularly vulnerable. The Cartiera Burgo by Pier Luigi Nervi and Gino Covre returned to production in 2020 after many years of dereliction, proving that industry and heritage can be fused in intelligent projects.

SCIENTIFIC KNOWLEDGE AND RESTORATION REVALUED: FROM RENOVATION TO CONSERVATION

As studies were being conducted for the renovation of the Pirelli Skyscraper, a dramatic accident led to the establishment of a technoscientific committee of experts in the discipline of conservation – eminent professors and directors of research from the *Politecnico di Milano* and *La Sapienza* in Rome, Conservation of the Regione Lombardia.[11] It required restoration to be a critical and scientific process that favored the path of monumental conservation resting on its solid theoretical and practical foundations, and abandoned the alternative that consisted of replacing facades with "identical" renovations, using more efficient technologies and materials. Far from the reconstruction of the Lever Building or the Phoenix Rheinrohr Tower, which is now undergoing its second transformation, over the past 15 years

11. Maria Antonietta Crippa (ed.), *Il restauro del grattacielo Pirelli*, Milan, Skira, 2007.

we have witnessed a veritable paradigm shift with regard to the preservation of the emblematic lightweight facades of the 20th century. This has evolved from the renovation of the facade of Nestlé's Administrative Headquarters at Vevey, for example, toward more respectful forms of intervention, such as that in the Bergpolderflat in Rotterdam and the Pirelli Skyscraper in Milan.

NEW OPERATIONAL ACADEMIC RESEARCH ON LARGE COMPLEXES AS MONUMENTAL HERITAGE

Georges Addor, Dominique Juillard, Louis Payot, and Jacques Bolliger, Cité du Lignon, Geneva, Switzerland, 1963–1971.

Franz Amrhein, Walter Maria Förderer, and Peter Steiger, Cité Avanchet-Parc, Geneva, Switzerland, 1969–1977.

Beyond an exceptional and sometimes spectacular output, during the age of *Les Trente Glorieuses*, housing was built on a massive scale, leading to an unprecedented expansion of the European city. Although this output was often sprawling and lackluster, certain developments are recognized as being of high quality, and even to have monumental value. Built before the oil-price shocks and unanimous support for sustainable development, their construction systems, naturally, do not comply with today's standards, in particular in respect to energy efficiency, and upgrading them involves extensive work for the vast majority of existing buildings. The issues of heritage and energy both support sustainable development through the preservation of cultural and natural resources, but lead to positions generally considered to be irreconcilable. In pursuit of a wider reflection on this major topic of restoring post-1945 heritage, research has been undertaken by our laboratory in recent years on building envelopes in the Cité du Lignon in Geneva. This is a remarkable residential complex from the 1960s designed by Georges Addor (1920–1982) for 10,000 inhabitants, whose heritage value is widely recognized.[12] The research aimed to define a specific strategy of intervention, resting on the material specifics of the buildings, in order to identify their deficiencies but also their potential. The energy usage of the building was examined in the same way as the other traditionally diagnosed parameters, supported by laboratory expertise. There is a need for further research to be conducted on other complexes with similar requirements, such as Avanchet-Parc, built 1969–1977 in Geneva.[13]

THE DISTANCE BETWEEN RESEARCH AND THE PROJECT: RECOGNITION, NEW IMAGE, DEMOLITION

Research on large complexes, as practiced in the history of architecture, has contributed to the recognition of their heritage value and avoided radical demolition or restructuring, as almost happened at the Cité de l'Étoile in Bobigny, where it was only prevented by an expert mission following its last-minute classification.[14] However, if history and project design remain two segments of knowledge that are unconnected or too far apart, there is a risk that we will see an increase in creative interventions by architects following cursory historical studies that pay insufficient attention to the material qualities of the buildings and, at best, produce outcomes

12. Franz Graf and Giulia Marino, "Modern and Green: Heritage, Energy, Economy," *Docomomo Journal*, No. 44 – "Modern and Sustainable," Barcelona, Docomomo International, 2011, 32–39; Franz Graf and Giulia Marino, *La cité du Lignon, 1963–1971. Etude architecturale et stratégies d'interventions*, special issue, heritage and architecture, Geneva, 2012; Franz Graf and Giulia Marino, "The Lignon. A silent restoration," *Casabella*, No. 918, 2021, 8–15.

13. Built for 7000 inhabitants, the Avanchets-Parc housing estate is the most important and last operation in the extension of the Geneva urban agglomeration, having been inaugurated in 1977. See: Franz Graf and Giulia Marino, *Avanchet-Parc "Cité de conception nouvelle et originale,"* Gollion, Infolio éditions, 2020; Franz Graf and Giulia Marino, "*Avanchet-Parc* in Geneva: an Experimental Housing Scheme, an Exemplary Complex," *Docomomo Journal*, No. 65 – "Housing for All," Lisbon, Docomomo International, 2021, 70–77.

14. Richard Klein (ed.), *La Cité de l'Étoile à Bobigny. Un modèle de logement social*, coll. "Lieux habités," Paris, éditions Créaphis, 2014.

like the "new faces" of Park Hill in Sheffield or Les Courtillières Housing Estate at Seine-Saint-Denis. Worse still, when the project is so remote that the only battle to be won is its classification as a historical monument, its rejection sounds the death knell for the whole complex, as shown by the demolition of Robin Hood Gardens in suburban London. To avoid these pitfalls, 20th century monuments and their conservation should benefit from operational academic research, which is now firmly established and rests on considerable experience.

PROFESSIONAL RESEARCH: FROM INDIVIDUAL EXPERIENCE TO SHARED METHODOLOGICAL KNOWLEDGE

Operational research is also being directly undertaken by knowledgeable professionals. Restoration informs both the design project and its history, situating the field of research clearly in the operative sphere. We can cite the work of John Allan (1945–) in establishing recent guidelines for the restoration of the Barbican and Golden Lane complexes in London. This drew on the office's considerable experience in safeguarding modern heritage, in particular the work of Berthold Lubetkin (1901–1990) – the Highpoint Building, the Penguin Pool, and Finsbury Health Centre in London – for which it wrote the reference monograph.[15] Similarly, Winfried Brenne's (1942–) work on the *Siedlung* Onkel-Toms-Hütte in Berlin led him to develop more general scientific studies on polychromy in the work of Bruno Taut.[16] Also in Berlin, what can we say about the work of David Chipperfield's (1953–) office? Nothing prepared it to deal with restoration, yet it has just brilliantly completed the restoration of the Neue Nationalgalerie.[17] And what great lessons there are to be learnt from the refurbishment of the Grand Auditorium of the Calouste Gulbenkian Foundation in Lisbon![18]

15. John Allan, *Berthold Lubetkin. Architecture and the Tradition of Progress*, London, RIBA Publications, 1992.

16. Winfried Brenne, *Bruno Taut. Meister des farbigen Bauens in Berlin*, Berlin, Braun, 2008.

17. Martijn Jaspers, "The Neue Nationalgalerie: the Refurbishment of a Modern Monument," *Docomomo Journal*, No. 56 – "The Heritage of Mies," Lisbon, Docomomo International, 2017, 78–85.

18. Ana Tostões, *Restauro e renovação do Grande Auditório*, Lisbon, Fundação Calouste Gulbenkian, 2015.

FOR A MATERIAL HISTORY OF THE PRESERVATION PROJECT

In the history of architecture, we need to consider the material history of the building, as this material history plays a substantial part in any preservation project. The material history of modern and contemporary buildings is a precious key for interpreting projects involving existing heritage, both in terms of method and their cultural implications. The development and reconsideration of projects to safeguard modern monuments and the "recent past" are taking shape very quickly in the European and even North American contexts. Lines of force have emerged in practice in recent years, pushing the issue into the rich debate that has run since the end of the 18th century. Not only does the enlarged notion of a "cultural asset" – a process begun in the 1970s – favor the attention that we now give to recent heritage, but a new consideration of the material substance of the built environment also marks a gradual change in attitude that is significant and most certainly beneficial. Set in the context of the notion of authenticity, a true material history of preservation projects today deserves to be written, and this task is already underway. This field of research has established an articulated and largely unprecedented understanding, on the one hand of the buildings of the 20th century, and on the other hand, of the history of their restoration.[19]

19. The studies recently conducted on the Vaudoise Assurances Headquarters in Lausanne give an explicit illustration of this, see Giulia Marino, "Jean Tschumi, l'architecte et le constructeur," and Franz Graf, "Actualité de l'œuvre de Jean Tschumi," in Jean-Baptiste Minnaert and Stéphanie Quantin-Biancalani (eds.), *Jean Tschumi Architecte*, Paris, Bernard Chauveau édition, 2021, 230–265 and 267–295.

Hence, the material history of the built environment embodies various modes of research into restoration, which produce cumulative understanding, multiplying knowledge and establishing architectural value. In addition, as the substrate of the project of intervention in an existing monument, it becomes "knowledge in action" and develops operative research through an approach that is a synthesis of technical and methodological factors with their cultural implications.

Jean Tschumi, headquarters of the Mutuelle Vaudoise Assurances, Lausanne, Switzerland, 1951–1956.

Conversely, the observation of projects and built work involving existing buildings, nurtures the material history of practices to preserve 20th century buildings and traces the lines of force and major developments. This will make it possible to reinterpret and understand architecture and its existence, not only by studying new buildings – which never stay new for long – but also by studying their alteration, stratification, or demolition, which are entwined with the permanence and mutation of the city, the territory, and the landscape, and also possess this character of a palimpsest, a permanent site of alteration and restoration.

THE MUSEUM AS ADVOCATE OF MODERNIST PRESERVATION: A CASE STUDY OF THE MUSEUM OF MODERN ART

BARRY BERGDOLL

The fame of New York's Museum of Modern Art (MoMA) as a champion of the new and as the promoter of the concept of the International Style from its inaugural architecture exhibition in 1932 is such that the museum's role in advancing architectural conservation and legal protection for significant buildings has long been forgotten.[1] Even if Viollet-le-Duc (1814–1879) said of architectural "restoration" – in a phrase premonitory of Michel Foucault (1926–1984) – that "both the word and the thing are modern,"[2] the architectural *avant-garde* of the early 20th century is associated more with creative destruction than with pious conservation of the historic. Yet, in the United States, the Museum of Modern Art played an integral role in the promotion of the very idea of historic preservation – as architectural restoration and conservation came to be called – embracing even the relatively recent present. The role of museums and exhibitions in creating the culture of preservation, out of which Docomomo emerged in the 1980s, has never been fully studied; here I can offer but one facet of a complex history that awaits its historian.

Museums had a paradoxical relationship from the outset with the idea of architectural preservation. While these temples of the muses acquired early on the dual – and sometimes conflicting – roles of displaying artistic treasures for public enlightenment and of conserving those treasures for future generations, the ability of bringing architecture into the purview of the museum was beset with even greater contradictions than the tension between display and conserve. The vociferous early critic of the very idea of the art museum, the French sculptor and art theorist Antoine-Chrysostome Quatremère de Quincy (1755–1849), underscored the conundrum that works of art created for specific places and purposes inevitably lost much, and not the least their "aura," when removed from their original context.[3] On the other hand, since the Enlightenment framing of the idea of the public gallery, proponents of the museum as an institution have maintained that the new context created by curators compensated for loss of original context. But what about architecture which first entered the museum through either fragments or representations in other media (models, drawings, engravings)? And what about modern architecture, which lacked even the patina of age, one of the qualities that Alois Riegl defined in his taxonomy of the values that cultures ascribed to monuments to qualify them for protection.[4]

The museum as treasure house, and the preservation movement with its focus on saving buildings *in situ* have nonetheless enjoyed occasionally an alliance at once natural and unnatural. Museums have at their heart conservation, but to preserve a building, a museum often must dismantle it for interior display or, as in open air museums dislocate it. In this sense, museums have often been treacherous allies in the campaigns of preservationists. Yet the ever-increasing role of temporary exhibitions – as opposed to permanent collections – in the practice of museums since the mid-20th century makes them often valuable collaborators in the publicity and newsworthiness, even sometimes in acts of protest and critique, in the very timeliness, that are key tools of the campaign for preservation.

Far from places of aesthetic detachment and neutrality, museums have often been places for advocacy. The zeal with which Quatremère de Quincy argued for dismantling Alexandre Lenoir's (1761–1839) *Musée des Monuments Français*, formed of fragments of sculpture and architectural elements salvaged from

1. See Barry Bergdoll, "Modern Architecture: International Exhibition," in David Hanks (ed.), *Partners in Design: Alfred H. Barr, Jr. and Philip Johnson,* New York, The Monacelli Press, 2015, 136–147, originally published as "Layers of polemic: MoMA's founding international exhibition between influence and reality," in *Modern Architects, Uma Introdução/An Introduction,* Lisbon, Babel (Athena), 2011.

2. "Le mot et la chose sont modernes," Viollet-le-Duc, "Restauration," in *Dictionnaire raisonné de l'architecture française du XIe au XVIe siècle,* Paris, Morel, 1858, Vol. 8., 14; here quoted from the translation by Kenneth D. Whitehead, *The Foundations of Architecture: Selections from the Dictionnaire raisonné of Viollet-le-Duc,* New York, Braziller, 1990, 195.

3. Antoine-Chrysostome Quatremère de Quincy, *Lettres sur le projet d'enlever les monuments de l'Italie,* Paris, 1796; reprint edition with scholarly introductions in French as *Lettres à Miranda sur le déplacement des monuments de l'art de l'Italie (1796),* Introduction by Édouard Pommier, Paris, Macula, 1989. And in English translation as *Letters to Miranda and Canova on the Abduction of Antiquities from Rome and Athens,* Introduction by Dominique Poulot, Los Angeles, The Getty Research Institute, 2012.

4. Alois Riegl, *Moderne Denkmalkultur: Sein Wesen und seine Entstehung,* Vienna and Leipzig, W., Braumüller, 1903. Published in English translation as "The Modern Cult of Monuments: Its Character and Its Origin," translated by Kurt W. Forster and Diane Ghirardo, *Oppositions,* No. 25, Fall 1982, 21–51.

ecclesiastical and aristocratic properties taken over as state property under the French Revolution, signaled the multiple risks the museum posed. For Quatremère de Quincy, Lenoir's theatrical display of medieval and renaissance sculpture and architectural elements rearranged in the disaffected Monastery of the *Petits Augustins* on Paris' Left Bank, not only celebrated the alienation of private property, it had also had sparked a new fashion for the art of the Middle Ages to the detriment of the reigning orthodoxy of classicism's revered status as the measure of excellence in the arts. He campaigned for the closure and dismantling – only partly achieved – of Lenoir's museum after 1815. No less was the founding over a century later of a Department of Architecture in the young MoMA tied to a mission to change taste among American audiences, chief among them, those in the position to commission new architecture.

Modern Architecture: International Exhibition, MoMA, New York, USA, 1932. View of Le Corbusier room.

THE PHENOMENON OF THE PERIOD ROOM

By the time the architectural historian Henry-Russell Hitchcock (1903–1987) and the wealthy young aesthete Philip Johnson (1906–2005) joined forces with MoMA's youthful director Alfred Barr, Jr. (1902–1981) to stage the survey *Modern Architecture: International Exhibition*, architecture had already gained a firm foothold in American museums through the paradoxical phenomenon of the period room which had achieved the height of its popularity in the 1920s. Inspired by the historic interiors installed in Zurich's *Schweizerisches Landesmuseum* and Munich's *Bayerisches Nationalmuseum*, American museums were in stiff competition with one another to install individual rooms ripped from the context of either a building on the brink of demolition or from the houses of families realizing that to spare a room's paneling and architectural features could command an impressive price on the burgeoning market for architectural elements.[5] Two spectacular events gained national headlines in the 1920s: the opening in 1924 of the Metropolitan Museum of Art's new American Wing with 15 period rooms housed in a structure fronted with the remounted neoclassical facade from the 1824 Assay Bank office from Wall Street, and the announcement in 1926 that John D. Rockefeller, Jr. (1874–1960) was funding the massive reconstruction of the 18th century city of Williamsburg, Virginia to create Historic Williamsburg, an American answer to the type of open air museum launched by Arthur Hazelius (1833–1901) with *Skansen* in Stockholm in 1891. Period rooms were inevitably paradoxical since they involved dismantling what they set out to preserve, even as they extricated a single room from both its place in a larger spatial design and from the physical and local context in which it had been created. Even if such rooms were generally meant to embody the lessons of both art and national history – signs of the evolution of style as an integral part of the social and political evolution of cultures – they also carried with them elements that modernists considered invitations to nostalgia. In a few rare instances museums were as keen on collecting the most up-to-date interiors as documents of contemporary taste, beginning with the acquisition of an *Art Nouveau* room at the Paris *Exposition Universelle* of 1900 by the Hamburg *Museum für Kunst und*

5. Kathleen Curran, *The Invention of the American Art Museum, From Craft to Kulturgeschichte, 1870–1930*, Los Angeles, Getty Research Institute, 2016, esp. pp. 9ff. John Harris, *Moving Rooms: The Trade in Architectural Salvages*, New Haven, Yale University Press, 2007.

Gewerbe and the unfulfilled project of the Philadelphia Museum of Art in the 1920s to include both an *Art Nouveau* interior and an *Art Moderne* (c. 1925) room among their impressive suite of period rooms once the museum opened in a monumental neo-Greek temple at the end of the Benjamin Franklin Parkway in 1928.[6]

6. Kathleen Curran, *op. cit.*, 197.

While period rooms often put museums at loggerheads with preservationists, museums also played from time to time strategic roles in promoting the preservation of significant buildings *in situ* and in the cultivation of support for local and national preservation of architecturally significant buildings in cities where the promise of the new and the resonant memories of the old would cohabitate. The oldest preserved historic city centers in the United States – in Charleston, South Carolina, and in New Orleans – were both given legal protection in the wake of museum exhibitions dramatizing the imminent peril of destruction of the historic urban fabric. While, in the 1920s, focus was on the colonial and 19th century past of the United States, in the post-World War II era the early history of modern architecture increasingly came into focus, even the early history of the skyscraper.

Exhibition *Early Modern Architecture, Chicago 1870–1910*,
MoMA, New York, USA, 1933.

THE ADVOCATE OF AMERICAN MODERNISM

Since its founding in 1932, MoMA's Department of Architecture (later Department of Architecture & Design) had been crafting a genealogy of Modernism, even as it advocated for the Modern Movement. Increasingly the trio of H.H. Richardson (1838–1886), Louis Sullivan (1856–1924), and Frank Lloyd Wright (1867–1959) were enshrined as the pioneers of American Modernism, even as Le Corbusier, Walter Gropius, and Alvar Aalto (1898–1976), along with Wright, remained figures to be followed on a regular basis in the museum's exhibition program. Here the medium was photography, from the outset a way of recording the state of things either to preserve them against the ravages of time or to document and protest the ravages of time. Just months after MoMA staged its first photographic display of early modern architecture often threatened with demolition, *Early Modern Architecture, Chicago 1870–1910*, was installed. These photographic exhibitions were meant to circulate not only to other venues but through press coverage. The press release announced, "The Museum's exhibition will (...) be the first record of a great architecture which is vanishing rapidly under the sledgehammer of the house wrecker."[7]

7. Press release, *Early Modern Architecture, Chicago 1870–1910*, January 1933, MoMA archives, https://assets.moma.org/documents/moma_press-release_324987.pdf?_ga=2.188709416.1618906106.1622752718-464908565.1577467034, accessed 3 June 2021.

The idea that the new itself might quickly become the old and be, in turn, imperiled first surfaced in a show mounted in 1958 to support the work of the young National Trust for Historic Preservation, founded in 1949 with a charter from the U.S. Congress with the express purpose of acquiring and administering historic sites. The trust began with the acquisition of the 1805 Woodlawn Plantation in Virginia in 1951 and only accidentally began to acquire modern architecture when it was bequeathed one of Wright's first Usonian houses, the 1940 Pope-Leighy House, threatened in the 1960s with demolition to make way for a federal Interstate highway through Virginia. To save it, Wright's house was moved to the vast estate of the 19th century Woodlawn and became the first of his houses to open as a house museum.

Large-scale photographs and texts dramatizing the accelerating loss of significant works of architecture in the United States, notably in the climate of post-war programs for urban renewal of city centers, not only marked MoMA's entry into the growing movement for preservation, but was an awakening for Arthur Drexler (1925–1987), director of the Department of Architecture & Design since 1956. "The preservation of America's 18th century architecture now enjoys public sympathy and support," he noted in the press release:

> But many great buildings of the 19th and early 20th centuries – too recent to seem romantic or significant – have not yet aroused public interest and are being ruthlessly destroyed. The Museum of Modern Art, which has always championed the cause of a creative modern architecture, is concerned with this problem because unless the habit of preservation prevails there can be no architecture at all, and today's great buildings will soon disappear in their turn.[8]

8. Press Release, *Architecture Worth Saving*, 1958, MoMA archives, https://assets.moma.org/documents/moma_press-release_326131.pdf?_ga=2.247470599.1618906106.1622752718-464908565.1577467034, accessed 3 June 2021.

Wright's Larkin Building in Buffalo had been demolished in 1950 to make way for a surface parking lot. The exhibition not only made the case for imperiled masterworks, including Wright's Robie House in Chicago, but also for the need for stronger legislation to provide buildings in the United States with the type of protection that was established in Britain and many European countries.

THE CASE OF THE VILLA SAVOYE

Exhibition *Villa Savoye: Destruction by Neglect*, MoMA, New York, USA, 1966.

Exhibition *Villa Savoye: Destruction by Neglect*, MoMA. Detail view.

The campaign was not to be limited however to American buildings, as just months after Le Corbusier's death in 1965, Drexler became increasingly alarmed over reports on the state of the architect's Villa Savoye at Poissy-sur-Seine (1928–1930), alerted by French architects dismayed at the lack of action by the French state even after the acquisition of the building in 1958. In the spring of 1966, Drexler received photographs of the house's lamentably decayed condition – images which had been exhibited at the *Musée des Arts Décoratifs* in Paris a few weeks earlier – and determined to make a polemical appeal for action. The show *Villa Savoye: Destruction by Neglect*, was only on the walls at MoMA for three weeks in July of 1966 but the press coverage was extensive. Drexler had nine of the images blown up to large size and staged them around the model of the Villa Savoye,[9] the exhibition space darkened and dramatically spot lit for a sense of drama and even danger. The architectural model was the very one that Le Corbusier had had made for inclusion in the museum's inaugural architecture exhibition in 1932, which had been shown in numerous contexts and traveled widely in the museum's circulating exhibition program ever since. With the juxtaposition of photographs from the early 1930s and those taken just a few weeks earlier, the museum departed from the ethos of presenting modern buildings as eternally new and pristine. "A classic that can be compared with the most brilliant achievements of the past," the wall text declared, "its slow destruction through neglect is scandalous." Although efforts were underway – only now being

9. Ironically enough, the model had itself been all but destroyed during the traveling show of *Modern Architecture: International Style* in the early 1930s and was almost completely rebuilt by the American model maker Theodore Conrad.

realized over a half century later – to "turn the Villa into a museum of Le Corbusier's work," not only had they made no headway, it was only saved from demolition by the intervention of André Malraux. The villa shared its formerly pastoral setting with a new high school building, "so close to the Villa as to deprive it irrevocably of the open landscape which gave its original point."[10] MoMA's widely circulated press release crafted the sentences to be taken up by the American press: "Last winter a heavy

10. Wall label for *Villa Savoye: Destruction by neglect*, 1966, MoMA archives, assets.moma.org/documents/moma_press-release_326459.pdf?_ga=2.249339527.1618906106.1622752718-464908565.1577467034, accessed 3 June 2021.

Exhibition *The Architecture of the École des Beaux-Arts*, MoMA, New York, USA, 1975.

snow load inflicted great damage. Unheated, its windows gone, the metal frames rusted, and the exterior stucco peeling away, the building is now completely vulnerable to the effects of structural strain. There is little reason to think it will still be standing by the end of this decade."[11] In the *New York Times*, Ada Louise Huxtable (1921–2013) declared that the show "may record the architectural crime of the century," although she was quick to point out that "the United States probably holds the all-time championship for landmark destruction." She went on to note that "there may yet be a happy ending to the story of the *Villa Savoye*. The Museum obtained these photographs in June, and shortly after deciding to exhibit them received word that workmen had appeared (...) to patch up the exterior stucco."[12] By 13 November 1966, the *Times* reported that the plans were afoot for a Le Corbusier study center in the Villa, a project that fell by the wayside as the *Fondation Le Corbusier* was established in the Maison La Roche and Maison Jeanneret in Paris after 1968. If the Villa Savoye museum project had quietly died, the building would live on, and was declared a "Monument Historique" in 1976.[13]

11. Press release for *Villa Savoye: Destruction by Neglect*, July 1966, MoMA archives, https://assets.moma.org/documents/moma_press-release_326458.pdf?_ga=2.243209986.1618906106.1622752718-464908565.1577467034, accessed 3 June 2021.

12. Ada Louise Huxtable, "Architecture: A Cultural Fable for Our Time," *New York Times*, Sunday, 24 July 1966.

13. Kevin Murphy, "The Villa Savoye and the Modernist Historic Monument," *Journal of the Society of Architectural Historians*, Vol. 61, No. 1, March 2002, 68–89. And Susanna Caccia Gherardini and Carlo Olmo, *La Villa Savoye: Icona, rovina, restauro (1948–1968)*, Rome, Donzelli Editore, 2016, 180–188. See also Fondation Le Corbusier, *Le Corbusier: L'oeuvre à l'épreuve de sa restauration*, Paris, Éditions de la Villette, 2017.

URBAN PRESERVATION

MoMA's new support for saving Modernist architectural heritage was not to be confined to the canon of masterpieces it had helped craft in exhibitions and publications. In Spring 1968, as college campuses across America were erupting in protests, MoMA mounted a small exhibition of the proposal of several architectural students, including the young American designer Joseph D'Urso (1943–) (later a

Kurokawa (1934–2007), Masato Ohtaka (1923–2010), and Fumihiko Maki (1928–) prepared the publication of the Metabolism manifesto that fused ideas about architectural megastructures with those of organic biological growth. The idea of architecture that Metabolism represented was different from the principles of the European Modern Movement, and its manifesto not only introduced new concepts for the creation of architecture, but also dealt with architectural culture in general. Traditional forms of monumentalism were a natural target of Metabolist critique, so it seems contradictory to apply the ideas of conservation and preservation to Metabolist architecture. However, many Metabolist buildings have unfortunately not managed to respond to social change (Utopian Metabolism) and, as they no longer met user requirements, have recently been demolished. Examples are the Izumo Grand Shrine Administrative Building (Shimane, 1963, Kiyonori Kikuta), the Miyakonojo Civic Hall (Miyazaki, 1966, Kiyonori Kikutake) and the Nakagin Capsule Tower (Tokyo, 1972, Kisho Kurokawa).

Kiyonori Kikutake, Izumo Grand Shrine Administrative Building, Shimane, Japan, 1963. Demolished in 2016.

Kiyonori Kikutake, Miyakonojo Civic Hall, Miyazaki, Japan, 1966. Demolition in 2019.

The world is changing dramatically in the face of the Covid-19 pandemic. Its effects can be felt in the rescheduling of the Tokyo Olympics 2020 (which were to be held in Tokyo again for the first time since 1964) and of the *16th International Docomomo Conference* “Inheritable Resilience: Sharing Values of Global Modernities,” also in Tokyo. While the architectural works of Utopian Metabolism were being destroyed, the Yoyogi National Gymnasium for the 1964 Olympic Games was designated an Important Cultural Property of Japan in May 2021 and, with the aim of registering it as a World Heritage Site, a symposium was held on 2 September 2021, at the closing ceremony of the *16th International Docomomo Conference*.

Two works by Kenzo Tange are among those selected for the Docomomo Rehabilitation Award. One of his most important buildings, the Yoyogi National Gymnasium, has been seismically strengthened and refurbished for the Tokyo 2020 Olympic and Paralympic Games to adapt it to today's performance requirements, such as disabled accessibility. It was also classified as an excellent example of sustainable refurbishment. The renovation project of the Yamanashi Press and Broadcasting Center, a non-utopian Metabolist building, had a specific approach to conservation. The owner of this building respects it as a work by Kenzo Tange, has continued to use it with care, and has refurbished it to meet the changing requirements of each period since its completion. The continuous work that has been done to keep the building viable may not be considered a conservation project from a European point of view but it presents an interesting example of a culturally grounded rehabilitation. Despite the international spread of the Modern Movement, in order to consider architectural work as cultural heritage it is important to respect the specificity of each architectural culture, country, and region, and to acknowledge its diversity in international debate. I hope that the discussions at Docomomo International, which began in the late 1980s, will not become like the doctrinaire debates that once led to the demise of CIAM, with its limited shelf life of 30 years.

DOCUMENTATION AND CONSERVATION OF MODERN MOVEMENT ARCHITECTURE IN EDUCATION

Since its foundation in 1988, Docomomo International has devoted more than three decades to the study, documentation, and conservation of the architectural heritage of the Modern Movement. Today it enjoys widespread recognition and prestige, with over 70 national or regional working parties located on the five continents consisting of academics and professionals from the fields of planning, design, engineering, and conservation. During this time Docomomo has developed many formats supporting the increase and dissemination of knowledge and awareness raising among students, professionals, and the public: fiches, conferences, seminars, workshops, books, dossiers, and the *Docomomo Journal*. Facing rapid digitization and globalization, Docomomo has fostered its role as an international network and platform by making the knowledge and information available online and by creating the

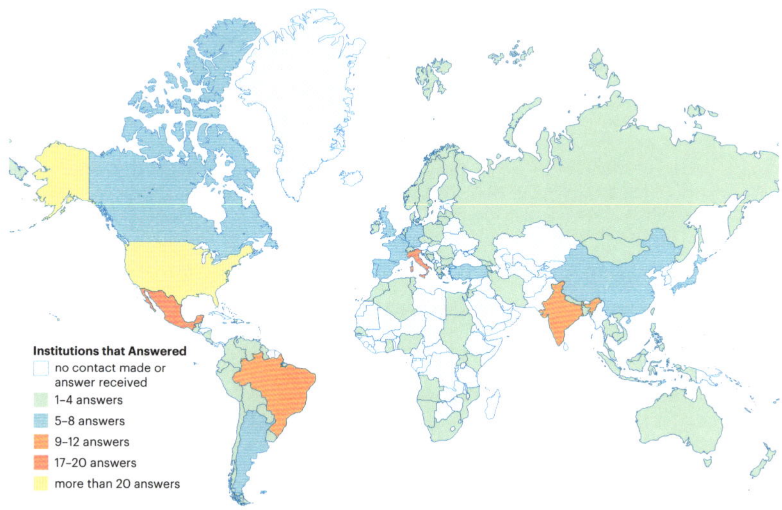

A total of 261 institutions from 84 countries responded to the *Global Survey on Education and Training*. The map represents in different colors the absolute number of institutions per country that responded to the survey.

Docomomo virtual exhibition (*MoMove*). Back in 2016, the International Specialist Committee on Education & Theory (ISC/E&T) decided to reestablish itself as the International Specialist Committee on Education & Training to support the involvement and training of students and young professionals by establishing a network between teaching and training institutions. As a joint effort between Docomomo International and the Getty Conservation Institute (GCI), the Global Survey on Education and Training for the Conservation of Twentieth-Century Built Heritage[1] provided a first basis for new international educational initiatives in 2020. At the same time, recent experiences around the world with digital online teaching and learning due to the COVID-19 pandemic have provided valuable insights into the opportunities and challenges for future educational approaches as part of open science, open scholarship, and open education.[2]

EXPERIENCING ACADEMIC EDUCATION AND TRAINING

As an organization, Docomomo International has established strong formats for knowledge exchange with the documentation homework (fiches) and the biannual

1. Margherita Pedroni, Cesar Bargues Ballester, Andrea Canziani, Wessel de Jonge, and Chandler Mccoy, *A Global Survey on Education and Training for the Conservation of Twentieth-Century Built Heritage, Research Report*, Los Angeles, Getty Conservation Institute, Docomomo International, 2020, also available online at: https://www.getty.edu/conservation/publications_resources/pdf_publications/global_survey_on_education_and_training.html
2. Jonathan Tennant et al., *A tale of two "opens": intersections between Free and Open Source Software and Open Scholarship*, SocArXiv. OSF, 2020.

UTA POTTGIESSER

International Docomomo Conferences (IDC). During the 9th *International Docomomo Conference* in 2006 in Istanbul (Turkey) the first student workshop was held. Since then, the workshops have become a tradition, and link the themes of the conferences with specific threatened buildings or ensembles at the conference location, uniting international docents and students. Due to the COVID-19 pandemic the 16th *International Docomomo Conference 2020* in Tokyo (Japan) had to be postponed and was finally held as the first Virtual IDC in 2021. The student workshop took place beforehand as a ten-day Online Docomomo School Tokyo 2020+1 – an oDOMO.

In addition to these biannual activities, the six International Specialist Committees (ISC) have established their own formats. The ISC/Technology has organized 16 technology seminars from 1996 to 2018 which are documented in 14 Docomomo *Preservation Technology Dossiers*, mainly focusing on the technologies and conservation challenges of building materials and components, but also exploring the interaction and collaboration of different disciplines in 20th century built heritage.[3] In parallel, the committee members are engaged with comparable international organizations such as the Association for Preservation Technology International (APT) and the International Association for Science and Technology of Building Maintenance and Monument Preservation (WTA International), and also collaborate in joint international publications comparing conservation approaches in different countries and regions.[4] Together the ISC/Technology and the ISC/Interior Design explored *Plastics in Modern Movement buildings* and *Plastics in Modern Movement interiors* in two joint seminars in Delft 2017 and in Antwerp 2018.

The ISC/Registers was created to engage national and regional working parties in the documentation of buildings and sites by providing documentary fiches every two years for the Docomomo council meetings. Since 2016, ISC/Registers set a new focus on "good conservation practices" to complement the documentary work with conservation work. The publication of the many hundreds of collected fiches is still pending and should be considered both as a rich source for further educational and training programs, and as the shared knowledge of the international Docomomo community. Part of this research is already accessible online in the Docomomo *virtual exhibition* (*MoMove*) available at the Docomomo website.[5]

The ISC/Education & Training aims at "creating a general awareness and appreciation of modern buildings in the younger generation, general public and the society at large"[6] and has produced a *Global Survey on Education and Training for the Conservation of Twentieth-Century Built Heritage* in collaboration with Getty Conservation Institute, conducted in 2018–2019.[7] A total of 758 institutions in 115 countries worldwide were contacted, and responses from 261 institutions in 84 countries were received. Of these responses 220 institutions in 71 countries offer educational activities and programs on 20th century-built heritage and conservation, the majority at undergraduate and graduate level, and much less at doctoral or professional level. The remaining 41 institutions confirmed they were considering establishing related activities in the future. However, the regional overview of responses shows the uneven distribution between countries, in particular the lack of responses from large parts of Africa, Asia, Oceania, and parts of Eastern Europe.

The survey also took a closer look at pedagogical approaches, teaching methods, and how the connection of these educational activities with "traditional

3. Jos Tomlow, Alex Dill, and Uta Pottgiesser (eds.), "Perceived Technologies in the Modern Movement 1918–1975," *Proceedings of the 13th International Docomomo Technology Seminar*, 25–26 January 2013, Karlsruhe. The seminar also figures as the *10. Karlsruher Tagung 'Das architektonische Erbe'/International Working Party for Documentation and Conservation of Buildings, Sites and Neighbourhoods of the Modern Movement, Preservation technology dossier 13*, Zittau, Graphische Werkstätten Zittau, 2014. Some dossiers are available online at: https://issuu.com/docomomoisctechnology/docs

4. Angel Ayón, Uta Pottgiesser, and Nathaniel Richards, *Reglazing Modernism. Intervention Strategies for 20th-Century Icons*, Basel, Birkhäuser, 2019.

5. http://exhibition.docomomo.com/

6. Quote from Docomomo International website, https://www.docomomo.com/about/organization/iscs

7. Margherita Pedroni et al., *op. cit.*

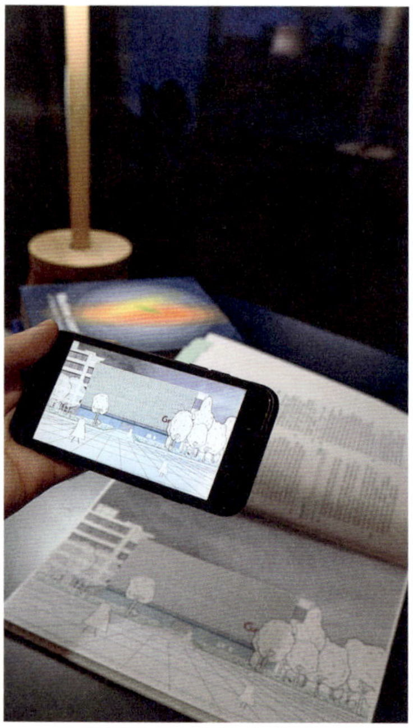

Augmented Reality used to partially immerse into the history of the Germia Department Store in Pristina, Kosovo (Lilijana Rasevski, 1972).

conservation curricula" is designed. The vast majority of educational activities at undergraduate and graduate level are taught as individual courses or as modules within other courses (over 60%). Other formats are workshops (18–22%) and just a few are degree, certificate, or diploma programs (15–16%). The subjects of education and training activities were subdivided into building conservation practice, material conservation practice, design, and others. At undergraduate level, building conservation practice, material conservation practice, and design were rather evenly distributed (24–34%); at graduate level, building conservation practice at 38% ranked above material conservation practice (27%) and design (24%). A similar distribution can be seen at PhD level, with building conservation practice (46%) dominating over material conservation practice (19%) and design (22%). Also, at professional training level, building conservation practice (39%) ranked ahead material conservation practice (31%) and design (22%), although the share in material conservation practice was higher. Teaching methods tended to employ traditional formats such as lectures and presentations (93%), followed by field exercises and case studies (77–76%) and readings (67%), while laboratory classes only accounted for 34%. Despite the important role that case studies already play in education, most respondents stressed the importance of case studies as educational tools and for decision-making processes in conservation. The survey highlighted that there is an "ambiguity of approaches" as to whether the "topic of conserving twentieth-century heritage is or should be taught separately from the teaching of traditional heritage conservation."[8] The respondents' additional comments gave further insight into the specific needs of particular areas and groups. The report clearly stated that, "distance learning was an underexploited resource" and that, "it is impossible now to predict how online education will impact this field in the long term."[9] Digital and distance learning, inclusive approaches and the provision of multilingual educational material need to be explored further. Some ongoing initiatives are mentioned here:

8. *Idem.*, 38.

9. *Ibidem.*, 39.

One example was the European Erasmus+ project *Re-use of Modernist Buildings (RMB),* coordinated by Michel Melenhorst from OWL, University of Applied Sciences (Detmold, Germany) from 2016–2019, which brought together six universities from Germany, Belgium, Portugal, Serbia, and Turkey, and Docomomo International to develop a curriculum for the growing field of reuse and rehabilitation of 20th century architecture as a joint master's program with digital components.[10] The accreditation of the master's program is in progress.

10. Michel Melenhorst, Uta Pottgiesser, Theresa Kellner, and Franz Jaschke (eds.), "100 Years Bauhaus. What Interest Do We Take In Modern Movement Today?," *Proceedings 16th* Docomomo *Germany, 3rd RMB Conference*, Lemgo, Hochschule Ostwestfalen-Lippe, Docomomo Deutschland e. V., 2019, https://www.th-owl.de/elsa/record/1101

Another example were the writing workshops of the African Studies Association of the UK (ASAUK) first run in 2009, and repeated and developed over time. In 2018 and 2019 they took place in Ghana, and in 2021 the workshops were entirely virtual, involving students from Ghana and Nigeria. Ola Uduku, one of the organizers, pointed out that the imperative for both workshops has been threefold:

- to support and work with young African students to develop their writing skills using the intensive workshop medium,
- to encourage the appreciation through the writing about and recording of contemporary and historical African built environment; comprising social infrastructure, public, commercial and private buildings,

- to disseminate the products of the workshop; comprising written material, images and other media.

The 2021 edition of the workshops directly links the students with their campuses, considered the "best examples of Africa's Modernist architectural heritage," which are still widely undocumented and deserve to be rediscovered.

The writing workshops also highlight the unequal distribution of production of and access to knowledge that still persists in 2021. In the article "The World Cannot Afford Any More Global Academic Jamborees," its authors state that, in the context of COVID-19 pandemic, "this pandemic should make us look hard at our paradigms of knowledge production and call into question how structures in the university sector have intensified global inequalities."[11] The initiative Modern Heritage of Africa (MoHA), started in 2020, aims to build university networks across Africa and raise awareness of modern heritage – conferences are planned for 2021 and 2022. A further collaboration between Docomomo International, Germany, and the Accra chapter with universities in Nigeria, Uganda, and the UK, is addressing this issue by developing the idea of the writing workshops and adding visual and digital skills to it. Under the title of *Shared Heritage Africa. Rediscovering Masterpieces* the project (started in 2021) will announce so-called Digital Fellowships, and combine writing, photography, and desktop publishing in collaboration with the online platform Architectuul and photographer Jean Molitor, to allow a holistic and interdisciplinary approach to the documentation of Africa's Modernist architectural heritage.

11. Ambreena Manji, Carli Coetzee, Ola Uduku, and Toby Green, "The World Cannot Afford Any More Global Academic Jamborees," *Times Higher Education Supplement*, 21 May 2020, https://www.timeshighereducation.com/opinion/world-cannot-afford-any-more-global-academic-jamborees?fbclid=IwAR0mpUs2GQhPUWwj8xJJ3NEPWOADc7V3ohAc6tDxEudGW0Xu7bsPaGAhykc

EVOLVING EDUCATIONAL EXPERIMENTS

Augmented Reality used to compare the functionalities of two Frankfurt Kitchens (Margarete Schütte-Lihotzky, 1926) located in Detmold and in Frankfurt.

Altogether, the national and regional working parties and their members have organized manifold activities and events and produced a wide range of publications, often linked to academic institutions and programs. The involvement of new and digital technologies can complement the experience of conferences, seminars, and workshops. Consequently, the course Conference and Communication (ConCom) at OWL, University of Applied Sciences addresses students of the Master's in Integrated Architectural Design (MIAD) and Master's in Integrated Design (MID). In collaboration with Docomomo Germany and the Bauhaus Dessau Foundation, the course served as a platform for students to explore the achievements of Modern Movement architecture around the world, with a thematic focus on infrastructure, the 2021 conference theme of Docomomo Germany. Students were asked to think about how they could communicate academic findings (resulting from their literature research in the previous semester) and how the findings could contribute to society and reach a larger audience in the form of non-written (NWO) or non-traditional outputs (NTO). In introductory sessions, students analyzed the state of the art of digital archives, depots, exhibitions, and museums in order to evaluate positive and negative aspects and formulate pros and cons. Students were also asked to identify the technologies, software, and sources used, and to understand their potentials and limits.

12. Uta Pottgiesser, Anica Dragutinovic, and Marzia Loddo (eds.), *MoMove Modern Movement and Infrastructure*, Detmold, OWL University of Applied Sciences, 2021, https://www.th-owl.de/elsa/record/5491

Tools and technologies identified by the students were: websites, apps, short movies, films, as well as 360-degree image applications, augmented and virtual reality, and online platforms to display their exhibits. Originally intended to be a physical exhibition in the Bauhaus building in Dessau, it turned into a completely virtual exhibition.[12]

The ConCom course enabled a great variety of subjects to be investigated and tools to be applied, depending on the students' educational and cultural backgrounds and interests. The approaches and outputs were diverse and were mostly developed in teams in an iterative process involving feedback from individual docents and peer groups from online teaching in video conferences. The students' work offered an advanced experience through in-depth virtual and visual representation and interpretation. With regard to the target audience, students made

Germany's first branded large petrol station in Hamburg around 1927. Illustration as part of a historic video.

different choices, but all of them were able to communicate their new knowledge to a wider and non-expert audience. The course also raised the students' awareness of their responsibility as future designers and engineers for shaping the livability of our cities, sites, and buildings, and allowed the 40 students to engage in interdisciplinary, international, and cross-cultural research and collaboration.

EXPLORING OPEN SCIENCE

There has been a long-lasting scholarly discussion on how to disseminate research output in general, and non-written output in particular, how to introduce new knowledge into educational programs, and how to connect research and education. With regard to the goals of Docomomo International to contribute to the documentation and conservation of our recent built environment and heritage – landscapes, cities, sites, buildings, and interiors – the same questions arise.

13. BOAI, *Budapest Open Access Initiative (BOAI)*, 2002, https://www.budapestopenaccessinitiative.org/read

Since the early 2000s and the publication of the *Budapest Open Access Initiative,*[13] open access publishing has developed into a movement adopted by academia, professional publishers, and non-governmental institutions to promote various types of work (images, text, audio, video, data, databases, source code, etc.). By publishing its policy guidelines on open access, UNESCO supports the goal of giving "universal access to information and knowledge, focusing particularly on two global priorities: Africa and Gender equality."[14] The *San Francisco Declaration on Research Assessment*[15] expressed the general skepticism felt in the research community toward the dominant use of indicators such as journal impact factors (JIFs). Since then, universities and research institutions worldwide have been changing their policies and including alternative categories such as design, exhibition, media, and performance and qualitative indicators into their policies. Finally, the new open-science policy links science to society – specifically the general public and lay people – and established the term Citizen Science (CS) in 2014.

Also Docomomo International with its committees, national and regional working parties and members will digitally strengthen the existing international academic collaborative network. Docomomo may further converge with universities, foundations, museums, and in general, with any kind of public or private, international, or local institution with which it shares objectives, to support educational formats and disseminate open educational resources. Analysis of the digital challenges and potentials of the recent online learning period has just started, and different conclusions might be drawn for the Global North and the Global South.[16] In any case, digitization in the form of Open Access (OA), Free and Open Software and Sources (FOSS), and Open Educational Resources (OER) should be part of Docomomo's future educational agenda to foster the documentation and conservation of recent built heritage worldwide.

14. Alma Swan, *Policy guidelines for the development and promotion of open access*, Paris, UNESCO, 2012.

15. DORA, *The Declaration on Research Assessment (DORA)*, 2013, https://sfdora.org/read/

16. See Evelyn Lami Ashelo Allu-Kangkum, "Covid-19 and Sustainable Architectural Education: Challenges and Perceptions on Online Learning: Challenges and Perceptions on Online Learning," *IJRDO – Journal of Educational Research*, Vol. 6, No. 2, March 2021, 7–12, http://ijrdo.org/index.php/er/article/view/4179; and Aleksandra Milovanović, Miloš Kostić, Ana Zorić, Aleksandra Đorđević, Mladen Pešić, Jovana Bugarski, Dejan Todorović, Neda Sokolović, and Andrej Josifovski, "Transferring COVID-19 Challenges into Learning Potentials: Online Workshops in Architectural Education," *Sustainability* [online], 28 August 2020, Vol. 12, No. 17, 7024.

MODERN WORLD HERITAGE – BLINDSPOT TECHNICAL INFRASTRUCTURE?

Next year, the UNESCO World Heritage Convention adopted in 1972 will celebrate its 50th anniversary. The commemorations will provide an occasion for both a self-confident and self-critical look back. Probably no other program has brought UNESCO's world cultural policy to the attention of the general public more than the World Heritage Convention signed on 23 November, to which almost 200 states have now acceded and whose World Heritage List had grown to over 1100 natural and cultural sites by mid-2020.

The impressive outcome of these first 50 years is thus a source of pride for both UNESCO and its Advisory Bodies, the International Union for Conservation of Nature (IUCN), International Centre for the Study of the Preservation and Restoration of Cultural Property (ICCROM), and International Council on Monuments and Sites (ICOMOS), which UNESCO calls upon for advice regarding World Cultural Heritage and World Natural Heritage. However, the anniversary is also an appropriate time to undertake an interim review to identify weaknesses in the implementation of the World Heritage Convention to date, and to highlight positive development opportunities for the future. From the point of view of Docomomo, initiated in 1988 and internationally established in 1990, and of the International Scientific ICOMOS Committee on 20th Century Heritage Conservation (ISC 20C), launched in 2005, this interim review should pay special attention to the young heritage of the Modern Movement from the 20th century.

THE DOCOMOMO TENTATIVE LIST FROM 1998

The most revealing starting point for examining the importance that the UNESCO Convention has attached to the heritage of the 20th century over the last 50 years is probably the pilot study "The Modern Movement and the World Heritage List," which was presented back in 1998 by Hubert-Jan Henket (1940-) on behalf of Docomomo. Already raising the issue in the late 20th century, this document was probably one of the earliest discussion papers to consider the eligibility of this young architectural and urban heritage for World Heritage status. Sometimes abbreviated to the "Docomomo Tentative List" and compiled at the invitation of ICOMOS (1992), this first overview of potential World Heritage candidates from the modern era emerged from a survey involving all of Docomomo's national experts and international working groups, and yielded some 100 proposals for future World Heritage nominations.[1] In the mid-1990s, the World Heritage List numbered about 350 items, of which only three were clearly attributable to 20th century architectural history: Brasília (Brazil), added in 1987; the Woodland Cemetery Stockholm, Sweden (added in 1993); and the Bauhaus sites in Germany (added in 1996), accounting for less than one percent of all listings.

The Docomomo list comprised around 100 proposals (dating from 1897 to 1977) and already incorporated the idea of nominating the complete oeuvre of certain heroes of Modernism as a package, such as the masterpieces of Le Corbusier and Frank Lloyd Wright, or selected buildings from the life's work of others, such as Mies van der Rohe (1886–1969) and Alvar Aalto. In retrospect, there was a notable absence of outstanding technical testimonies to the art of civil engineering or the technical infrastructure created and left behind by the Modern Movement, which

1. The Modern Movement and the World Heritage List. The Docomomo Tentative List by Hubert-Jan Henket, from December 1998. Cf. Ana Tostões and Liu Kecheng (eds.), *Docomomo International 1988–2012: Key Papers in Modern Architectural Heritage Conservation*, Xian, China Architecture & Building Press, 2014.

JÖRG HASPEL

were, at best, only marginally reflected in the list of proposals. The vast majority of the sites proposed as World Heritage candidates were distributed among the UNESCO regions of Europe and North America, while those of Latin America, the Caribbean and the Asia/Pacific region were hardly represented, and African and Arab states were not included at all. Essentially, the Docomomo Tentative List of 1997 embodied a geographic and thematic imbalance, and the need to correct this Eurocentric List of World Heritage was recognized a few years later by ICOMOS and UNESCO in the so-called Gap Report (2005).[2]

2. ICOMOS (ed.), *Monuments & Sites* – "The World Heritage List: Filling the Gaps – an Action Plan for the Future. An Analysis by ICOMOS," No. XII, Paris, ICOMOS, 2005. Compiled by Jukka Jokilehto, with contributions from Henry Cleere, Susan Denyer, and Michael Petzet.

UNESCO'S MODERN HERITAGE IS GAINING GROUND

The 1997 Docomomo Tentative List also marked the beginning of successful efforts to redress the lack of 20th century examples on the World Heritage List. This is even more the case if one looks beyond the narrow category of 20th century world architectural history, to a broader definition of the heritage of the last century, thus including historical sites such as the Nazi concentration camp at Auschwitz-Birkenau (Poland, inscribed in 1979), or Robben Island prison (South Africa, inscribed in 1999). In 2001, UNESCO's World Heritage Centre, ICOMOS, and Docomomo jointly initiated a program to identify, document, and promote modern architectural heritage, because properties and sites under this category were considered to have been underestimated in general and underrepresented on the World Heritage List in particular.[3] A series of international meetings followed from 2002 to 2005, covering UNESCO regions worldwide (Latin America, Asia/Pacific, Sub-Saharan Africa, and the Mediterranean Basin).

3. Ron van Oers and Sachiko Haraguchi (eds.), *World Heritage Papers* – "Identification and Documentation of Modern Heritage," No. 5, Paris, UNESCO World Heritage Centre, 2003.

Africa's modern World Heritage City Asmara in Eritrea was added to the UNESCO list in 2017: the Fiat-Tagliero Building (Giuseppe Pettazzi, 1938) served as a petrol station and as a futuristic symbol of modern transport and traffic technology.

The inscription of Le Corbusier's oeuvre, which was successfully completed in 2016 and included 17 sites in seven countries on three continents, and the inscription of a series of eight works by Frank Lloyd Wright on the 2019 UNESCO list, fulfilled the mandate of the first Docomomo Tentative List and UNESCO's heritage program to some extent. The 2017 inscription of the capital of Eritrea, entitled "Asmara: A Modernist African City," which documented close to a half-century of architectural history (1893–1941) up to World War II, also shed new light on the colonial and post-colonial legacy of Modernism on the African continent. In Germany alone, where there were still 43 heritage sites bearing the UNESCO label in 2020, more than ten entries can be attributed in whole or in part to 20th century heritage. In fact, for years now, not a session of the World Heritage Committee has gone by without the nomination and confirmation of Modern Movement monuments and sites, and many tentative lists include further candidates. Against the background of human history stretching back thousands of years, one can no longer claim that the 20th century is particularly underrepresented on the World Heritage List.

Today, the question is no longer a general one of whether the World Heritage List of monuments and sites of the 20th century should be better balanced in historical-chronological or geographical-regional terms, but above all: which architectural, urban planning and technical achievements and successes of the last century have made an outstanding contribution to the recent history of mankind and of the planet, and in which heritage sites can this extraordinary universal contribution be credibly affirmed and conveyed. Put bluntly, it should not primarily be a matter of expanding the list of possible architectural masterpieces of the last century in the UNESCO register, or of drawing up back-up lists for the oeuvre of underrepresented heroes of Modernism (including late- and post-Modernism), but of taking into account values and achievements without which the 21st century and the world in which we live today would be unthinkable.

IDENTIFYING THE GAPS IN MODERN WORLD HERITAGE

Social and cultural infrastructures of the 20th century, such as sports and recreational facilities, also deserve more attention in the World Heritage List. Cover of the latest ICOMOS Journal of the German National Committee on the heritage of the modern Olympic Games.

In looking back on the almost 50-year history of the World Heritage Convention, and making a cursory review of the more than 1100 World Heritage nominations, and almost 1800 proposals by signatory states for new nominations, what is notable is not any statistical underrepresentation of Modernism or the 20th century, but rather the conspicuous lack or even absence of outstanding examples of modern infrastructure, something that has determined the reality of modern life in the last century and will probably continue to do so in the next. This is true, in large part, for social, cultural, and ecological infrastructures – for example, the heritage of sports facilities or of the modern Olympic movement have been missing from the UNESCO list so far, as have more recent testimonies to social and health care or even green-blue infrastructures – but it is particularly striking with respect to the broad spectrum of technical and transportation infrastructure that the last century has brought forth and shaped extensively. Four heritage categories for technical and transport infrastructure of the last century can be used to identify a *desideratum* of World Heritage policy that will do greater justice to the cultural diversity of Modernity in the future.

ENERGY SUPPLY

To identify gaps in the World Heritage List, one does not only have to think of the testimony of nuclear energy generation, whose disastrous legacy in Chernobyl (Ukraine) or Fukushima (Japan) is likely to outlive mankind. Monumental gas tanks and historical gas production facilities – mostly shut down – are now listed as monuments in various countries, but are not yet represented on the UNESCO list. Examples of other forms of grid-based energy, such as electrical or long-distance heating networks, are also almost completely absent from the World Heritage List. The production and spread of electric power radically changed the world in the 20th century, not only in the energy sector but also in everyday life – from work to housing to leisure activities and, not least, metropolitan traffic, but the second Industrial Revolution has only exceptionally found its way into World Heritage. A rare example is the Rjukan-Notodden Industrial Heritage Site in Norway, registered

"Elektropolis Berlin": the Buchhändlerhof Substation, today called E-Werk (Hans Heinrich Müller, 1924–1928), is a prominent component of the local electricity network, related to heritage sites of energy supply and global players of the historic electrical industry.

in 2015, which includes hydro-electronic power plants to supply heavy industry, settlements, and transportation systems in the neighborhood. The legacy of power supply and the electrotechnical industry in Berlin, brought together as a whole under the label "Elektropolis,"[4] – from Peter Behrens' (1868–1940) AEG Turbine Hall, to the factories of Siemensstadt, and its power plants and substations – is internationally considered to be unique, but its nomination was ultimately unsuccessful because of the economic concerns of certain major companies.

4. Jörg Haspel and Hubert Staroste, "Das Erbe der Elektropolis Berlin," *ICOMOS – Journals of the German National Committee* – "Weltkulturerbe und Europäisches Kulturerbe-Siegel in Deutschland. Potentiale und Nominierungsvorschläge," Vol. 51, Berlin, ICOMOS, 2011, 74–78.

COMMUNICATION

In 2004, the Varberg Radio Station (Sweden), a working long-wave transmitter station of the early 1920s, and in 2019, Jodrell Bank Radio Observatory (UK) from the 1950s, were added to the World Heritage List as technological installations of radio and radio transmission. Radio and television towers have long accentuating cityscapes and landscapes – think of Vladimir Shukhov's (1853–1939) legendary hyperboloid grid net towers from the interwar period in Russia or the slender reinforced concrete structures of television and telecommunications towers after 1945 – but are not represented on the list, nor are radio facilities, broadcasting stations or television studios. The great inventions and developments in communications technology that revolutionized the world and brought it closer together in the 19th and 20th centuries, from telegraphy and telephony to digital media, have left behind architectural and technical testimonies that are worthy of preservation, but are a rarity on the World Heritage List.

SUPPLY AND DISPOSAL

Modern water supply and drainage systems as well as waste disposal and processing have decisively shaped how mankind has lived together in the 20th century, especially in large metropolises, and they have made possible the dense settlement types and urban structures of the modern age. The role of modern water management and its potential as World Heritage was recently comprehensively examined by James Douet in his study "The Water Industry as World Heritage"[5] for The International Committee for the Conservation of the Industrial Heritage (TICCIH) and ICOMOS, and was substantiated with 14 comparative case studies. Exceptions, such as the recent inscription of the "Water Management System of Augsburg," which includes 22 listed elements dating from the late Middle Ages to the last century, only serve to highlight how underrepresented this category of technical infrastructure is on the UNESCO register. Much the same can also be said for the field of waste disposal and processing.

5. James Douet, *The Water Industry as World Heritage. Thematic Study*, TICCIH, 2018, https://ticcih.org/wp-content/uploads/2018/05/TICCIH-Water-Report.pdf, accessed 13 July 2021.

TRAFFIC AND TRANSPORT SYSTEMS

Transport routes have now been examined in various thematic studies and bibliographies by TICCIH and ICOMOS, and are increasingly represented on the World Heritage List. Among them are historic rail routes, as well as man-made waterways and bridge structures, some of which date well into the 20th century. The old city center of Budapest, inscribed on the World Heritage List in 1987 and expanded in 2002, does incorporate a section of the subway, which entered operation in 1896 as the first metro on the continent. But none of the major cities in either Europe or America in which modern subways were founded are represented, such as London, Paris, and Moscow, or New York and Buenos Aires. The unique achievements in the history of intercontinental traffic and transport, mostly dating from the 20th century, have rarely found their way onto the World Heritage List. This is particularly true of the architectural and technical heritage of aviation and aerospace, which has not only rapidly accelerated and multiplied the worldwide interchange of people and goods, but also – in the case of aerial and satellite photography and space exploration – enormously expanded our knowledge of the planet and the whole solar system.

Aerospace heritage: the concrete structures of the vertical wind tunnel and motor-testing laboratory (1934–1936) in the aerodynamic park of the former Berlin-Johannisthal Airfield represents a gap in the list of modern World Heritage Sites.

FILLING THE GAPS WITH LANDMARKS OF TECHNICAL INFRASTRUCTURE?

The reasons why the technical infrastructure of the 20th century is so poorly represented on the World Heritage List are manifold. It cannot be because modern energy, communication, supply, and transport facilities are unimportant for the world today. Rather, this lacuna in the World Heritage register probably reflects an approach by architectural and urban planning historiography to Modernism that places greater emphasis on style, so that even outstanding works of engineering and epochal scientific and technical innovations are often only discussed in the margins. Secondly, technical infrastructure systems, for example in the fields of energy supply or metropolitan transportation, are often difficult to grasp visually and functionally, particularly when they owe their groundbreaking effect to extensive spatial connections and interconnections, i.e., they are highly complex and multi-layered, and cannot be condensed to be perceived or conveyed at a glance. Thirdly, the description of urban engineering as the "invisible intelligence" of urban planning[6] reminds us of the extent to which infrastructural facilities and services are removed from public perception when they are created and mediated because, for example, they are underground, difficult to access, or are non-material in nature anyway. And finally, technical infrastructures provide services in the general interest over generations, whose requirements change rapidly and therefore, not only need continuous care and maintenance, but also require ongoing renewal and modernization. Permanent technical infrastructure can only perform optimally if it can be continuously improved and adapted to changing needs.

6. Robert Kaltenbrunner, "Die unsichtbare Intelligenz," *Telepolis* [online], 18 October 2020, https://www.heise.de/tp/features/Die-unsichtbare-Intelligenz-4916182.html, accessed 13 July 2021.

The "metro" has become the epitome of modern metropolitan transport worldwide – the crossing under and accessing of cities by subways for local public transport promoted metropolitanization and the formation of urban agglomerations in the 20th century, but is scarcely represented as a category in the World Heritage List. Cover of a recent ICOMOS Journal of the German National Committee on post-war underground architecture in Europe.

UNESCO and its World Cultural Advisors – Docomomo, TICCIH, and ICOMOS, as well as ICCROM – understand that the World Heritage Convention is not merely an aesthetic concept, and that the World Heritage List is not merely a collection of the best-of the world's architectural history. They, and those like them, are committed to recognizing the achievements and cultural heritage of human history in all its broadness and diversity, and therefore, they also claim a place on the World Heritage List for the epochal achievements of modern infrastructure in the 20th century. The current updating of many national Tentative Lists for future nominations for World Heritage provides an opportunity to reflect on this gap identified within the UNESCO List, and to work more intensively toward a representative, balanced, and credible World Heritage List of Modernism.[7]

7. This article is an abridged version of a keynote address given by the author on 26 February 2021, as part of the Bauhaus Foundation Dessau's "Infrastructure" theme year at Docomomo Germany's 18th annual meeting, "Modern Movement, Infrastructure and Utilities."

LINA BO BARDI'S CASA DE VIDRO AND THE CHALLENGES OF MODERN ARCHITECTURE PRESERVATION

The Bardis' Casa de Vidro (Glass House) was designed in 1949–1951 and built in Morumbi, a suburb of São Paulo. It represents an international case of the architectural preservation of a modern residence, which is also associated with the institutional framework created by its owners, the couple Lina Bo Bardi (1914–1992) and Pietro Maria Bardi (1900–1999). This essay seeks to clarify the specificities of this framework, in both the Brazilian and the international contexts, and to discuss its current challenges, especially in regard to the current political and economic situation, which is unfavorable for the preservation of any cultural heritage.

THE PRESERVATION OF MODERN ARCHITECTURE IN BRAZIL AND DOCOMOMO

Lina Bo Bardi, Casa de Vidro, São Paulo, Brazil, 1951.

Brazil contains an extensive production of modern architecture, urbanism, and landscaping that dates back to the second decade of the 20th century and that reached its peak in the late 1950s, with the inauguration of Brasília in 1960. Unlike many countries that abandoned the postulates of Modernism after the 1960s, in Brazil they endured and were renewed in the work of new generations. The preservation of modern architecture coincides with the acknowledgment of its historicity, and an acceptance of the need for adaptations to the conditions of use and urbanity of the contemporary city.

The history of the preservation of this kind of architecture contrasts with its extent and quality. Although some of these constructions were listed after their inauguration in the 1940s, as a strategy of cultural affirmation in the disputes of the time, the preservation of the modern gained momentum with the creation of Docomomo Brazil in 1992. The first step of its affiliates – most of them professors and university researchers, who grew in number as graduate programs in the history of architecture and urbanism expanded – was to catalog this production.

This work expanded knowledge on the diffusion of modern architecture on Brazilian soil, identifying its presence in the most diverse regions. It showed the emergence of an architecture that was disseminated and reproduced throughout the country, and contrasted with a historiography centered on examples located either in Brasilia or large cities in the south-east region, such as Rio de Janeiro and São Paulo. Action to address its conservation, on the other hand, advanced more slowly, in the face of resistance to recognize its importance by preservation agencies, which prioritized the listing of constructions from the colonial period.

THE INSTITUTO BARDI AND THE CASA DE VIDRO

In this Brazilian context, the initiative by the Bardis, in 1986, to preserve their own residence must be understood as an exceptional effort, as should the couple's creation of an institution to continue their intellectual legacy, and their endowment of it with resources for this purpose. Although exceptional, the initiative was consistent with the pioneering path of the couple, both in widening the horizons of Brazilian art history and architecture, and in introducing new parameters for the restoration and adaptation of buildings of historical and cultural importance. In 1961–1962, Lina

RENATO ANELLI

had applied the principles of critical restoration in her adaptation of the Solar do Unhão as the seat of the Museum of Modern Art in Bahia. In 1977, she had proposed the conservation of an unlisted 1936 modern factory, to house the SESC Pompeia Leisure Center.[1]

1. Renato Anelli, "Bauhaus and Lina Bo Bardi: From the Modern Factory to the Pompéia Leisure Center," *Docomomo Journal*, No. 61 – "Education and Reuse," Lisbon, Docomomo International, 2019, 42–49.

In a memorandum to CONDEPHAAT (the Portuguese acronym for the Council for the Defense of the Archaeological, Artistic and Tourist Heritage of the State of São Paulo), Pietro Bardi argued for the dual action of listing their residence and creating a cultural institution:

> Allow me to complement my wife Lina's idea in terms of the possibility of designating our house and art objects for a foundation capable of transforming it into a curious example of a dwelling of immigrants who contributed to the promotion of the arts in Brazil in the fields of architecture (the residence in Morumby, the MASP building on Avenida Paulista, the restoration of the Pompeia Factory, and the restoration of the Politeama Theater in Jundiaí), museography (the creation of MASP and notable donations), journalism (the magazines Habitat, Mirante das Artes, and Vogue Arte) and publishing (a vast bibliography). I think that the Morumby House, once restored at our expense, with its forest-garden, could be adapted with a series of works of art of a certain value, to one day be visited by a public interested in experiencing a portion of the history of the renovation of national museography. *(...)* In practical terms: the Foundation's responsibility will be the conservation, and custodianship of a collection of works of art *(...)*. The entire project should be studied by a representative of the foundation and the undersigned.[2]

2. Pietro M. Bardi, Letter addressed to Modesto Carvalhosa (25 October 1985) in CONDEPHAAT. Landmarking process, No. 24.938, 1 July 1986, São Paulo, 1986.

The state listing of the Casa de Vidro, proposed in 1985, was approved in 1986. The Quadrante Institute, in turn, was created shortly after, in 1990, and renamed *Instituto Lina Bo e P. M. Bardi* in 1993, a year after Lina's death in 1992. Its goals are defined in its founding minutes, "the objectives of the Institute are exclusively cultural and artistic, and also related to the history of art and architecture, capable of both promoting and practicing any activity inherent to its ends."[3]

3. Minutes of the general meeting of 3 May 1990, in which the Institute Quadrante was created.

The couple sold a painting by Francisco Goya (1746–1828), from their collection, to provide an endowment to preserve the Casa de Vidro and achieve their goals. These resources made possible the restoration of the house in 1993, and also supported several cultural projects.

Among the most significant of these were the organization of Lina Bo Bardi's collection, and the mounting of an exhibition, accompanied by a catalog and video, which honored the architect at the Museum of Art of São Paulo (MASP) in 1993. Then a publishing house was created that produced finely printed and abundantly illustrated books on Brazilian architects such as Affonso Eduardo Reidy (1909–1964), Vilanova Artigas (1915–1985), and João Filgueiras Lima (Lelé) (1931–2014). The Bardi Institute had taken its first steps toward achieving its primary objectives.

In 1995, sick and retired from MASP, Pietro Bardi donated the house to the Institute, who used it as its headquarters after his death and maintained its original characteristics. With his death, in 1999, the couple's wish was thus fulfilled. Nevertheless, over the years enthusiasm for the original project cooled. Due to its constructional characteristics and its aggressive garden environment, the house required constant interventions to preserve it. In 2008, new conservation actions were needed, to restore slabs, roofing, frames, and glazing – all of which was carried out by Marcelo Suzuki (1956–), a former collaborator of Lina, who was responsible for the 1993 restoration.

The Institute's mission focused on conserving the collection and making it accessible to researchers, whether Brazilians or foreigners. A specialized team was formed to conserve the drawings, photos, and documents. With resources from cultural initiatives by state-owned companies, and a research support agency, it was possible to provide the collection with special furniture, to partially digitize it, and make it available for online consultation. Thanks to these improved conditions, the Institute and the Casa de Vidro was able to satisfy the growing international interest in Lina's work, resulting in exhibitions and publications in several countries, especially in 2014, when her centenary was celebrated.

Nonetheless, the original endowment was becoming depleted, making the institution dependent on the support of cultural initiatives by state-owned companies, copyright fees from new editions of its furniture, the distribution of images, and loans of items from the collection.

THE CONSERVATION MANAGEMENT PLAN

Cover of *Casa de Vidro – Lina Bo Bardi architect: Conservation Management Plan* (2019), supported by the Getty Foundation.

Obtaining support from the Getty Foundation, in the 2016 edition of the Keeping it Modern program, opened new perspectives for both the Casa de Vidro and the Institute.[4] The methodology of the Conservation Management Plan (CMP) incorporated the symbiotic relationship between architecture and institution. Thus, a policy was established that associated institutional development with the conservation of the property, and covered the building, the garden, and the collection.

The work of developing the CMP was carried out by researchers from the Institute of Architecture and Urbanism of the University of São Paulo, through a partnership with the Bardi Institute, under the coordination of this author. This work was organized on four fronts: cataloging historical documents, digital surveys, diagnosis of buildings, and diagnosis of the garden.[5] The coordinator was also responsible for analyzing the studies and creating, in conjunction with the Bardi Institute, a Target Plan capable of guiding the group's management. The work started in 2016 and was completed in 2019 – a three-year period during which Brazil changed a great deal.

As already mentioned, after the endowment had become depleted, the main source of funds for the operation of the Bardi Institute were cultural projects undertaken with the Ministry of Culture. Petrobras' support started in 2014 and was renewed in 2016, but was abruptly interrupted after the change of government in the second half of that year. The impact of this interruption led to a drastic reduction in the workforce and the prioritization of the search for resources to maintain the institution. Nonetheless, with support from the Getty Foundation, the research work was carried out as originally planned.

One of the activities foreseen in the project was a seminar, held in 2017, with the curators of three houses located in the USA: Philip Johnson's Glass House, Mies van der Rohe's Farnsworth House, and Charles (1907–1978) and Ray Eames'

4. Renato Anelli (ed.), *Casa de Vidro – Lina Bo Bardi architect: Conservation Management Plan*, São Paulo, Instituto Bardi Casa de Vidro, 2019, also available at: https://www.getty.edu/foundation/initiatives/current/keeping_it_modern/report_library/index.html

5. Project Team coordinator: Renato Anelli, Adjunct coordinator: Ana Lúcia Cerávolo, Supervisor: Marcelo Suzuki. Task coordinators: Aline Coelho Sanches (historic documentation), Márcio M. Fabríccio (Digital documentation), Marcelo Balzani (3D scanning), João A. Rossignolo (Structure and pathology), Ricardo Couceiro Bento (Structural report), Luciana B. Schenk (Historical Garden), Darkon Roque (Graphic design). Sol Camacho as Cultural Director of Instituto Bardi.

(1912–1988) Eames House. In addition to technical issues concerning the conservation of these houses, aspects of their institutional frameworks and financial sustainability were also shared.

The first two houses, although donated to the National Trust for Historic Preservation, have survived thanks to private donations, entrance tickets, and hosting of events. The Eames House, on the other hand, became the property of the Eames Foundation, which raises resources for its maintenance by means of copyright fees from the reproduction of the couple's collection and furniture, which is still in regular commercial production.

Superimposition of the drone image with the Casa de Vidro site plan.

It was observed that none of them preserved the collection of projects by their authors, which were donated to university libraries and museums. The Glass House and the Eames House maintain their collection of furniture and works of art displayed in their original layout, while the interior of the Farnsworth House was recreated according to the architect's designs, as the first owner had furnished it independently.

By the time Petrobras support was interrupted, the Casa de Vidro had already started a management plan based on a trinomial of: admission tickets, rental from hosting events, and copyright fees. The exchange of experiences with the curators of the three houses enabled this approach to be further developed. Thematic exhibitions of items from the collection, which started in 2013 with the exhibition *Anhangabaú, Jardim Tropical* (Anhangabaú, Tropical Garden), became more frequent and longer, occupying the main hall and altering its configuration, which still maintained its characteristics from the 1990s. Despite expanding visits and generating income for the Institute, this practice was widely criticized for frustrating visitors who wanted to see the interior of the Bardi couple's home.

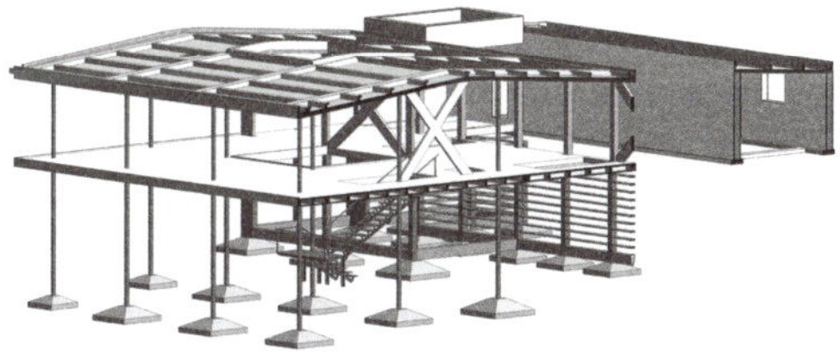

Axonometric view of the structure of the main house of Casa de Vidro.

CONSERVATION OF THE CASA DE VIDRO

As to physical conservation, the CMP had the good sense to understand the significance of the garden for the architecture of the house, and to adopt an integrated approach to it. The lush tropical greenery, which currently surrounds the house, was almost entirely planted by Lina after its construction. The presence of the garden was conceived as part of the architecture; the transparent living room opened toward the suburban surrounding, still empty at the time. The room appears to blend with the treetops that hide the disorderly urbanization of the Pinheiros river valley from view. Thus, it creates the impression of being in a lush forest, an idyllic vision of living in the midst of tropical nature.

In the CMP, the landscaping team was just as important as that of the civil engineers and architects. They surveyed, and cataloged, and the management plan they drew up for the tree vegetation and understory occupies 70 of the 230 pages of the architectural inventory.

With regard to construction, the CMP addressed the four existing buildings on the property: the main house, the caretaker's house, the garage, and the studio. Built in different periods, they embody the transformations Lina went through in her life. While the main house and the caretaker's house represent her approximation to the modern Brazilian architecture of the period, the masonry garage, covered with a mass of rolled pebbles, represents her first inflection, in 1958, toward the organic architecture propagated by Bruno Zevi (1918–2000). The studio, from 1986, was built with a wooden structure and cladding, and had a tiled roof, incorporating into the Casa de Vidro complex, her interpretation of popular architecture.

Among various technical aspects concerning preservation, the main house presented two special and interrelated challenges: analyzing its structure and finding out why the glass broke so frequently. The structure was first designed by Pier Luigi Nervi (1891–1979), an old friend of Pietro Bardi. According to the survey carried out in the *Fondo Nervi*, at the *Centro Studi e Archivio della Comunicazione* (CSAC), in Parma, the structure of the room was to be entirely in steel, with tubular columns and laminated "C" profile beams. Nervi himself found it difficult to produce this system in Brazil and recommended some adaptations to the owners. The project was developed by an engineer of Italian origin, Túlio Stucchi (1914–1989), who kept the very thin tubular columns, filled with reinforced concrete. However, the rest of the structure was made up of beams, columns, and reinforced concrete slabs. Stucchi applied the system commonly used in the work of other modern architects in São Paulo: alveolar reinforced concrete slabs for the raised floor of the living room; a reinforced concrete structure inside masonry walls in the bedrooms, bathrooms, and kitchen; and structural masonry in the laundry area. In other words, the construction actually had three structural systems, and not just the two usually reported by historians.

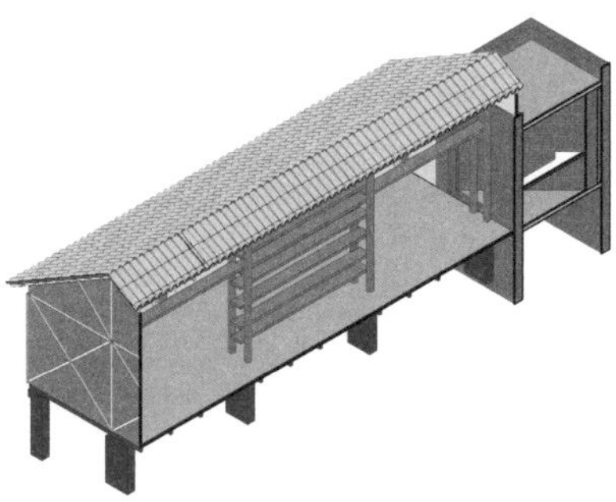

Lina Bo Bardi, studio at Casa de Vidro,
São Paulo, Brazil, 1986. Axonometric view.

The structural report, based on the design drawings and on the carbonation test of the concrete, attested to the stability of the buildings, even today. The evaluation of the structural elements made it possible to identify a potential horizontal displacement in the roof slab of about 0.27 centimeter, and a displacement between floors of up to 0.15 centimeter. Although these displacements are acceptable for structural stability, they could have been the cause of the glass breakage, since the glazing pockets of the frames had no expansion joints. It is assumed that the professional responsible for the structural calculations predicted different horizontal displacements between the slabs, and to reduce them, created two X-shaped interlocks between the columns, inserted into internal masonry walls next to the stairs and the courtyard.

However, the temperature difference between the roof slab, which is exposed to the sun, and the floor slab, that is permanently in the shade, aggravated the difference in the amplitude of the horizontal movements of the two slabs, and may have contributed to the frequent breakage of the glass. Consequently, elastomers will be inserted between the glass and the glazing pocket, and between the frames and the slabs, designed to absorb these movements and avoid breakage.

PLAN OF GOALS, ACTIONS, AND PROJECTS

The CMP required a Declaration of Significance, a statement agreed between all stakeholders to guide the next steps. In this case, it is a Matrix of Significance, in which the Aesthetic Value, Symbolic Value, Authenticity, Degree of Irreplaceability, and Overall Significance of the main components of the complex are evaluated. This matrix serves as a reference for interventions, especially to identify opportunities to replace some of them, whenever necessary.

The Management and Preservation Policy is structured into six goals, which are broken down into actions and projects. The goals are divided into:

- Preserve the aesthetic integrity of the main house;
- Preserve the adjoining buildings;
- Make the garden an object of enjoyment for visitors;
- Institutional – consolidate its use as a house museum;
- Provide the Casa de Vidro with adequate facilities, infrastructure, and routines;
- Plan new buildings and expand their urban/social insertion.

The institutional goal permeates all the others, from those aimed at the conservation of physical/aesthetic characteristics to that of creating conditions for the necessary adaptations to the proposed use, as a house museum. The proposal of a Master Plan for expansion and urban integration expresses the persistence of the Bardi Institute's outlook of subsistence and growth, despite the clear signs of the worsening of the country's political, economic, and cultural situation. To establish the guidelines for expansion, studies for annexes to host the Institute have been evaluated, dating back to the first known sketch, made by Pietro Bardi in a 1976 letter to his friend Ettore Camisasca (1922–1995), then in Italy.

The physical interventions in the architectural complex and the house's garden were ranked in terms of priorities. The Tree Management Plan, the change of roof tiles and the maintenance of gutters, the elaboration of a universal accessibility plan and a fire safety plan should be the first steps. In 2019, after the conclusion of the CMP, the first projects were developed and presented to preservation agencies for their approval.

SUSTAINABILITY OF THE INSTITUTO BARDI

In 2020, the Bardi Institute had begun to restore its financial balance, in accordance with the guidelines established in 2017: with receipts from visits, copyrights, and the promotion of events in the house. However, the outbreak of the COVID-19 pandemic, in March 2020, completely changed this situation. The disastrous policy to combat the virus adopted by Brazil ended up extending the peak of contamination, creating a long and growing level of fatalities.

With insufficient visitors to generate income, without exhibitions for loaning the collection, and without a publishing market to distribute images to, the Bardi Institute was forced to reduce its activities and staff to a minimum, to preserve its few existing funds and get through the pandemic. This situation contrasts with the enormous international recognition of the architect Lina Bo Bardi.

GENESIS AND RECONSTRUCTION OF VLADIMIR MÜLLER'S VILLA IN OLOMOUC

I am very familiar with the "Loosian cube"[1] villa in Olomouc. I visited it for the first time in 2007, in order to write about it for the book *Slavné vily Olomouckého kraje* (The Famous Villas of the Olomouc Region).[2] On that occasion, it was Jitka Hynková, Vladimir Müller's (1889–1967) daughter, who introduced me to it. I returned for the second time, four years later, with a paint brush in my hand to help the new owner, a friend from my art studies, with preparations for moving in. That was how I came to spend several hours repainting in white an area with illogically positioned walls. We took the opportunity to discuss the building's architect, Paul Engelmann (1891–1965), his architecture, and his concept of the house. The main things I learnt about were the wonderful, almost fateful, coincidences which led his family to purchase the house. After the death of Vladimir Müller, the first and original owner of the villa, his daughter, who lived abroad at the time, put the house

Paul Engelmann, Villa Müller, Olomouc, Czech Republic, 1927–1928. View from the historic city center, 1930.

up for sale. The house had sentimental value, and the daughter was worried that new owners would not show much respect for the protected property, and would change it to suit a 21st century aesthetic, ignoring the subtleties of Engelmann's architecture. This led to the intervention of the head of the Olomouc Museum of Art, Pavel Zatloukal, who recommended David Voda (1976–) and his wife Sabine as buyers. They were an obvious choice, as German literature and the arts were not only their passion, but also the subject of their research. In exchange for certain financial benefits, they committed themselves to the property and accepted that the genius *loci* of the house must remain, including: "sundry objects, books, crockery, and miscellaneous items collected since the 1920s."[3] This meant, in the later words of David Voda, a rather odd transition and "under the influence of the house's myriad *objets d'art*, the need to change everyday habits and rituals."[4] This would have been impossible without gaining an understanding of the architect's character, and what they learnt about the architect, philosopher, and poet Paul Engelmann, born on 14 June, 130 years ago, led to an "almost lifelong program"[5] and was a key element in the restorative reconstruction of the house.

1. Looking at Vladimir Müller's villa in Olomouc, the exterior similarities with Adolf Loos' Villa Müller in Prague (1928–1930), his typical cube house, are evident.
2. Pavel Zatloukal (ed.), *Slavné vily Olomouckého kraje*, Prague, Foibos, 2007.
3. David Voda, "Žít Raumplan," *Stavba*, No. 3, 2020, 8.
4. Conversation between Jakub Potůček and David Voda, Olomouc, 15 August 2021.
5. David Voda, *op. cit.*, 8.

*translated by Alec Solomon

JAKUB POTŮČEK*

ARCHITECT PAUL ENGELMANN AND HIS FAMILY

Paul Engelmann was born into a Jewish family in Olomouc. The family raised creatively talented children. Paul's brother Peter (later known as Peter Eng) (1892–1939) shot to fame as a painter in Britain, and a pioneer of Austrian animated films. His sister Anna (1897–1942) became a famous illustrator of children's books. Having completed his high-school education at the German-speaking school in Olomouc, Paul enrolled to study the Viennese technique in architecture in 1909. However, he soon interrupted his studies and joined the services of the journal *Die Fackel* led by playwright, poet, literary critic, and journalist Karl Kraus (1874–1936), and became its secretary. Indeed, it was in this magazine, in 1911, that he published his poem "Das Haus auf dem Michaelerplatz," in which he unhesitatingly called the Goldman & Salatsch Department Store, "the first sign of a new era." It is more than apparent from the verses that he was deeply impressed by the scandalous and ground-breaking work of Adolf Loos (1870–1933). Indeed, he delighted in the personality of its creator. It was, therefore, logical that, when the famous inciter of riots and *bon-vivant* opened a private school of architecture in the Austrian capital in 1912, Engelmann became one of his first and most loyal students. An equally important moment in his life was his acquaintance with Ludwig Wittgenstein (1889–1951), whom he first met in 1916 in Olomouc, where Wittgenstein was attending a preparatory school for artillery officers. "One afternoon the maid told me," Engelmann later recalls, "that there is a gentleman who wishes to speak with me. I went to the back room (...) where we sat with friends in the evening. The afternoon sun shone upon the young man in uniform. Wittgenstein brought me greetings from my then teacher, and prominent Viennese architect, Adolf Loos." From that day on, Wittgenstein, who allegedly also longed to stay in the tower of Olomouc's town hall, became a favorite guest of the Engelmann family, whom he fell in love with after they lovingly cared for him when he became seriously ill. Young intellectuals met regularly in the house where the siblings Anna, Paul, and Peter lived. Friends of the house began to refer to it by the nickname "Palais am Mauritzplatz," and Wittgenstein, who was already working on a major philosophical work later known as *Tractatus logico philosophicus*, was at the center of the so-called Engelmann circle until he was deported from the city.

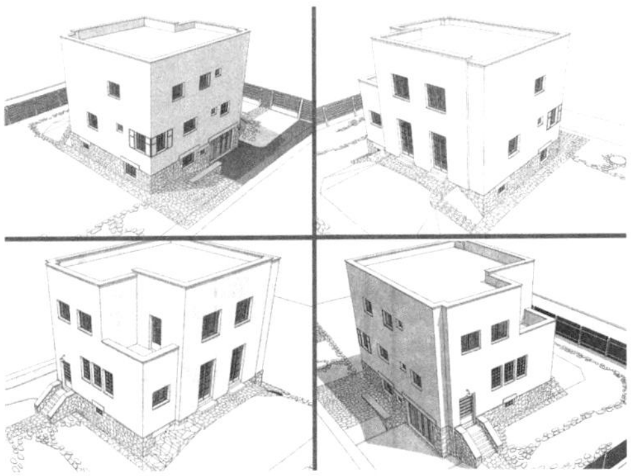

Restoration of Villa Müller in Olomouc by Michal Sborwitz, 2016–2019. Axonometric views.

PAUL ENGELMANN AND ADOLF LOOS

Before both friends met once again in Vienna, at the outset of the 20th century, Engelmann cooperated with Loos in the design of a villa in Olomouc for the state railway inspector Hermann Konstandt. The project, designed between 1916 and 1919, already showed evidence of Loos' experiments with *raumplan*. Surprisingly, he considered decorating the villa, but this was never realized. Along with a student project for a classical-themed villa from 1912, the project commissioned in 1925 by Ludwig's sister Margaret Wittgenstein-Stonborough (1882–1958), served as a starting point for Engelmann. The architect became more engaged in designing the urban villa, or new-age palace, the following year. As Margaret wanted to involve her family in the project, Engelmann moved to Vienna, and Ludwig Wittgenstein was persuaded to cooperate in the design. Despite the architect's wishes, the villa did not follow *raumplan* principles, and the final version, whose construction began at the turn of 1926–1927, was attributed to "P. Engelmann & L. Wittgenstein Architekten," and only completed in their absence two years later by Jacques Groag (1892–1962), who took over the work. He was another pupil from Olomouc of Loos' private school and, as a close friend of Engelmann, was invited to represent him in supervising the work. Although Wittgenstein was fanatical about each and every detail, Engelmann's departure was not prompted by any disagreement with him, but by a new commission in his native Olomouc.

Entrance front before the restoration.

Entrance front after the restoration.

THE CLIENT VLADIMÍR MÜLLER

Vladimír Müller, a sportsman and head of Olomouc's State Land Office (which had given Müller the plot and a mortgage), commissioned a family house in 1927. It was to be built in the new Letná area. It was designed and built relatively quickly between the summer of 1927 and the following July. This was thanks to the generally modest and economical design of the house. As Engelmann wished to avoid any ostentation, he went for the "Loos cube" design with an area of garden. He and his teacher considered the garden to be of primary importance. Thus, the garden, particularly the alpinum at ground level, can be considered an integral part of the interior, divided by *raumplan*. This concept, unique in terms of architecture, is visible in both floors and is most prominent in the central living space, which the architect connected to a low-lying study, and indirectly connected to the dining room and kitchen. An odd corner space, along with a veranda, occupying a single square meter, is found adjacent to the logically situated kitchen and larder. This is one of the many "Dadaistic" elements which lends the design a certain level of irony. "The entrance and exit points of the villa are areas of curiosity. The staircase at the entrance starts just before the threshold. Thus, when exiting, one is forced to pull the door handle on the first step. Otherwise, it is impossible to open the door."[6] The floor plan of the first floor is also quite odd, as is the garage. It is necessary to turn the car through 90 degrees to drive it into the garage. This is one of the many odd elements in a house where pretty much everything is odd. For example, there are window frames, with flowery wallpaper, which are actually built-in cupboards. These windows serve to enlarge the space visually, and provide a pleasant, homely atmosphere thanks to functional and symbolic elements. Built-in bookshelves, benches and plug sockets, tiles and fittings, wooden staircases and bathroom tiling add to the ambience. All of this has remained intact within the house, but would have been lost under any other owners. After all, the house has survived a war, changes in society, and major flooding.

6. *Idem.*, 9.

THE 2016–2019 RENOVATION BY MICHAL SBORWITZ

After some time had elapsed, the new tenants realized that they had been living amongst "perpetually started but unfinished pieces of work."[7] This led to a decision to take drastic action. They moved out of the house and began a complete restoration. After a number of years of research on Engelmann, they now had a clear idea of what was needed, and just had to find a suitable designer. Michal Sborwitz was a logical choice for the task. David Voda was well-acquainted with the Prague-based architect's work, in particular, his renovation of the Olomouc Museum of Arts in the 1990s. Furthermore, the architect had extensive experience and a rich portfolio of renovations of well-known modern monuments, namely: Josef Gočár's (1880–1945) Villa Bauer (1912–1914) in Libodřice, and Vladimír Grégr's (1902–1943) functional Schauer Mansion (1933–1934) in Jevany.

7. *Ibidem.*, 8.

Along with staff from the National Heritage authority, Müller's granddaughter Šárka was present during discussions in which Voda set out his proposal for the "heritage site and for the repair of Vladimir and Helena Müller's villa." The first third of the work, between 2016 and 2019, revolved around the restoration of the interior, following the partial replacement of the building services, the renovation of the bathroom and the restoration of the stucco. The second stage involved the removal of the garage area from the 1930s, the non-original roofing above the entrance, the massive staircase guardrail, and the wooden pergola in the loggia. This pergola was attributed to Zdeněk Hynek (1922–2006), Müller's son-in-law, who served as Olomouc's chief architect between 1966 and 1971. Once the outdoor stucco had been restored, paths in the garden and, later, fencing were taken care of in the final stages of the work. Following the guiding principle of retaining original elements intact, the work was limited to restoration, conservation, and the finishing

Living room after the restoration.

Bedroom on the first floor after the restoration.

of specific details. Certain features of suitable style were added, such as switches, lighting, bathroom tiles, a bathtub, and radiators. The original exterior façade from the 1960s and 1970s was preserved, but complemented by a layer of white modern mineral stucco, typical of the period, while the high, quarry-stone masonry plinth was repointed. The new fencing was, naturally, based on the original, and consisted of concrete foundations, posts in the same material, completed with wooden slats. The neglected garden paths and the paved areas around the house, much increased after the demolition of the garage, were complemented with limestone pavers. The new "break between the garden and the entrance has been articulated by a ramp on the facade, and a wall with a bench,"[8] i.e. elements typical of Loos.

8. Michal Sborwitz, "Památková a stavební obnova vily Vladimíra a Heleny Müllerových," *Stavba*, No. 3, 2020, 2.

What most fascinates me is the fact that, thanks to the owners' knowledge of central European modern culture, the house still serves its original purpose, despite the restoration. This is in sharp contrast to Mies' Villa Tugendhat in Brno or Loos' Villa Müller in Prague, which have been transformed into museums.

SAVING A GEM OF MODERNIST ARCHITECTURE IN SLOVAKIA

The Jaromír Krejcar Society is a non-profit organization named in honor of the prominent Prague architect Jaromír Krejcar (1895–1950), who was one of the most talented Czech architects of the interwar period. The "poet of construction," as his companions used to call him. Along with the philosopher Karel Teige (1900–1951), poets Jaroslav Seifert (1901–1986), and Vítezlav Nezval (1900–1958), he was a member of the cult *avant-garde* group Devětsil. He was a student of the significant Czech architect Ján Kotěra (1871–1923), and even in one of his first works, the Olympic Palace in Prague from 1926, won the admiration of Le Corbusier himself. In 1937, Jaromír Krejcar also built the Czechoslovak Pavilion at the World Exhibition of Art and Technology (Expo) in Paris. With its glass and steel pavilion on the banks of the Seine, in the immediate vicinity of the Eiffel Tower, he paid tribute to constructivist architecture. The pavilion won a Gold Medal at the exhibition in Paris.

However, his most significant and last intact work is the Machnáč Sanatorium in Trenčianske Teplice, a town in Western Slovakia. It is located at the end of the park of this picturesque spa town, situated on thermal sulfur springs. The Machnáč Sanatorium was established through a competition in 1929 and was subsequently built in 1932. After its commissioning, the building was described by Karel Teige as the most remarkable work of Modern Movement architecture in the country.

THE JAROMÍR KREJCAR SOCIETY

The establishment of the Jaromír Krejcar Society was initiated after ten years of intensive efforts to save the Machnáč Sanatorium. Due to the privatization in 1997, it found itself in a complicated and obscure tangle of ownership rights, and after 2002, it fell into disrepair. Exactly ten years ago, the art group Abandoned (re)creation was established by photographer Andrea Kalinová and architect Martin Zaiček. Apart from initial attempts to draw attention to the significance and unjust fate of the Machnáč Sanatorium, such as a series of student workshops and several artistic interventions in the building itself, since 2015 they have also been busy producing a series of publications. Among them, just to mention a few, are the pocket guide *C20: Guide to the architecture of Trenčianske Teplice*,[1] a monograph about the Machnáč Sanatorium entitled *OFF SEASON*,[2] and the book *Architecture of Care: Slovak Spas in the Second Half of the 20th Century*.[3] In 2018 they also brought out a documentary film *Po sezóne* (Off Season).[4] In addition to film festivals at home and abroad, it was repeatedly broadcast by the National Slovak Television. These efforts, naturally, resulted in the need to establish a new legal entity with the sole goal of saving and renovating the Machnáč Sanatorium in Trenčianske Teplice. The Jaromír Krejcar Society brought together experts, cultural and educational institutions, the government, business, and banking sectors, grant schemes, and the media, and united them all at the national "Czechoslovakian" and international European levels, to save the Machnáč Sanatorium.

The founders of the Jaromír Krejcar Society are the rector of the Academy of Fine Arts and Design in Bratislava, Bohunka Koklesová, and both founding members of Abandoned (re)creation, Andrea Kalinová and Martin Zaiček. The Jaromír Krejcar Society put particular emphasis on the importance of strong representation, and therefore, the members of its Management Board also include

1. Martin Zaiček, *C20: Guide to the Architecture of Trenčianske Teplice*, Bratislava, Archimera, 2016.
2. Petra Hlaváčková (ed.), Martin Zaiček and Andrea Kalinová, *OFF SEASON*, Bratislava, Archimera, 2017.
3. Martin Zaiček, Andrea Kalinová, and Petra Hlaváčková, *Architecture of Care: Slovak Spas in the Second Half of the 20th Century*, Bratislava, Archimera, 2020.
4. Documentary film *Po sezóne* (Off Season), directed by Andrea Kalinová, 2018.

MARTIN ZAIČEK

the former dean of the Faculty of Architecture in Bratislava and current vice-rector of the Slovak University of Technology in Bratislava, architect Ľubica Vitková, the director of the Slovak working party of Docomomo International, Henrieta Moravčíková, as well as the mayor of Trenčianske Teplice, Zuzana Frajková Ďurmeková. All the major educational scientific institutions in Slovakia and the Czech Republic, such as the Slovak University of Technology, and the Academy of Fine Arts and Design in Bratislava, but also the Academy of Arts, Architecture and Design in Prague, and the Brno University of Technology, support the activities of the Jaromír Krejcar Society.

WHY SAVE THE MACHNÁČ SANATORIUM

One might with some justification pose the question why the Jaromír Krejcar Society decided to save the Machnáč Sanatorium in Trenčianske Teplice when many other monuments are also falling into disrepair in Slovakia? A number of arguments in favor of the sanatorium come to mind.

The Machnáč Sanatorium is an exceptionally valuable example of functionalist *avant-garde* architecture built between the world wars in the Czechoslovak Republic. This iconic Functionalist building – the Slovak equivalent of the famous Villa Tugendhat in Brno by Mies van der Rohe, or other UNESCO monuments such as the Bauhaus Dessau by Walter Gropius and the Paimio Sanatorium by Alvar Aalto – is considered a gem of European Modernism. Moreover, with its typology as a medical facility, and innovative organization of space, it represents a unique example of social thinking in the architecture of the Modern Movement in the 1930s.

Jaromír Krejcar, Machnáč Sanatorium, Trenčianske Teplice, Slovakia, 1929–1932. Metal facade with balconies facing the park.

FUTURE USE OF THE MACHNÁČ SANATORIUM

It is planned to return the Machnáč Sanatorium to its role as a spa facility, with a café and restaurant services, as well as accommodation for the general public. It will be complemented by an international residency center for artists and architects. A new institution is to be established here – the Documentation Center of 20th Century Architecture – with a library and a space for hosting smaller cultural activities, which Trenčianske Teplice currently lacks. The purpose and entire cultural program of the Machnáč Sanatorium were conceived as part of the region's cultural development, and the candidacy of the nearby town of Trenčín as European Capital of Culture in 2026. To renovate the sanatorium, the Jaromír Krejcar Society is working with a team of young architects and experts on monument restoration from the Slovak design studio "ô".

AUTHENTIC RESTORATION

The Machnáč Sanatorium is a unique world monument, and therefore, it must be restored as a UNESCO World Heritage Site and be rigidly and uncompromisingly preserved rather than simply adjusted for reuse. The form of the building must not be adapted to new functions that do not respect its layout, materials, and operating limits. The Jaromír Krejcar Society is convinced that this unique work should not be forcibly adapted to new purposes but, on the contrary, potential functions should be adapted to enable the original building to be fully retained – inverting the initial Modern Movement slogan of "Form follows function" into "Function follows form." Of course, some people may be put off by a lack of ensuite bathrooms, but many examples from around the world suggest otherwise. For instance, the world-famous Bauhaus in Dessau offers a similar type of accommodation in a former student dormitory, and complaints are rare.

CURRENT STATE OF THE SANATORIUM

Unfortunately, the sanatorium is currently in a state of neglect, due to issues of ownership. The Machnáč Sanatorium is currently owned by Keorlen Trade, s.r.o., based in Uherské Hradiště in the Czech Republic. The only statutory member of the company – one Milan Baláž from Trenčín in Slovakia – is an executive whose connection to the property is unclear. However, since 2008, ownership of the Machnáč Sanatorium has already changed five times, mostly to mailbox companies whose owners have personal connections to each other. These owners have left the monument unprotected and unmaintained since 2012. Thus, the Machnáč Sanatorium has been left to the mercy of vandals, with the resulting loss from its interior of a number of valuable original objects and materials (brass railings, cast iron radiators, electrical and plumbing components, sanitary and kitchen equipment, etc.). The Regional Monuments Board in Trenčín has repeatedly demanded redress, and imposed numerous fines, none of which have yet been paid. Even after repeated calls, the owner has not responded to the Jaromír Krejcar Society and has ignored its efforts to solve the problem.

Exterior view of the sanatorium's current state.

Exterior visualization of the sanatorium after the proposed restoration by studio "ô" (Martin Varga and Martin Kvitkovský).

MISSION OF THE JAROMÍR KREJCAR SOCIETY

The Jaromír Krejcar Society is dedicated to the preservation, restoration, and subsequent protection and maintenance of Krejcar's buildings, in particular the former Machnáč Sanatorium in Trenčianske Teplice. The building is emblematic of the construction of modern Slovakia in the interwar period, and an architectural image of its nascent urban and civil society. It represents social and humanistic values that cross borders and link Slovak architecture with the best that emerged in the European environment. Few of Jaromír Krejcar's architectural works have been preserved. The Machnáč Sanatorium is probably the last building where the mastery of this exceptional architect can be admired, moreover, in its original state. By saving and restoring the Machnáč Sanatorium building, Slovakia would acquire a world-class architectural monument returned to its original authentic form.

The primary goal of the Jaromír Krejcar Society is to reach an agreement with the building's owner, and since 2020 we have repeatedly contacted him to negotiate a buyout but, unfortunately, our efforts have gone unanswered. In May 2021, we sent the owner our last direct offer to buy the building for the considerable sum of 416,000 Euro. This was the amount determined by an independent authorized expert to be the general value of the building. The Jaromír Krejcar Society finally initiated officially in September 2021 expropriation proceedings in the public interest pursuant to Act no. 282/2015 Coll as amended, regarding the expropriation of land and buildings and the forced restriction of the right of ownership in the public interest.

Machnáč Sanatorium. View of the sanatorium's staircase hall in its current state.

Machnáč Sanatorium. Visualization of the sanatorium's staircase hall after the proposed restoration. The original color scheme was unknown until the renovation proposal. It was investigated by Peter Szalay as part of the restoration proposal.

This expropriation procedure has never before been applied in Slovakia for the purpose of protecting a monument. However, it is an established legal procedure and its application was also supported by the District Court in Trenčín, and by the Regional Court of Appeal. In 2020, it prohibited the owner from transferring ownership to third parties, thus paving the way for our procedure. Further, the Constitution of Slovakia enshrines, as well, the protection of cultural heritage which, in some cases, takes precedence over private property. This is the case if extreme neglect of care or dereliction of responsibility lead to the extinction of cultural heritage. Being thus possible that the legal process takes several years, the condition of the national cultural monument may deteriorate further.

Poster for the documentary film *Po sezóne* (Off Season), directed by Andrea Kalinová, 2018. The film comprises footage of the Machnáč Sanatorium.

RENOVATION COSTS AND FINANCING

Rigorous restoration and conservation approaches should preserve and enhance all the original qualities of the building. Reference costs, calculated from similar renovations in Europe such as the Villa Tugendhat in the Czech Republic, and the Zonnestraal Sanatorium in The Netherlands, suggest that the price-parity construction cost of a comprehensive renovation in Slovakia starts at 3000 Euro per square meter, which would come to approximately 15 million Euro for the Machnáč Sanatorium. If the Jaromír Krejcar Society manages to acquire ownership of the building, as a non-profit organization, it would apply for subsidies. It already has promises from several international institutions ready to help with the restoration of the monument. The renovation of the building would be significantly boosted by the fact that the nearby city of Trenčín is officially declared as the European Capital of Culture 2026 and whose program includes the renovated Machnáč Sanatorium. This challenging project will also seek further strategic partnerships at the global level, and the Jaromír Krejcar Society believes that Docomomo International will play an important role in this process.

OUTSTANDING IN-DEPTH INTERVENTIONS IN RENOVATING MODERN MOVEMENT MASTERPIECES, WHILE KEEPING THE PRINCIPLES AND CHARACTER OF THESE JEWELS.

NEUE NATIONALGALERIE

An invisible imprint is left on the Neue Nationalgalerie by this project for the technical and functional renovation of a world-renowned masterpiece. Thinking as Mies would have done, the renovation project by David Chipperfield Architects has managed to faithfully bring the Neue Nationalgalerie into the present day, transforming it into a contemporary museum for art, while enhancing its Miesian spatial performance.

YOYOGI NATIONAL GYMNASIUM

Cherished as one of Japan's national symbols, the renovation of the Yoyogi National Gymnasium for the 2020 Olympic and Paralympic Games is an example of how to make structural and technical improvements to such an emblematic creation. Tange Associates and Kume Sekkei's renovation has respectfully and surgically reinforced the original structure and updated its spaces, which are now able to respond to the contemporary demands of its flexible use.

ENHANCED MASTERPIECES

ENHANCED MASTERPIECES

The Neue Nationalgalerie is the only building that Ludwig Mies van der Rohe realized in Europe after his emigration to the USA. Together with Hans Scharoun's (1893–1972) Philharmonic Hall and State Library, it was one of the key buildings of the West Berlin Cultural Forum that had been built since 1960 and that is located not far from Potsdamer Platz, which had been divided by the Berlin Wall in 1961. In 1962, without a prior architectural competition, the Berlin Senate directly commissioned 67-year-old Mies van der Rohe to design the Neue Nationalgalerie "as a gallery of the 20th century."[1]

1. Martijn Jaspers, "The Neue Nationalgalerie: the Refurbishment of a Modern Monument," *Docomomo Journal*, No. 56 – "The Heritage of Mies," Lisbon, Docomomo International, 2017, 78–85.

Mies based his concept for the gallery building on two unrealized designs for the administration building of the rum manufacturer Bacardi in Santiago de Cuba (1957) and on the design for the Museum Georg Schäfer in Schweinfurt (1960–1963). Both designs comprise a roof supported by eight exterior columns and a column-free interior in the sense of the universal space developed by Mies. His solution, with its latent classicism, is thus a modern realization of the ancient podium temple, the Neue Nationalgalerie being the first significant museum built for a 20th century collection in Europe. The building has been described as radiating "a sense of static tranquility," in order to avoid "distraction of the viewer," as Mies noted.[2]

2. Carsten Krohn, *Mies van der Rohe – The Built Work*, Basel, Birkhäuser, 2014, 209.

The outstanding importance of the Neue Nationalgalerie, representing the climax and conclusion of late Modernity, and the requirement for its almost undisturbed material and visual preservation, placed high demands on the compatibility of the intervention to preserve the monument. The perfection of this "temple of Modernity" affords precious little leeway and is unforgiving.

The building measures focused on a general overhaul of the structure, including the removal of toxins, and compliance with current technical and energy-related standards, in so far as this was compatible with the demands of the monument. The goal defined by the client, that is to enable "as much Mies as possible," as well as the building's intrinsic limits and potential, left little room for maneuver. Firmly in the spirit of the task and in a holistic approach, David Chipperfield Architects Berlin, adopted the strategy of becoming "invisible architects," planning and implementing the required adaptations and measures in the service of, and with a responsibility toward the original designer, Mies van der Rohe, rather than incorporating their own preferences.

The general overhaul had the aim of giving the building a new lease of life of around 40 to 50 years, in keeping its original role as an art museum and venue for special exhibitions. For this time period, appropriate building maintenance should suffice to ensure the building's operations, without making fundamental or structural changes necessary. Often, the desired sustainability of the general overhaul conflicted with efforts to retain as much of the original material structure as possible.

The starting point for all planning considerations was the built structure, which had aged over time and been partially changed: the large glass panes of the hall had been replaced with two-pane glass; the curtains in the hall had been removed; the checkroom had been relocated from the hall to exhibition areas of the basement; a new bookshop was installed in the lower foyer; the sculpture garden had been closed to visitors: defective original furniture had been stored in the public area. The approach to the monument was subject to the familiar questions, criteria, and methods similar to the ones generally applied to high-ranking monuments

2012–2021
DAVID CHIPPERFIELD ARCHITECTS BERLIN

1965–1968
LUDWIG MIES VAN DER ROHE

BERLIN, GERMANY

1. Facade of the main exhibition hall with the new large single glass panes identical to the original ones, after refurbishment.

elsewhere. In a first phase, lasting over a year, extensive archive research work was undertaken, studying the large volume of preserved original sources, which provided a virtually complete picture of the building's planning and history. In the following years, these guidelines provided a solid basis for all planning decisions.

The need to extensively repair the reinforced concrete shell and completely renew the technical building services required an in-depth intervention. In order to expose the shell construction, around 35,000 original building components, such as the stone cladding and all the interior fittings, were dismantled. After their restoration and modification, when necessary, they were reinstalled in their precise original positions.

Mies' design for the Neue Nationalgalerie and its structural implementation were defined by principles and typical characteristics. The underlying motif of a temple upon a podium is timelessly modern, as are the high degree of abstraction of its exterior appearance, the modular design principle, the eschewing of ostensible functionality for the exhibition hall, as well as the use of natural stone (granite and marble), brown oak, steel, bronze, and glass. In contrast, the aesthetic expression of the period when it was built can be seen in the modular suspended ceilings in the basement, the illumination of the spaces using down-lights and wall washers, the warm tone of the artificial light, the design of the restrooms, the woodchip wallpaper together with the fitted carpet flooring in the collection rooms, the use of curtains, and the floor-flex tiles in the back-of-house area. Both aspects were regarded as equally important by David Chipperfield Architects, having therefore preserved or reinstated them wherever they were missing. Also, the architects deliberately refrained from visually "refreshing" the monument or reinterpreting it by "updating" colors, materials, or details according to contemporary tastes.

Despite the necessary optimizations and improvements to meet technical standards, increase the safety of people and objects, enhance the comfort of use and reduce operating costs, the architects chose not to eliminate every defect or imperfection (from today's point of view). In order to avoid profound material losses and severe visual impairment, in some cases, such as condensation on the single glazing, the causes were not eliminated, but only the consequences were mitigated. In some cases, such as that of condensation, the situation was merely alleviated to a tolerable level. Such aspects, typical for buildings from the 1960s, form a significant element of the building's character and are a genuine part of the historical evidence that was preserved as far as possible.

2. Exterior view toward the Matthäuskirche, after refurbishment.

3. Foyer in the basement, after refurbishment.

4. East elevation with the main entrance to the Potsdamer Straße, after refurbishment.

7

5

8

6

9

5. Detail of the main hall roof structure, before refurbishment. 6. View from Sigismundstraße, before refurbishment. 7. Sculpture garden at the basement level, before refurbishment. 8. Exterior view toward Potsdamer Straße, 1968. 9. View from Potsdamer Straße, 1968.

10

11

12

10. Main exhibition hall in the basement, 1968. 11. West view from the sculpture garden, 1968. 12. Piet Mondrian exhibition at the upper floor exhibition hall, 1968.

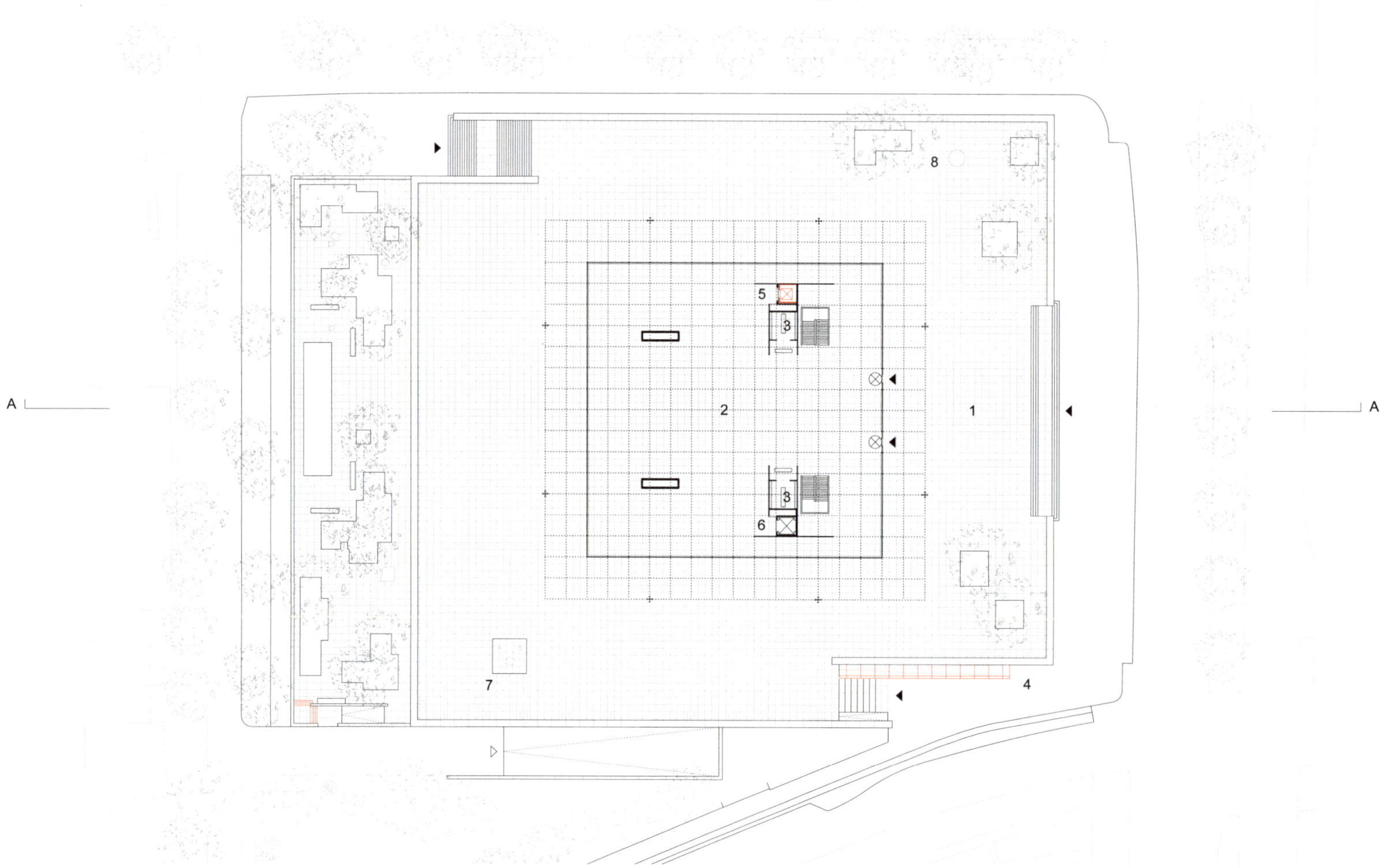

13

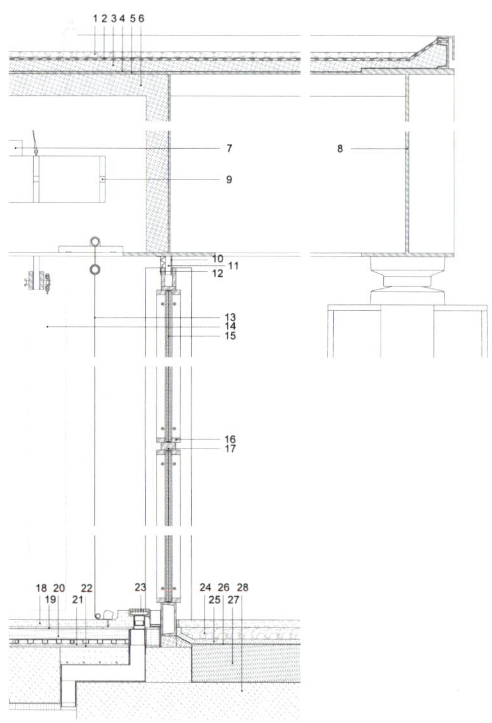

14

1 Gravel
2 Two-layer bitumen sheet sealing
3 60 mm foam glass insulation
4 Bitumen
5 Steel roof (existing)
6 120 mm foam glass interior insulation
7 Light fixture (existing)
8 500/1800 mm steel beam (existing)
9 250 mm aluminium grating (existing)
10 Steel cover profile 100/6mm, between joint profiles, welded to bottom flange (existing)
11 Steel joint profile 100/35/300 mm at vertical curtain wall profile
12 EPDM membrane seal
13 Additive hangings / black-out (temporary)
14 Curtain (optional)
15 Laminated safety glass of 2 x 12 mm partially tempered white glass, glued with Sentry Glass interlayer
16 25/55 mm glazing bead (cut)
17 Frame of 40/80 mm solid steel profile (existing)
18 1200/1200/400 mm granite slabs (existing)
19 10 mm mortar layer
20 80 mm heated screed
21 10 mm systemic insulating floor heating 10 mm
22 Leveling pin
23 Aluminium ventilation grille (existing)
24 60 mm grit sheet
25 16 mm drainage
26 Two-layer bitumen sheet sealing
27 60–210 mm foam glass gradient insulation
28 Reinforced concrete slab (existing)

Refurbishment project: 13. Ground floor plan. In red are marked the new elements. 1 – terrace, 2 – exhibition hall, 3 – cloakroom, 4 – new barrier-free access, 5 – new visitor elevator, 6 – goods lift, 7 – sculpture “Tetes et Queue” (Alexander Calder, 1965), 8 – sculpture “The Archer” (Henry Moore, 1964–1965). 14. Structural detail section of the facade.

15

N
20 m

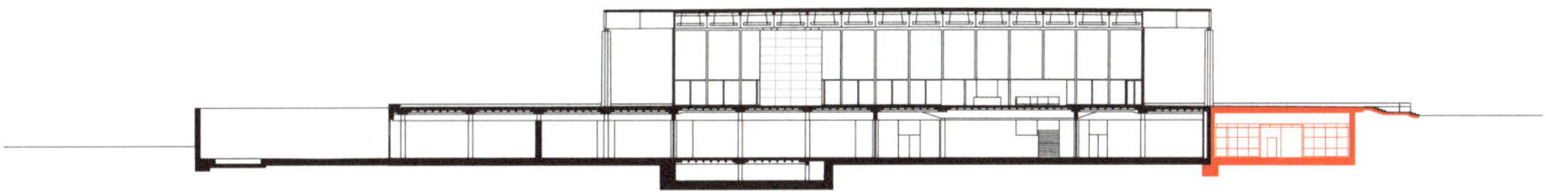

16

Refurbishment project: 15. Basement floor plan. In red are marked the new elements. 1 – staircase hall, 2 – graphics art gallery, 3 – smaller exhibition hall, 4 – large exhibition hall, 5 – sculpture garden, 6 – museum shop in the former sculpture storage space, 7 – cloakroom in the former painting storage space, 8 – visitor toilets, 9 – café, 10 – management, 11 – deliveries, service entrance, 12 – exhibition preparation, 13 – new art storage space, 14 – central ventilation plant room. 16. East–west section A–A. In red is marked the new art storage space.

YOYOGI NATIONAL GYMNASIUM

Specially designed for the 1964 Summer Olympics in Tokyo, the Yoyogi National Gymnasium complex is recognized as one of Kenzo Tange's most outstanding works and has been cherished for the emblematic "suspended roof structure" of its two stadiums (the first and the second gymnasium). The roof "skin" is suspended from one or two reinforced concrete masts, resulting in the world's largest suspended roof span at the time. It consists of a prestressed steel net with welded and painted steel plates attached.[1] Their massive spaces not only encouraged both spectators and athletes to share the excitement and thrills of the Olympics, but also technically and intuitively enabled the smooth circulation of 15,000 spectators.[2]

Since its construction, the building has continued to actively serve the community and has been renovated several times over the decades, not only due to deterioration over time, but also to changes in use, as in the case of the first gymnasium (originally a swimming pool, now converted into an events stadium).

After 56 years, the Yoyogi National Gymnasium was once more chosen to accommodate the Olympic Games – the Tokyo 2020 Olympic and Paralympic Games –, consequently requiring updates and adaptations. The new renovation project was designed by the consortium of Tange Associates and Kume Sekkei Co., Ltd. and had two main goals: on the one hand, the structural and full-scale seismic reinforcement of the building, as Tange Associates had already carried out a seismic diagnosis and survey years before (between 2010 and 2012). Secondly, the accessibilities systems for a barrier-free environment for users had to be updated.

Bearing in mind the building's historical significance, great care was taken to ensure that the renovation works were always coordinated with the key architectural features of the gymnasium, such as its space, form, materials, and colors.[3] The structural reinforcement and improvement of the building's earthquake resistance was implemented based on the current earthquake resistance standards and with deep respect for the building's original appearance and avoided affecting its distinctive exterior image in any way. The work included: the placement of additional concrete elements inside the double wall of the main tower's structural skeleton; increasing the number of concrete piles at the main tower to reinforce soil bearing capacity; and strengthening the steel frame of the large roof with reinforcing plates and stiffeners.

In order to achieve a barrier-free environment for users – which was especially important since it was to host the Paralympics – interventions both on the outside and the inside of the building were necessary: on the exterior, ramps were installed in areas where previously there were only steps, stone-paved surfaces were smoothed, and handrails were added; while in the interior areas the number of wheelchair spaces was increased and wheelchair-accessible toilets were built in. No less important were repairing works undertaken during the intervention. The retaining stone wall in the exterior was mended, the roofs and outer walls were painted, the floor of the arena was refurbished and the electricity and machinery facilities updated.

1. Udo Kultermann, *Kenzo Tange 1946–1969. Architecture and Urban Design*, Zurich, Verlag für Architektur – Artemis, 1970, 200–204.
2. See: *a+u, Drawings from the Kenzo Tange Archive – National Gymnasiums for Tokyo Olympics*, No. 589, October 2019.

3. Japan Sport Council, *Management Plan for Preserving the Yoyogi National Stadium as a Living Heritage*, Tokyo, Japan Sport Council, 2019.

2018–2020
TANGE ASSOCIATES AND KUME SEKKEI CO.

1963–1964
KENZO TANGE & URTEC AND TANGE LABORATORY

TOKYO, JAPAN

1. Arena of the first gymnasium, after renovation.

2. Exterior view of the first gymnasium, after renovation.

3. Exterior view toward the entrance of the first gymnasium, after renovation.

4

5

6

7

4. Interior of the first gymnasium, before renovation. 5. Exterior view of the second gymnasium, before renovation. 6. Exterior view toward the entrance of the first gymnasium, before renovation. 7. Arena of the first gymnasium, before renovation.

8

9

10

8. Entrance of the first gymnasium, 1964. 9. View toward the entrance of the first gymnasium, 1964. 10. Interior of the first gymnasium, serving as swimming competitions venue, 1964.

11

12

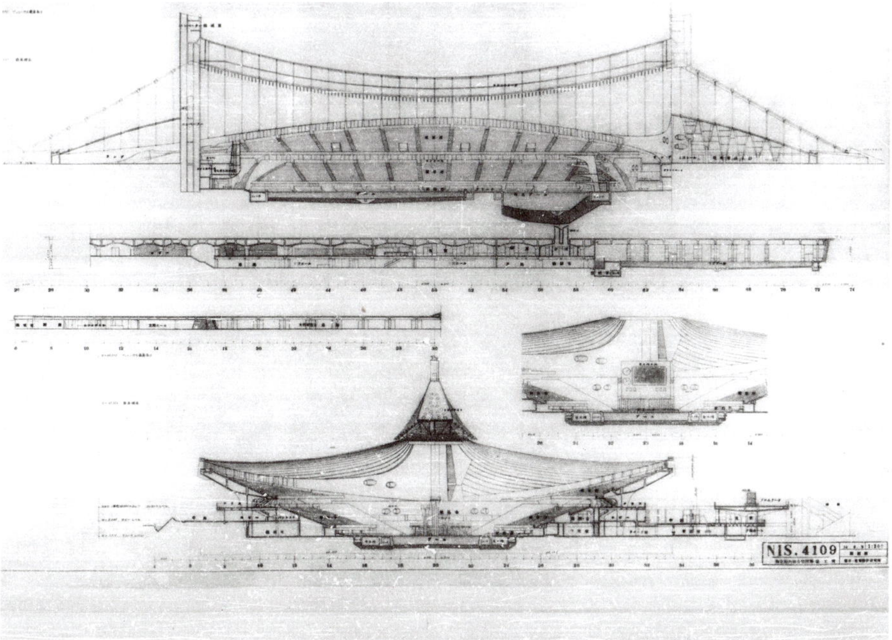

13

11. Aerial view, 1964. 12. Interior of the first gymnasium, serving as swimming competitions venue, 1964. 13. Longitudinal and cross sections (first gymnasium).

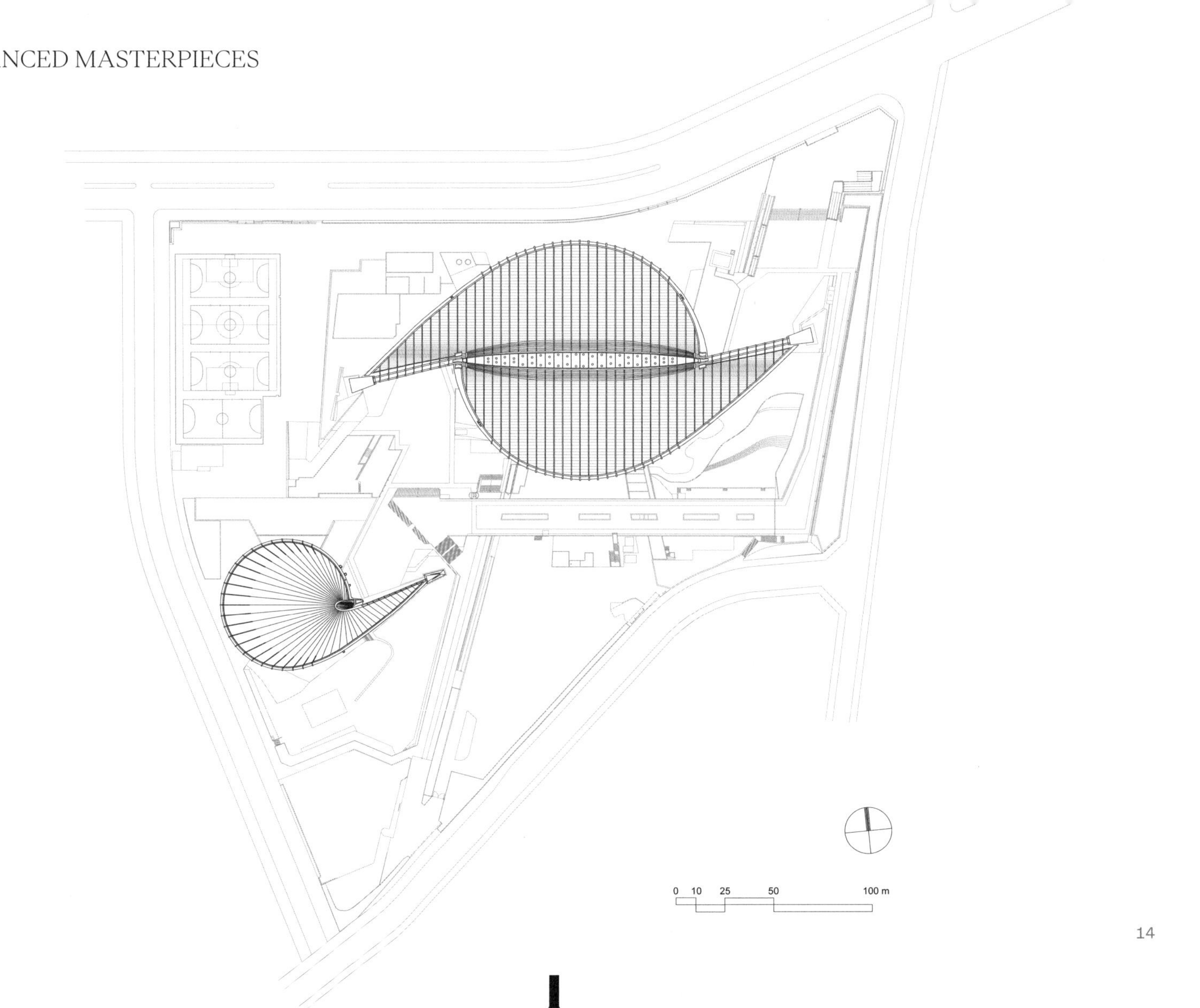

14

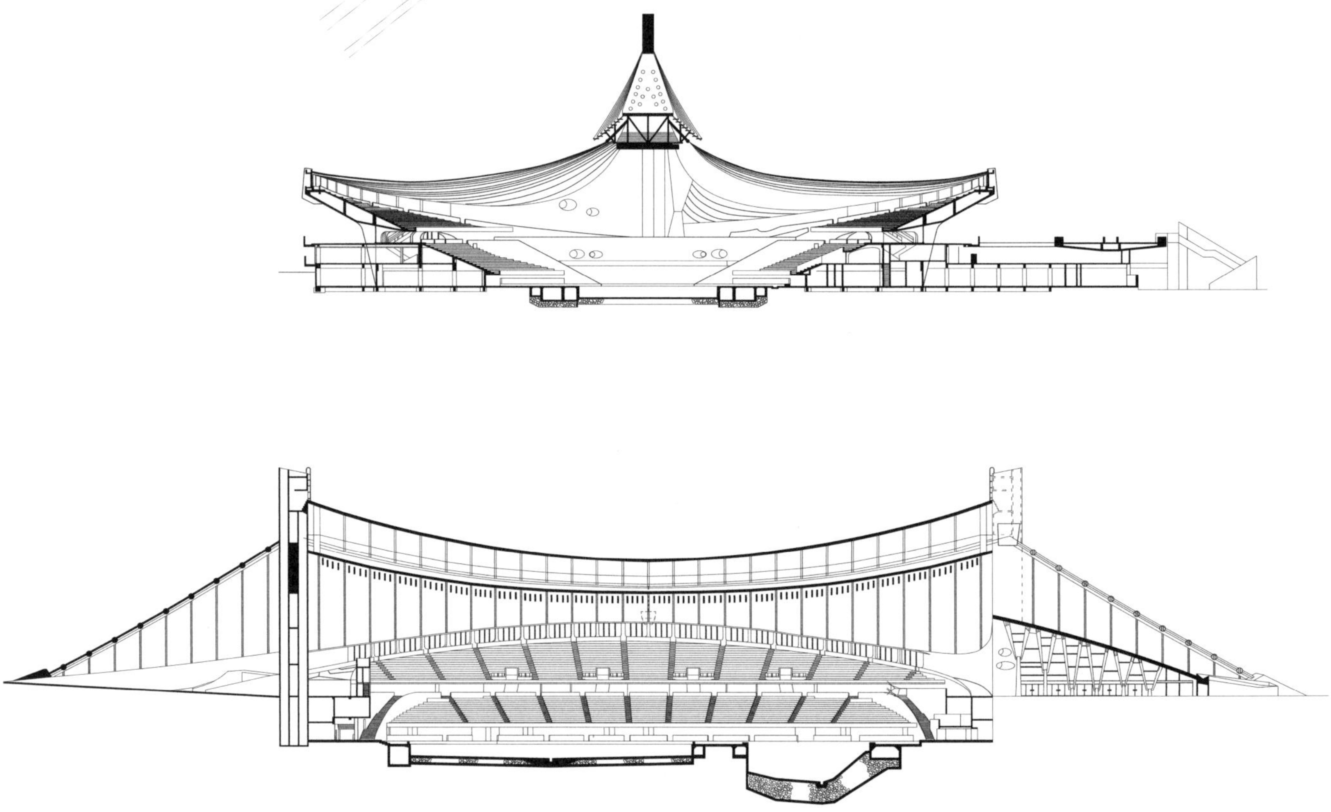

15

Renovation project: 14. Site plan showing both the first and the second gymnasiums. 15. Longitudinal and cross sections (first gymnasium).

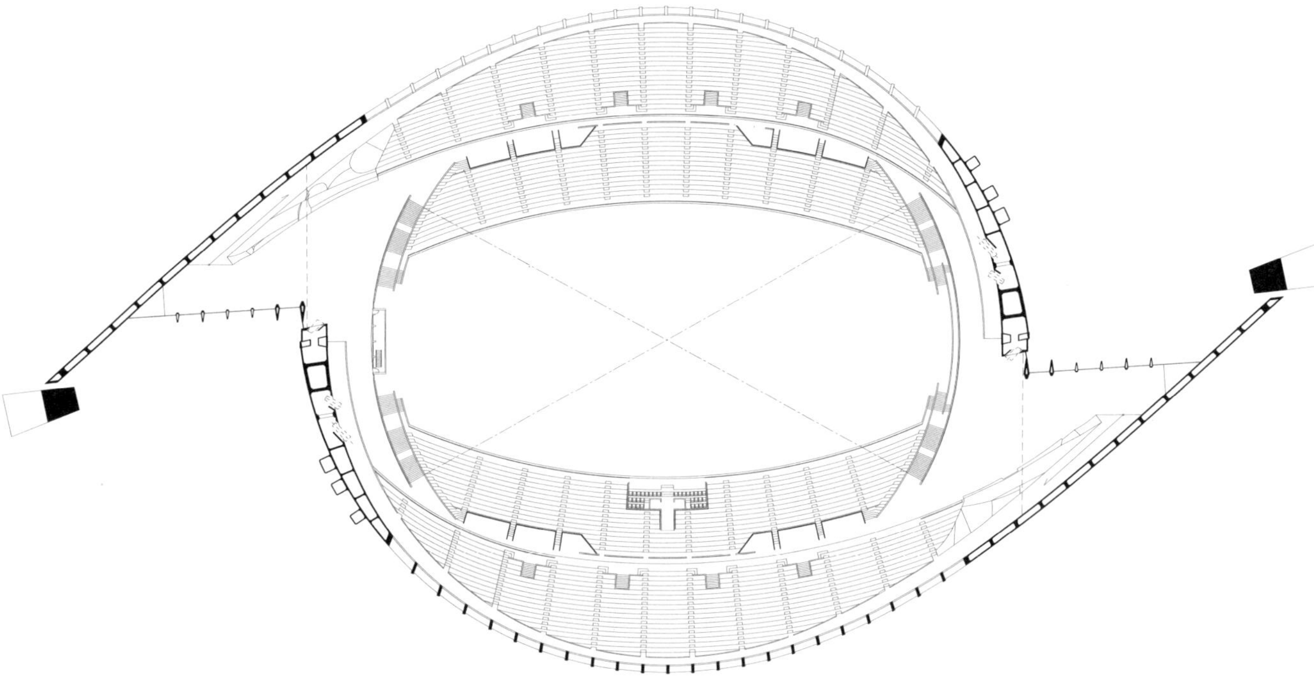

16

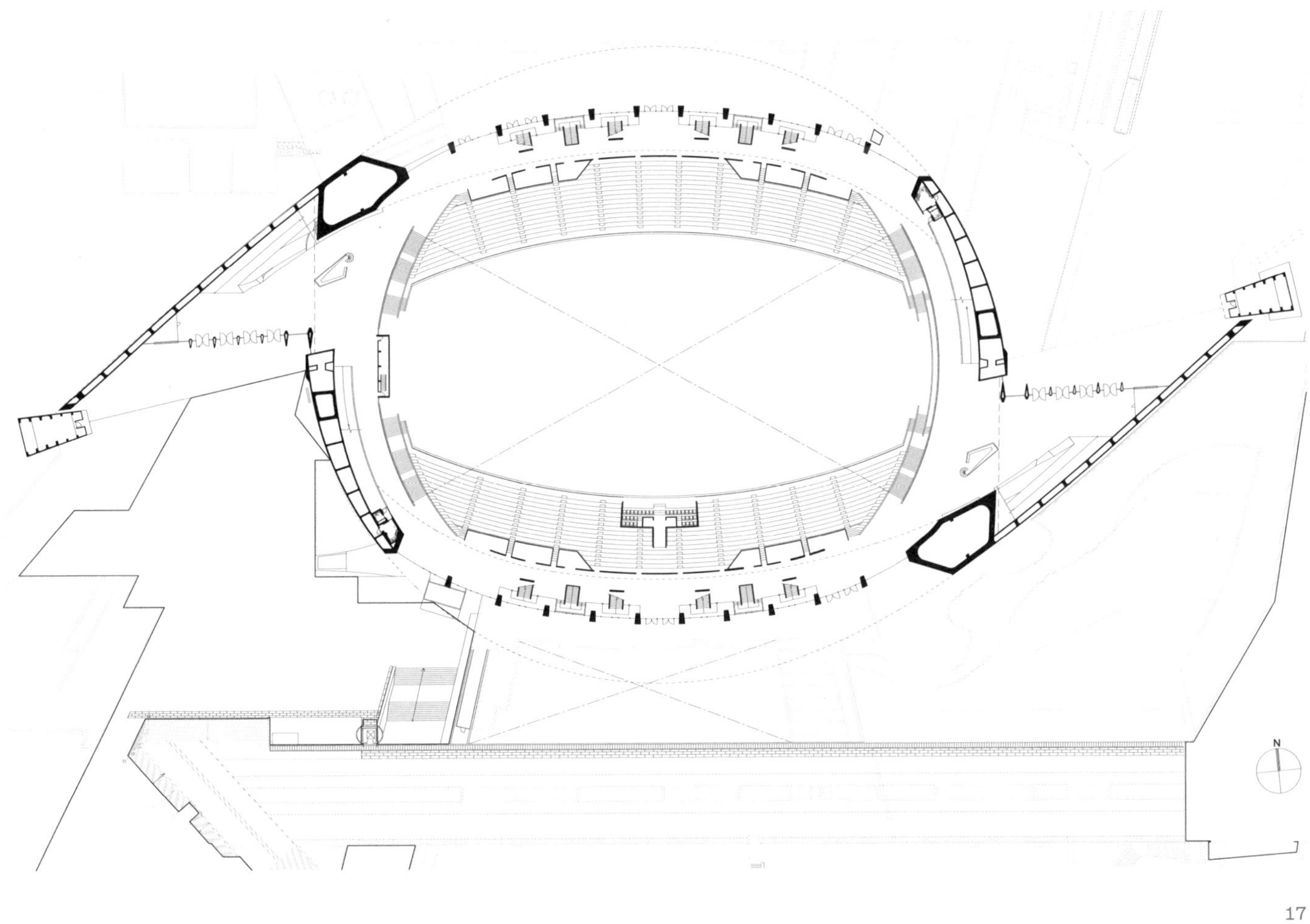

17

Renovation project: 16. Upper floor plan, tribunes (first gymnasium). 17. Ground floor plan, entrance and arena level (first gymnasium).

PRACTICES THAT CONSIDER CONSERVATION AND MAINTENANCE PLANS AS KEY TOOLS FOR DEFYING THE EFFECTS OF TIME.

SYDNEY OPERA HOUSE

The Sydney Opera House is the epitome of a work still in progress, continuously evolving in accordance with the design principles of its creator. Rightfully updating the guidelines of the previous three conservation-management plans to the contemporary demands made of the building, Alan Croker's conservation-management plan succeeds in securely perpetuating Utzon's founding design principles.

YALE CENTER FOR BRITISH ART

The symbiotic relation between the Yale Center for British Art's management plan and conservation project represent a paradigm of how to efficaciously delay the unescapable action of time over a building's lifespan. The almost natural synchronization between Peter Inskip and Stephen Gee's conservation plan, establishing the guidelines for approaching the building, and Knight Architecture's detailed conservation project, has led to the rigorous and transcendent safekeeping of Khan's presence in the building.

LASTING HERITAGE

LASTING HERITAGE

Built on Bennelong Point on Sydney Harbour, and adjacent to the Royal Botanic Gardens, the Sydney Opera House is one of the world's greatest 20th century buildings. It was designed by Jørn Utzon (1918–2008), as his proposal was selected in 1957 as winner of the international competition for the design of an opera house in Sydney. His proposal consisted of a complex with two theaters side by side on a large podium, covered by interconnecting concrete "shells," which acted as both wall and roof, complemented by a third smaller separate "shell" for the restaurant.

However, the construction of the Opera House was difficult and controversial. While the construction of the podium started in 1959, the design of the shell-shaped roof was still unresolved, since they were of undefined geometry in the competition entry. Therefore, Utzon started working together with engineer Ove Arup (1895–1988), spending the following years in search for an acceptable and economically feasible solution to build them. Based on Utzon's drawings, Ove Arup & Partners had to express the shell shapes mathematically. In 1962, they finally found a viable solution, having evolved the design of the "shells" through various iterations: from parabolic to ellipsoid, and finally to spherical geometry to derive the final form of the shells,[1] which became a timeless expression of the fusion between architecture and engineering. Herewith, it was possible to begin the construction of the roof in 1963. However, cost and scheduling issues, as well as government pressure, ultimately led to Utzon resigning from the project in 1966. An Australian architectural team headed by Peter Hall (1931–1995) – of Hall, Todd & Littlemore – had been appointed to the project following Utzon's departure, working chiefly on the interiors of the building, and the building was opened in October 1973.

Comprised of four main structures – a broad platform composed of the Forecourt and Broadwalks, the Concert Hall, the Joan Sutherland Theatre (Opera Theatre), and the Bennelong Restaurant – the Sydney Opera House has six internal venues[2] and is therefore a very complex site: "Utzon's vision created a truly remarkable place, a structure that elevates and celebrates the human experience of the performing arts, as well as of the place itself."[3] The three groups of soaring curved, ribbed concrete and white ceramic-tiled shells, supported by a massive, pink granite-clad podium, with Monumental Steps, and surrounded by the flat open Forecourt and Broadwalks orchestrate a sequence of public spaces from the approach to the arrival, entry and circulation, internally and externally, creating a sense of anticipation and joy. Further, to achieve a unified theme that remains flexible, economic, and incremental, prefabrication was used extensively: it was employed for the concrete ribs that support the shells, for the mass production of the ceramic tiles of the shells, and for the molded granite blocks of the podium, as well as inside, where prefabricated plywood elements were used to clad walls and ceilings and molded plywood elements for the seating and fit-outs.

Balancing the roles of the building as an architectural monument and as a state-of-the-art performance center, the Sydney Opera House Trust considered it necessary that an updated Conservation and Management Plan (CMP) would be drawn up. Since the 2003 publication of the CMP's third edition[4] by James Semple Kerr (1932–2014), the Sydney Opera House had not only been included in UNESCO's World Heritage List (2007), but also in the State (2003) and National (2005) Heritage lists. Alan Croker[5] was commissioned to develop this fourth edition of the CMP,

1. In his *Yellow Book*, from 1962, Utzon submitted the plans, sections, and elevations setting out the shells, details of the precast ribs and the tiling, showing on the cover the principles of the spherical geometry.

2. Concert Hall, Joan Sutherland Theatre, Utzon Room, Drama Theatre, The Studio and Playhouse.
3. Alan Croker, *Respecting the Vision: Sydney Opera House – a Conservation Management Plan*, Sydney, Sydney Opera House, 2017, 39.
4. James Semple Kerr, *Sydney Opera House: A plan for the conservation of the Sydney Opera House and its site*, Sydney, Sydney Opera House, 2003.
5. Alan Croker is principal architect of the office Design 5 Architects.

2017
ALAN CROKER 4TH CONSERVATION PLAN

1959–1973
JØRN UTZON FIRST PHASE
HALL, TODD SECOND PHASE
& LITTLEMORE

SYDNEY, AUSTRALIA

1. Aerial view from the east, at sunrise.

titled *Respecting the Vision: Sydney Opera House – a Conservation Management Plan*. Guided by the goal of "Treasure and inspire, conserve and renew,"[6] the CMP sets out the method for conserving and caring for the vision of the architect evidenced in the place itself and described by himself in the *Utzon Design Principles*.[7] This fourth edition includes a greater understanding of the contributions of those who completed the Sydney Opera House. It also graded the various components according to their significance from exceptional (A) to intrusive (int). This grading was then used as a base for the definition of a conservation approach for each element. Two new concepts were introduced in this edition: the Tolerance for Change and Opportunity for Change translated in tables for each space. The Tolerance for Change tables provide a more nuanced understanding of each component and the role each of its particular attributes (form, fabric, function, location) plays. The Opportunity for Change tables identify those aspects of the place that could be improved and provide direction for any change so that the significant values are retained and enhanced. Together with Utzon's *Utzon Design Principles*,[8] this fourth edition of the CMP has become the main source of guidance for renovation works at the Sydney Opera House.

Part of a decade of renewal works, started in 2013, the Sydney Opera House embarked on a series of projects that will replace machinery, open new areas to the public, and ensure the Opera House can welcome all visitors, namely through accessibility improvements for people with mobility issues. Following a priority analysis, a staged suite of five projects was developed: Entry and Foyers (May 2019–early 2020); Joan Sutherland Theatre (May–December 2017); Concert Hall (February 2020–); Function Centre (February 2018–April 2019); Centre for Creativity (February 2020–January 2022). These interventions represent the biggest upgrade in the history of Sydney Opera House. Further, an additional project to improve accessibility at the southern entry to the site was carried out in 2019.

6. Alan Croker, *op. cit.*, vii.

7. Jørn Utzon, *Sydney Opera House: Utzon Design Principles*, Sydney, Sydney Opera House Trust, 2002.

8. Utzon himself set out the main vision by intervening in the building: "As the architect of the Sydney Opera House, as the creative force behind its character, I sincerely believe that a large multipurpose structure such as this building, in time will undergo many natural changes. The ideas as they were developed in the sixties, evolved as the result of the needs and technique at the time. As time passes and needs change, it is natural to modify the building to suit the needs and technique of the day. The changes, however, should be such that the original character of the building is maintained," *idem.*, 48.

2

2. Interior sitting area.

3. Entrance to the Stalls Room.

4. Aerial view of the north facades, after renovation. The creation of the Yallamundi Rooms (Function Centre) from separate spaces within the north end of the podium, originally occupied by the former Harbour Restaurant, enabled the removal of the intrusive marquee on the Northern Broadwalk, restoring the building's original facade.

5. Re-paved Forecourt and Monumental Steps, after renovation. Preceded by the completion of an underground loading dock in 2015, the renewal project of the Entry and Foyers and of the Monumental Steps of 2019, carried out by Scott Carver architects, combined a number of upgrades. They improved pedestrian access and safety at the entrance and transformed the area under the Monumental Steps into a vibrant, welcoming, car-free entrance and meeting place. The main box office foyer was provided with better accessibilities and connection to the Concert Hall and Joan Sutherland Theatre.

6. Foyer of the Joan Sutherland Theatre, after renovation. In 2017, the Joan Sutherland Theatre underwent essential renewal and upgrade works to replace theater machinery that had reached end of life and to make improvements to the orchestra pit, acoustics, safety, and audience facilities.

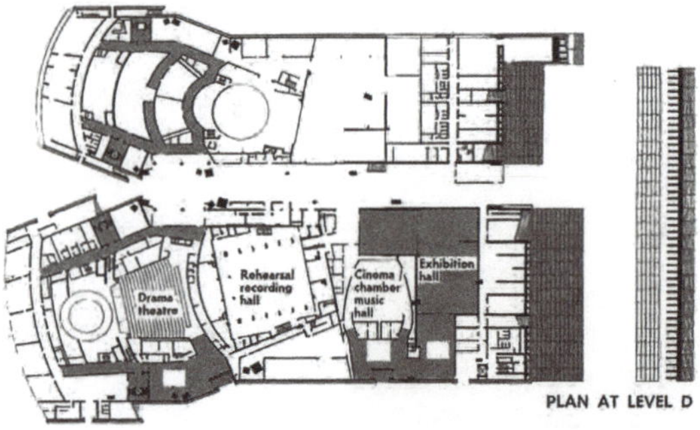

7

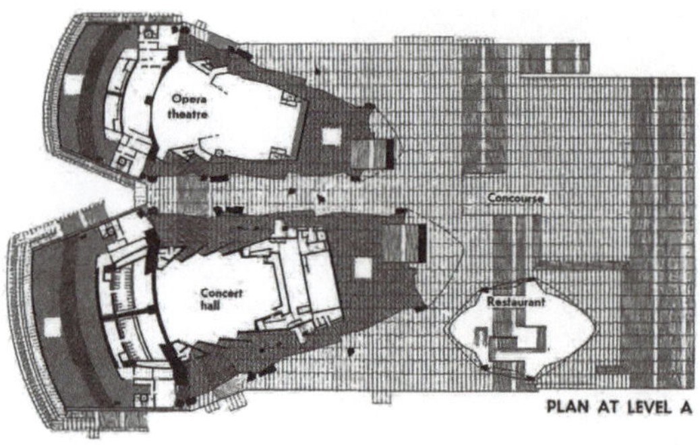

8

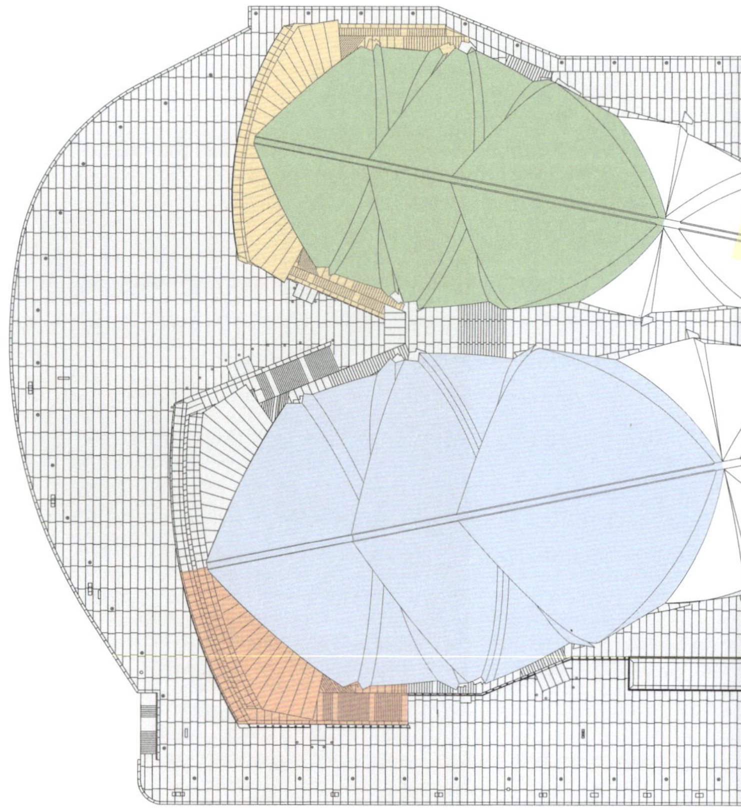

9

7. Plan at Level D, ground level. 8. Plan at Level A, upper auditorium level. 9. Concert Hall, interior before renovation. As the heart of the opera house and its largest internal venue, the Concert Hall is undergoing major renewal works to improve its acoustics, theater machinery systems, accessibility, and to provide it with an automated stage configuration, extension system, and a new theater flying system, designed by ARM architecture, 2020–in progress. The intervention is guided by the Tolerance for Change and Opportunities for Change tables of the CMP.

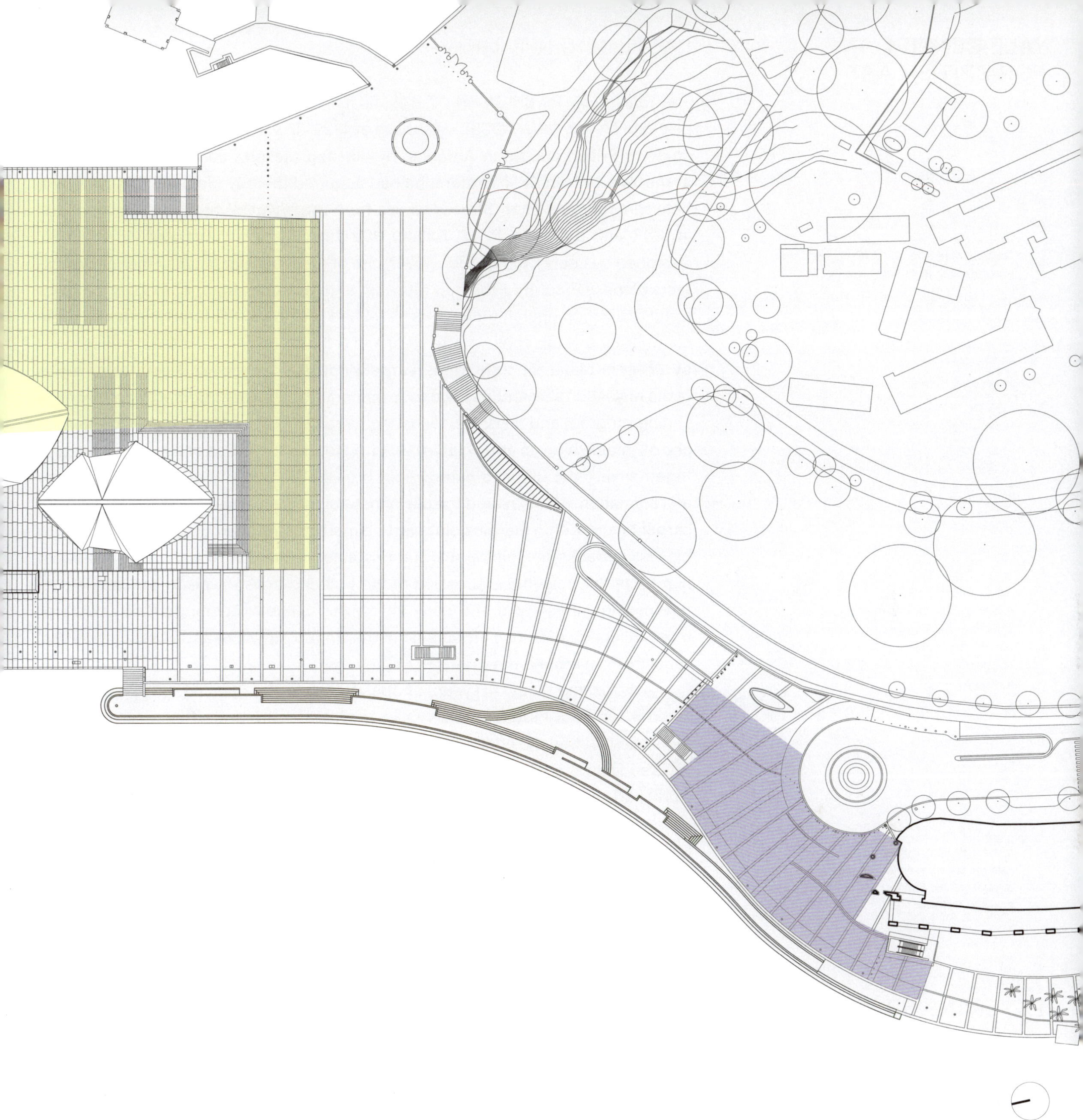

10

10. Site plan with the main refurbishments, undertaken according to the CMP. Yellow: Entry and Foyers (May 2019–early 2020); green: Joan Sutherland Theatre (May–December 2017); orange: Yallamundi Rooms (February 2018–April 2019); red: Centre for Creativity (February 2020–January 2022); blue: Concert Hall (2020–in progress); violet: southern site entry (2019).

YALE CENTER FOR BRITISH ART

LASTING HERITAGE

The Yale Center for British Art (YCBA) and its collection were the gift of philanthropist Paul Mellon (1907–1999), Yale Class of 1929. It was to become a center for the study of British culture in America, by housing Mellon's collection of British Art at the Yale University. Therefore, he had acquired the city block on Chapel Street between York and High Streets across from the Yale University Art Gallery, built in 1953, and the old Yale Art Gallery (1927) by Egerton Swartwout (1870–1943).[1] Designed by Louis I. Kahn (1901–1974), one of the most significant American architects of the 20th century, the new museum and research center embodies the masterful realization of architectural ideas he had previously explored in other notable commissions. Kahn chose matte steel and reflective glass to infill bays delineated by a cast-in-place concrete frame. Large windows offer visitors breathtaking views of the majestic Yale campus beyond. Interior materials were selected "as a means of coding program and uses, of delineating hierarchies of served and service spaces, and of establishing an aptly stable backdrop for the exhibition of the collection" and together with the diffused natural light provide the building its sense of intimacy and animation. Kahn favored the use of natural materials, namely warm-toned wool carpeting set within margins of travertine marble, stretched Belgian linen to ennoble wall surfaces presenting art, and unstained white oak to trim and paneling to humanize the powerful expression of the building's cast-in-place concrete structure, ceilings, shear walls, and iconic stair tower.[2] Since its opening it "holds the foremost collection of British art outside of the United Kingdom and hosts visitors and scholars from around the world."[3]

Following nearly 40 years of operation since its opening in 1977, the YCBA faced a series of mounting pressures: ingeniously integrated infrastructure systems had reached the end of their practical life; architectural finishes (such as linen walls and carpeted floors, concrete cast-in-place finishes, American white oak millwork) had become tired and worn; existing teaching spaces within the Center were oversubscribed and underequipped; nowadays' patron amenities and life safety measures standards no longer were met; contemporary conservation standards demanded far more robust environmental controls; and the growing collection required increased space for exhibition, storage, curation and study.

In response to escalating conservation pressures and to preempt deferred maintenance or an imprudent renovation, Amy Meyers, YCBA's former director, commissioned conservation architects Peter Inskip and Stephen Gee to create a detailed study of the building, which ultimately resulted in the publication *Louis I. Kahn and the Yale Center for British Art: A Conservation Plan.*[4] This pioneering document, the first of its kind in the United States for a building completed after World War II, identified the YCBA's most culturally significant attributes, established policies for the future care of the building, and formed the basis for the building conservation project.

Led by Knight Architecture LLC, the multi-phase 33 million Dollar building conservation project began in 2008, though the majority of construction was completed in an ambitious ten-month period during 2015. The project was phased strategically to meet the institutional mandate that the staff and the collection remain in the building during construction. The YCBA epitomizes Louis Kahn's design philosophy that all building systems be deliberately organized and rationally integrated

1. Heinz Ronner, Sharad Jhaveri, *Louis I. Kahn Complete Work 1935–1974, Second revised and enlarged edition*, Basel, Birkhäuser, 1987, 378.

2. George Knight, "The Yale Center for British Art: a Building Conservation," *Docomomo Journal*, No. 58 – "Louis I. Kahn – The permanence," Lisbon, Docomomo International, 2018, 50–59.
3. *Idem.*, 51.

4. Peter Inskip, Stephen Gee, and Constance Clement, *Louis I. Kahn and the Yale Center for British Art: A Conservation Plan*, New Haven, Yale Center for British Art, 2011.

2012
PETER INSKIP AND STEPHEN GEE — CONSERVATION PLAN

2008–2016
KNIGHT ARCHITECTURE LLC — CONSERVATION PROJECT

1971–1977
LOUIS I. KAHN

NEW HAVEN, CONNECTICUT, USA

1. Fourth floor gallery 02, featuring new demountable partition ("pogo") walls, whose design was based on Kahn's drawings of 1974, after conservation.

into the architectural form. Consequently, the inevitable replacement and upgrade of the center's building systems jeopardized the clarity of the building's formal order. Collaborating rigorously with a group of specialized consultants and technicians to ensure that any infrastructural improvements acknowledged and obeyed the order established by Kahn's original design, the project team undertook a comprehensive renewal of the building's electrical, mechanical, security, communications, and fire suppression systems.

The public galleries on the first, second, and third floors were refurbished to preserve Kahn's vision of intimate viewing spaces, echoing the domestic setting of an English country house. The building envelope was disassembled back to the "pewter" stainless steel panels. The exterior wall assembly was refortified with mineral wool insulation, a reestablished air barrier, corrosion treatment at structural members, and a new fire-retardant substrate beneath new Belgian linen stretched over the gallery walls. Existing demountable partition walls, known as "pogo" panels, were replaced with new pogos based closely on Kahn's original design.

The refurbishment project returned the layout of the center's sky-lit Long Gallery – one of the great undiscovered spaces of the 20th century – to Kahn's vision recalling linear galleries of English country houses with artwork hung salon-style. Existing partition panels which previously subdivided the Long Gallery into cellular spaces were removed, doors were reorganized for improved circulation, and finishes were revived to match those in the main galleries.

Original materials were reused whenever possible, and any new items were sourced prudently to match the quality and appearance of the existing. Undyed wool from New Zealand was used to create the new tufted carpet installed throughout the galleries and study spaces. Natural undyed Belgian linen, treated with a fire-resistant coating, covers the gallery walls. The honey-colored white oak millwork was refinished within the galleries and interior courts using Greenguard certified products. In the Lower Court, all brick pavers and bluestone treads were removed, cleaned, and reset instead of replaced with new materials. The cast-in-place concrete was selectively cleaned while ensuring that the patina remained undisturbed.

The revitalization of the Lecture Hall, with new seating, revived finishes, advanced audiovisual and lighting systems, and expanded simulcasting and teleconferencing capabilities, helps the Center to shape its rich cultural offerings with renewed vibrancy.

2. Long gallery, after conservation.

3. Study room, featuring new white oak paneling, whose design was based on Kahn's drawings of 1974, after conservation.

4. Library court, after conservation.

5

6

7

8

5. Long gallery, before conservation. 6. Long gallery, under intervention. 7. Lecture hall, before conservation. 8. Exterior wall refurbishment: fourth floor "Turner Bay," air barrier layer under intervention.

9

11

10

12

9. Exterior view from the corner of Chapel and High Streets. 10. Entrance court, showing the sun bleached white oak paneling, before conservation. 11. Aerial view of the building under construction, 1974. 12. Sketch of the second program, library court looking east, 1971: on the sketch, the rotated square stair shaft and the use of the space is visible, originally intended as exhibition court.

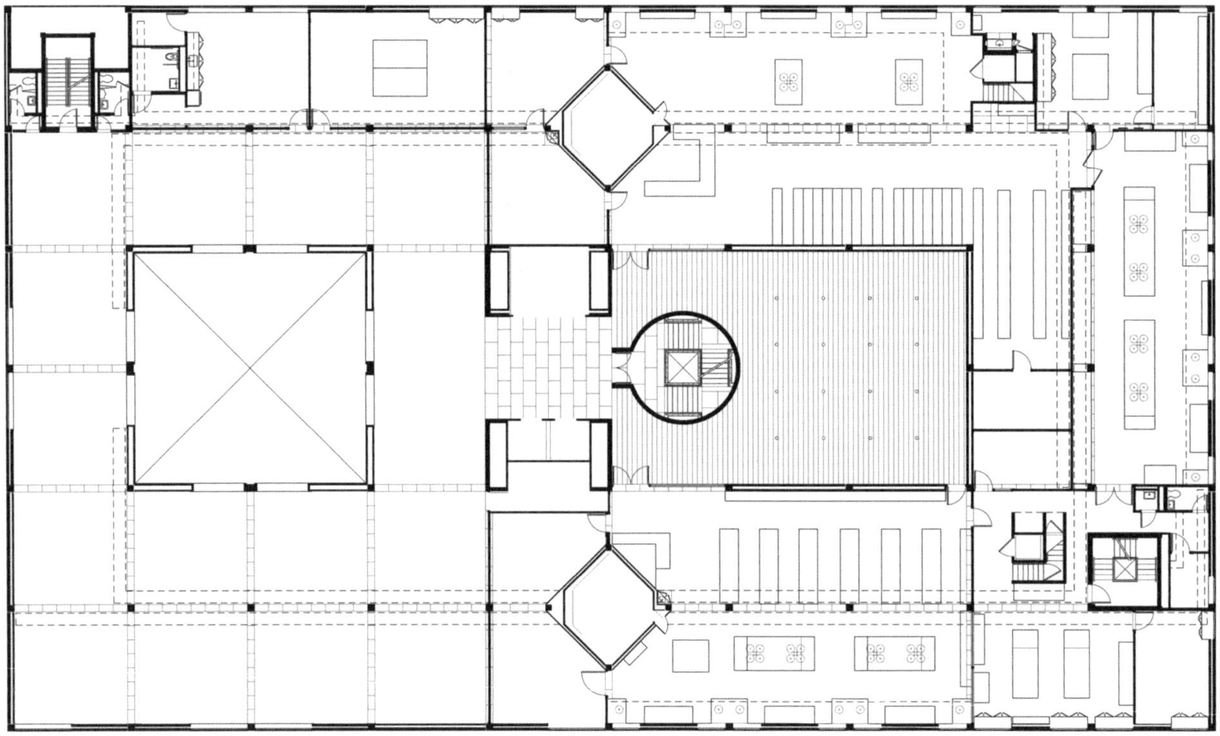

13

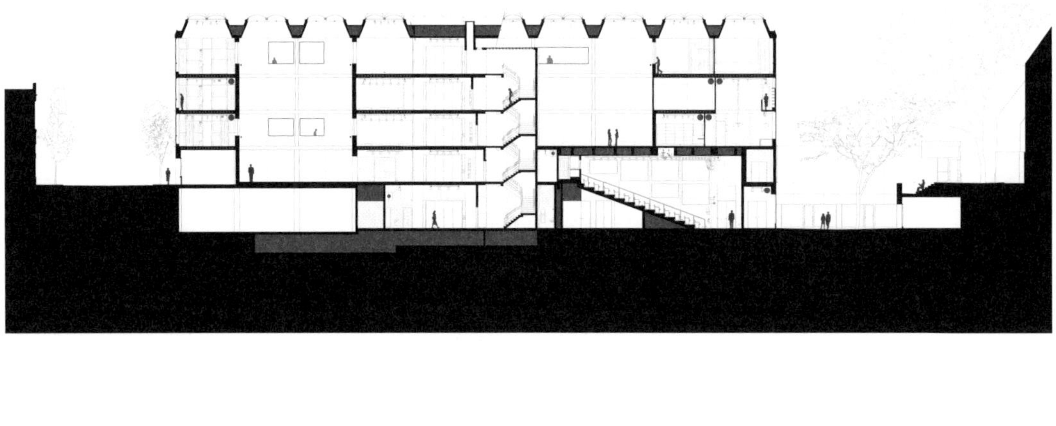

14

Conservation project: 13. First floor plan. 14. Longitudinal section.

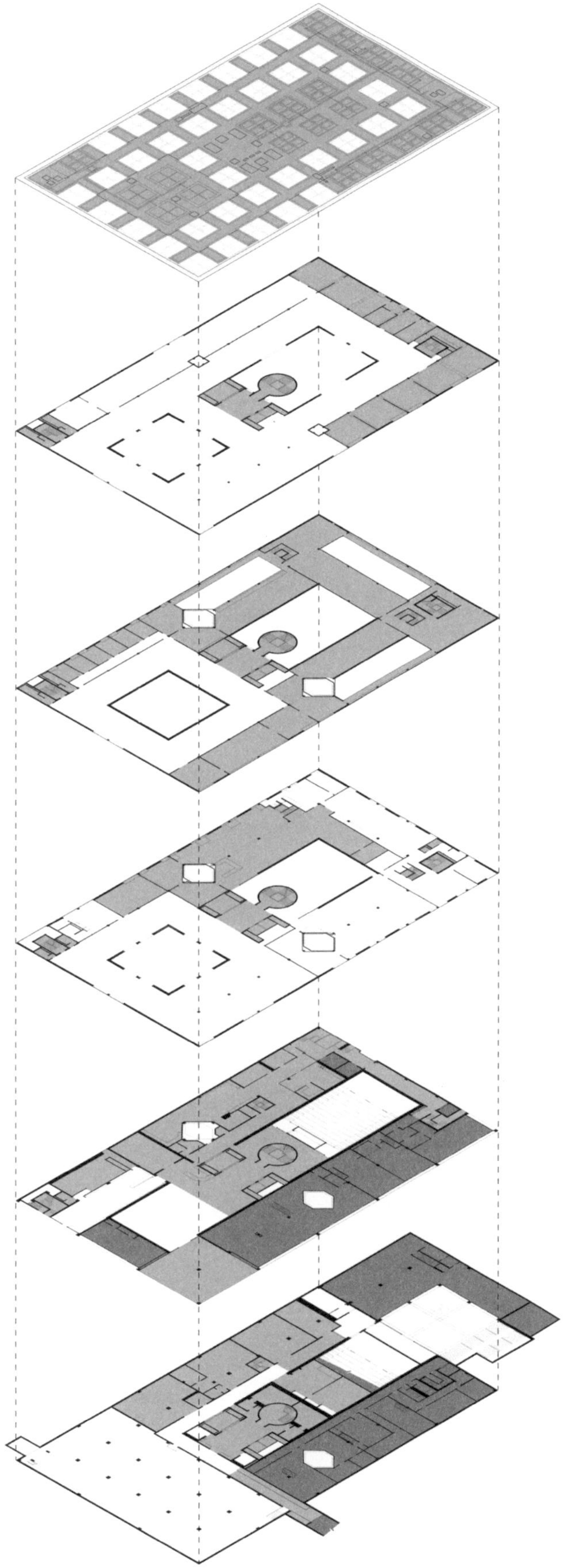

15

Conservation project: 15. Axonometric floor plans diagram (basement to roof) depicting the areas of conservation. Dark gray – primary building conservation area; light gray – secondary building conservation area.

INNOVATIVE RESEARCH APPLIED TO CURRENT ARCHITECTURE, SUCH AS HOUSING COMPLEXES, INVOLVING INSTITUTIONAL AND COMMUNITY ENGAGEMENT.

CITÉ DU LIGNON

The TSAM project for the Cité du Lignon is a pioneering research project to ensure the longevity of an example of the often-despised program of mass housing. In close dialogue with public authorities and representatives of the private owners, the project team managed to develop a "catalog" of solutions for the refurbishment of its curtain wall windows, and improving energy efficiency, and demonstrated the advantages of preservation over demolition.

SERPENTINE HOUSE

The Serpentine House is a representative case of the proper management of state-owned housing, which involved inter-disciplinary and intra-communitarian commitment. Despite the building's humble origins, Helsinki city council was quick to recognize its inherent qualities, and the success of the restoration, carefully crafted by Kati Salonen & Mona Schalin Architects, is a result of close collaboration between the architects, the Helsinki City Museum and the city's planning and building control departments.

ENGAGED SOCIETIES

Designed by Georges Addor, Jacques Bolliger, and Dominique Julliard – Addor & Julliard – together with Louis Payot to house 10,000 inhabitants, in two towers of 26 and 30 floors, respectively, and a linear volume that extends for more than one kilometer, the Cité du Lignon is a project of exceptional originality. In particular, apart from the lamellar structure in reinforced concrete, constructed for the first time in Switzerland using the "tunnel form" technique, the 125,000 square meters of curtain wall paneling in aluminum and glass reflected the logic of industrialized construction typical of the architecture of the 1960s.

Its formal recognition as a cultural asset, which took place in 2009 with measures of protection on an urban scale, has not exempted the complex from the inevitable pressure for significant energy adaptations. It was in this context of preliminary discussions – often animated by the presence of strongly diverging interests – that the architectural and energy study of the Cité du Lignon took place, conducted by the architects Franz Graf and Giulia Marino of the Laboratory of Techniques and Preservation of Modern Architecture at the École Polytechnique Fédérale de Lausanne (TSAM-EPFL).[1] Supported by a working team that brought together the cultural heritage authorities, the department of energy and representatives of the owners of the Cité du Lignon, the project had the goal of developing intervention strategies that could strike the right balance between the variables of culture (the imperatives of conservation), energy (the need to reduce consumption), and economics (the investment capacity of the individual owners).

Based on solid deontological foundations, but also on the pragmatism that is indispensable when intervening in 20th century constructions, the research – after a long, in-depth phase of surveying and diagnostics – defined a series of "typical solutions." Starting with the material, architectural, and functional specificities of the complex, design solutions were studied and then tested at the site, with the creation of many prototypes to evaluate technical feasibility and worksite timing. The project variants were subjected to painstaking "cost-benefit" analyses in keeping with different criteria: a synthetic vision of the variables involved – heritage, energy, economy – aimed at orienting the investment choices of the owners while guaranteeing that the coherence of the original project and its material substance will be conserved.[2]

The research yielded the encouraging result that energy consumption could be reduced by about 70 percent. The design choices, based on a principle of minimum invasiveness, especially on the scrupulously conserved outer surfaces, have made it possible to comply with the parameters of the heritage listing since all interventions are invisible from the outside. As an operative tool that includes detailed recommendations on implementation, the repertoire *ad operandum* defined during the research is attached to the heritage listing, and now offers a clear, unambiguous design reference point, a plan of programmed conservation that is indispensable in the management of a district where a wide range of ownership types coexist. To tackle the problem of decay connected with abandonment or lack of maintenance, the application of the plan can effectively be seen as a measure based on incentives for the owners: by utilizing the solutions already authorized by the proper authorities, the owners can benefit from simplified administrative procedures and easy granting of building permits, whether for ordinary

1. Franz Graf and Giulia Marino, *La cité du Lignon 1963–1971. Étude architecturale et stratégies d'intervention*, Patrimoine et architecture, Gollion, Infolio éditions, 2012. See also Franz Graf and Giulia Marino "Modern and Green: Heritage, Energy, Economy," *Docomomo Journal*, No. 44 – "Modern and Sustainable," Barcelona, Docomomo International, 2011, 32–39; "Il Lignon. Un restauro silenzioso/The Lignon. A Silent Restoration," *Casabella. Rivista internazionale di architettura*, No. 918, 2021, 3–15; "Heritage, Energy, Economy: Planned Preventive Conservation and Thermal Improvements to Building Envelopes at the Cité du Lignon Satellite Precinct, Geneva (1963-1971)," in Andrea Canziani (ed.), *Conserving Architecture. Planned Conservation of XX Century Architectural Heritage*, Milan, Electa, 2009, 216–227.

2008–2012 (RESTORATION PROJECT)
LABORATORY OF TECHNIQUES AND PRESERVATION OF MODERN ARCHITECTURE, EPFL, ENAC FRANZ GRAF AND GIULIA MARINO

IN PROGRESS (CONSTRUCTION PROJECT)
JACCAUD & SPICHER ARCHITECTES ASSOCIÉS
AND OTHER ARCHITECTS

1963–1971
ADDOR & JULLIARD WITH LOUIS PAYOT

GENEVA, SWITZERLAND

1. Facade, after restoration. All interventions are invisible from the exterior.

maintenance or for wider-ranging projects. A streamlined procedure, accompanied by incentives provided by the national energy conversion program, now ensures a coherent intervention conducted on a large scale, and avoids the ubiquitous and indiscriminate application of inadequate standard solutions. A scientific committee led by TSAM researchers and the public body in charge of safeguarding the heritage, together with representatives of the owners ensures the follow-up of the project. The various architects commissioned to execute the project thus work within a clear framework, established beforehand and whose principles are widely shared.

The TSAM project affords an opportunity to look more widely at large-scale contemporary heritage and its future. In terms of its method, but also its results, the pilot study could be a valuable precedent, applicable to a broader corpus of similar objects, not least, to more routine examples of post-war building stock.

Its exemplary approach has sparked much interest in Europe and North America, and been positively received and described in numerous scientific publications. The project has won several awards, such as the European Heritage Awards/Europa Nostra Awards in 2013.[3] Since 2018, it has been recognized as a "CoE Strategy21 good practice" by the European Cultural Heritage Strategy for the 21st Century, Council of Europe.[4]

2. Giulia Marino, "Lignon," in Franz Graf, Mélanie Delaune Perrin, and Giulia Marino (eds.), *Addor architecte*, Geneva, Éditions MetisPresses, 2015, 286–303; Franz Graf and Giulia Marino, "Le projet de restauration des enveloppes de la cité satellite du Lignon (Genève, 1963–71). Enjeux patrimoniaux et impératifs énergétiques," in France Vanlaethem (ed.), *La sauvegarde de l'architecture moderne, défis de la patrimonialisation et mobilisation des savoirs*, Montreal, UQAM, 2014, 225–237; "Modern and Green: Heritage, Energy and Economy," in Ana Tostões and Liu Kecheng (eds.), *Docomomo International 1988-2012: Key Papers in Modern Architectural Heritage Conservation*, Beijing, China Architecture & Building Press, 2012, 183–193, 152–161; "Sanierungsstrategien für die Satellitenstadt Cité du Lignon (Genf, 1963–1971). Baukulturelle Herausforderungen und energietechnische Erfordernisse," in Elise Feiersinger, Andreas Vass, and Susanne Veit (eds.), *Bestand der Moderne. Kontinuität und Herausforderung*, Zurich, Park Books, 2012, 68–75; Giulia Marino, "Il plan de site come strumento di tutela dei quartieri residenziali del secondo Novecento. Il caso ginevrino," in Francesca Albani and Carolina Di Biase (eds.), *Architettura Minore del XX secolo. Strategie di tutela e intervento*, Santarcangelo di Romagna, Maggioli Editore, 2013, 212–227. See also: Richard Klein, "Un modèle pour le Lignon," *AMC-Le Moniteur*, No. 217, 2012, 143; Cristiana Chiorino, "La cité du Lignon a Ginevra. Il progetto di rinnovo e riqualificazione energetica degli involucri," *Archi*, No. 3, 2013, 27–28; Nott Caviezel, "Zur energetischen Sanierung der Grosssiedlung Le Lignon in Genf," *werk, bauen+wohnen*, No. 11, 2011, 62–66.

3. "Prix Europa Nostra 2013," *Heimatschutz-Patrimoine*, No. 2, 2013, 4; "La cite du Lignon, une cite de référence. Interview avec Franz Graf et Giulia Marino par Jennifer Covo," Télévision Suisse Romande, *Couleurs locales*, 2013; "Restauration du Lignon distinguée en Europe," *L'Agefi*, 2013; Laurence Bezaguet, "Le Prix Europa Nostra a été remis au Lignon," *Tribune de Genève*, 2014; Laurence Bezaguet, "Nouvelle distinction pour la cité du Lignon," *Tribune de Genève*, 2013; Laurence Bezaguet, "La Cité du Lignon sacrée championne d'Europe," *La Tribune de Genève*, 2013. See also: https://www.europeanheritageawards.eu/winners/

4. https://www.coe.int/en/webculture-and-heritage/-/the-housing-complex-of-lignon

2. Window, after restoration.

3. Aerial view.

8

4

7

5

6

4. Walkway level veranda. 5. General view. 6. Square between the towers. 7. General view with urban context. 8. Elevation of the west facade, 1963.

9

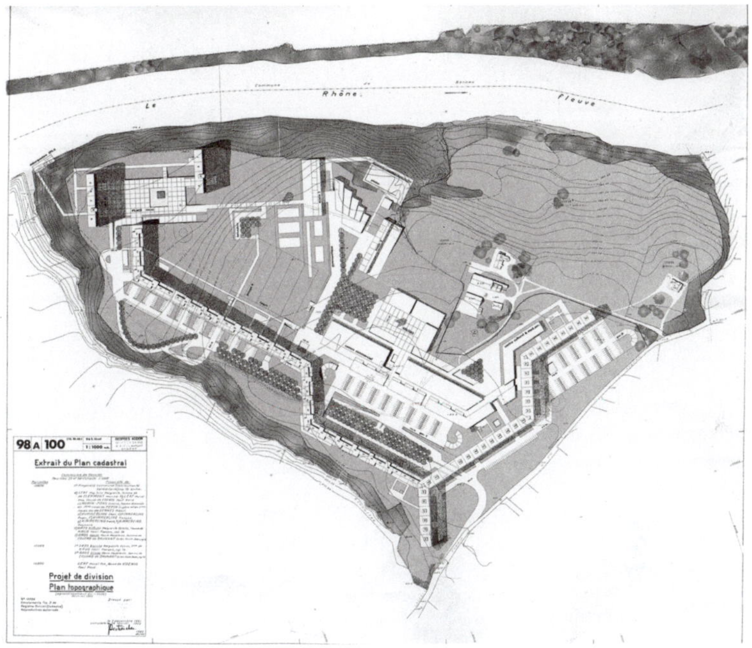

10

11

12

9. Masterplan, preliminary draft, October 1963. 10. Model. 11. Children playing at the playground, which is enhanced by sculptures by Costas Coulentianos. 12. Cité du Lignon under construction, 1960s.

13

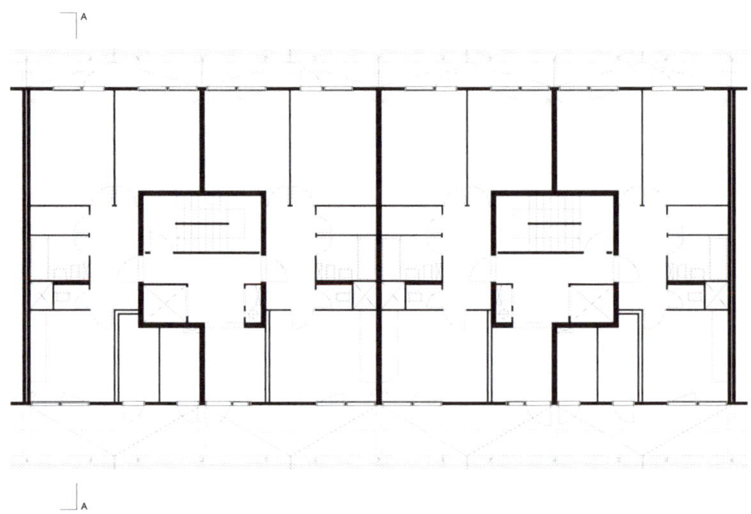

14

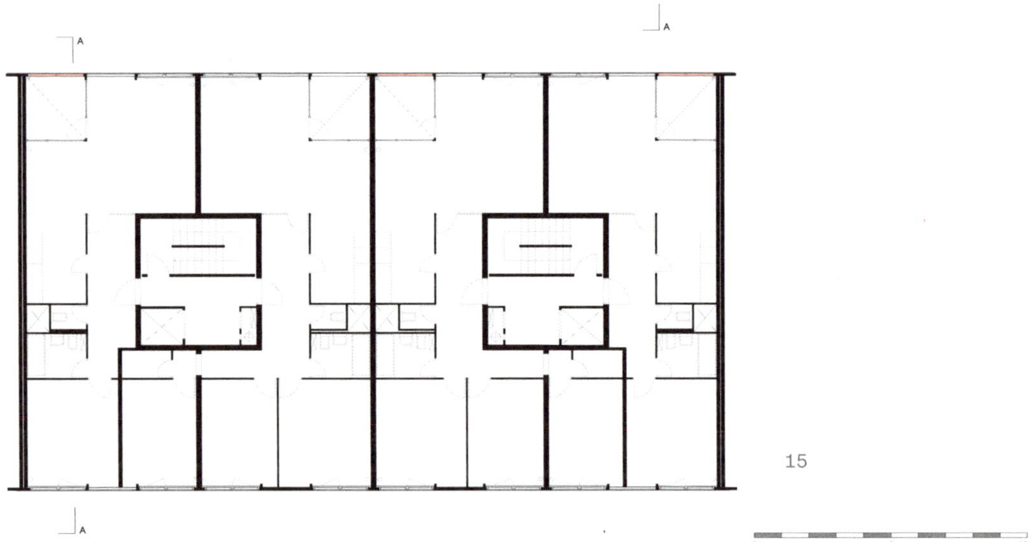

15

Restoration project: 13. Survey of the existing facades – transversal section A–A, north-west elevation, and south-east elevation. In red are marked the elements where intervention occurred. 14. Survey of a walkway level plan. In red are marked the elements were intervention occurred. 15. Survey of a typical floor plan. In red are marked the elements were intervention occurred.

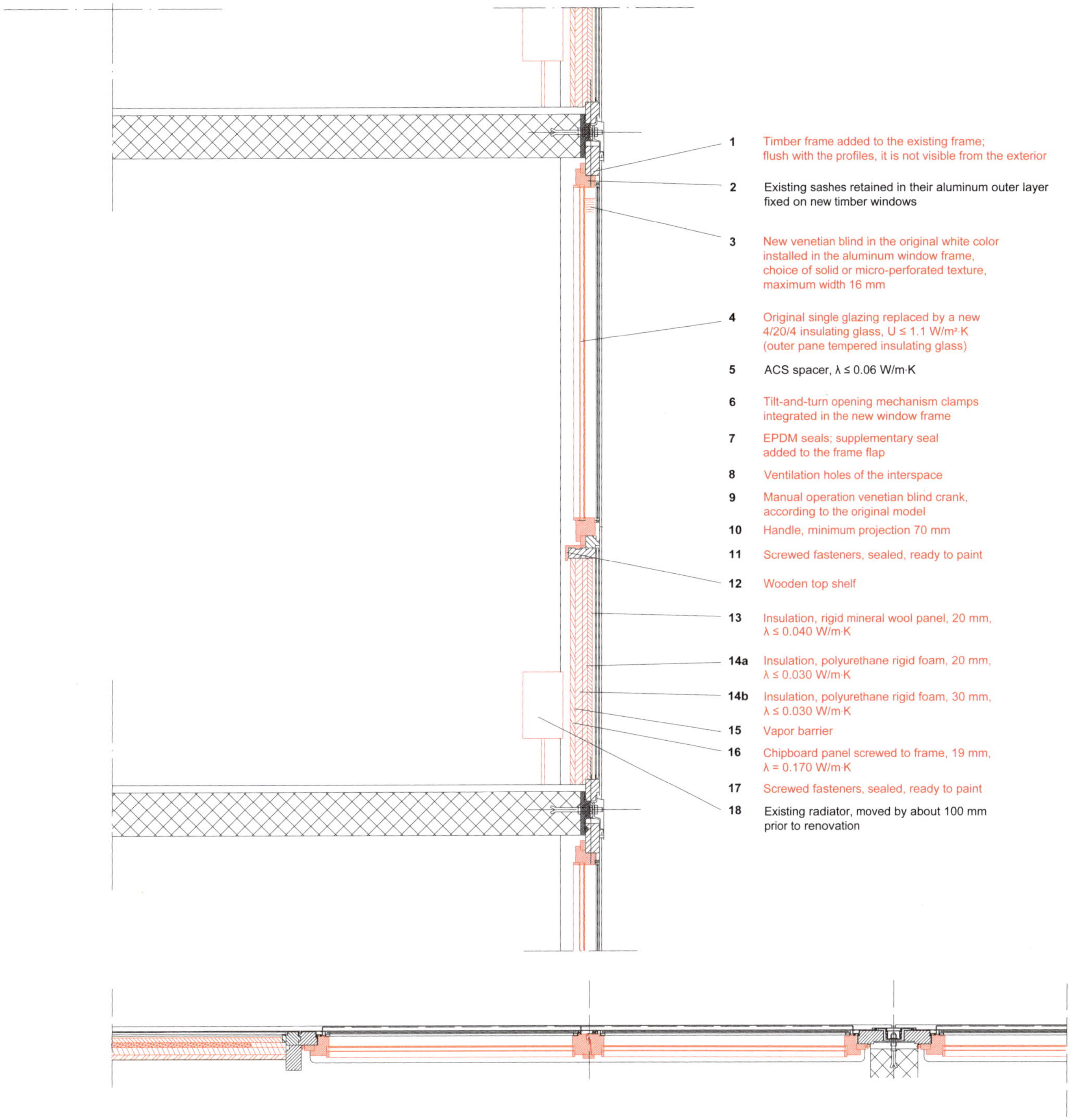

16

Restoration project: 16. Construction detail sections of the interventions on typical floor facades. In red are marked the new elements.

Architect Yrjö Lindegren (1900–1952) designed Serpentine House (Käärmetalo in Finnish) as a rental housing block for the City of Helsinki in the post-war rebuilding period. Ambitions were high and Hilding Ekelund (1893–1984), the architect in charge of the municipal housing committee, employed some of his most distinguished colleagues for the task of designing new housing. The undulating building, winding along its sloping site at the edge of an area of detached houses, forms an impressive overall composition. Designed in 1950, the Serpentine House comprises two separate, four-story residential buildings, completed in 1951, as well as a service building with a daycare center and swimming pool, finished in 1952. Originally, the buildings were designed to have 189 municipal apartments with a dwelling surface of in average 45 square meters. In the post-war decade, this was considered fully sufficient for a family with children. On each floor, three apartments were grouped around a stairwell, which allowed two of the three apartments to have windows and views toward both sides of the building.[1] Each apartment, ranging from one room to three rooms, had a bathroom, and a kitchen equipped with a small balcony. Inspired by Margarete Schütte-Lihotzky's (1897–2000) "Frankfurt Kitchen," the kitchens were manufactured by Enso as its "Teho" model.[2] The meandering form of the building was achieved by adding a small variety of trapezoid apartment blocks. The use of transverse load-bearing masonry walls, projecting from the facade like buttresses, became one of the most characteristic features of the Serpentine House.[3]

In 2016, when the renovation project was launched, the exterior spaces and the dwellings had long suffered from lack of funding for maintenance since the previous renovation in the 1980s. The public company in charge of managing and maintaining the municipal rental properties in the area had surveyed the condition of the buildings around 2010, concluding that the plinth, exterior plastering, balconies, roof structures, windows, bathrooms, kitchens, and ventilation system were in need of major repairs.[4]

Rejecting the initial renovation program, which was based on purely technical and functional priorities, the municipal authorities demanded greater focus on the significant architectural value of the Serpentine House. The City Planning Department commissioned a thorough building history survey, and eventually the site, buildings, and interior design of the Serpentine House, were all protected in a detailed town plan. Since the protection plan established strict boundaries for intervention, the preservation of the original architectural, spatial, and material characteristics clearly emerged as an objective shared by the client, the authorities, and the design team led by Kati Salonen & Mona Schalin Architects, notwithstanding the task to solve serious technical and structural problems and introduce functional improvements.

The main task of the refurbishment was the technical performance of the flat roof and the external walls, built of brick and *Betocel* blocks. Therefore, the roof slab was replaced by a ventilated construction; the concrete balcony slabs, produced at a time when steel and cement were scarce, were rebuilt and their delicate, painted steel railings were reconstructed; the characteristic, original rough render was restored, the original, wooden windows and balcony doors were repaired, and only details in poor condition were completely replaced.

The apartments, consisting mainly of two rooms, a kitchenette, and a bathroom, were upgraded with special attention to the bathrooms, fixtures, and fittings,

1. Yrjö Lindegren, "Asuntokortteli No 857 – Mäkelänkatu, Helsinki," *Arkkitehti*, No. 10–11, 1950.

2. Riitta Salastie, "Serpentine House/Käärmetalo," in Jonas Malmberg, Petteri Kummala, and Leena Makkonen (eds.), *Docomomo Finland – Register Selectionl*, Porvoo, Docomomo Finland, 2017, 92–93. Also available at: https://en.docomomo.fi/projects/serpentine-house/

3. Vilhelm Helander and Simo Rista, *Suomalainen rakennustaide. Modern Architecture in Finland*, Helsinki, Kirjayhtymä, 1987.

4. Arkkitehtitoimisto Koskinen & Schalin, *Käärmetalon rakennushistoriaselvitys*, 2011.

2016–2020
KATI SALONEN & MONA SCHALIN ARCHITECTS

1950–1951
YRJÖ LINDEGREN

HELSINKI, FINLAND

1 Aerial view, after renovation.

and the original kitchen cabinetry was repaired where possible. The integration of updated building engineering into these small apartments, while avoiding copious chasings in the thin dividing walls, required close cooperation within the project team: the electrical engineer collaborated with the architect in designing a new skirting board specifically for the Serpentine House, to be used alongside the preserved original skirting. The original color scheme for the Serpentine House was designed by artist Eino Kauria (1903–1997).[5] A study of the colors and surface layers revealed that, in each stairwell, a single wall and the steel parts of the handrail were originally painted in a vivid color. These tones of yellow, red, blue, and green were reconstructed in collaboration with a conservator, applying traditional paint methods, such as linseed oil paint.

5. Eino Kauria had cooperated with Alvar Aalto in the definition of the original color scheme of the interiors of the Paimio Sanatorium (1929–1933).

Since its renovation the Serpentine House has been regarded as a model for sustainable renovation – the wooden windows and kitchen cabinetry were skillfully repaired by the carpenters, the performance of the natural ventilation was improved, the common facilities and the courtyards were enhanced, and the tenants could all return to their apartments after the construction. The long road from preliminary condition surveys to the successful completion of the renovation provides an instructive example of a process that deliberately involved many stakeholders. The renovation project was awarded with the Finlandia Prize for Architecture in 2019.

2

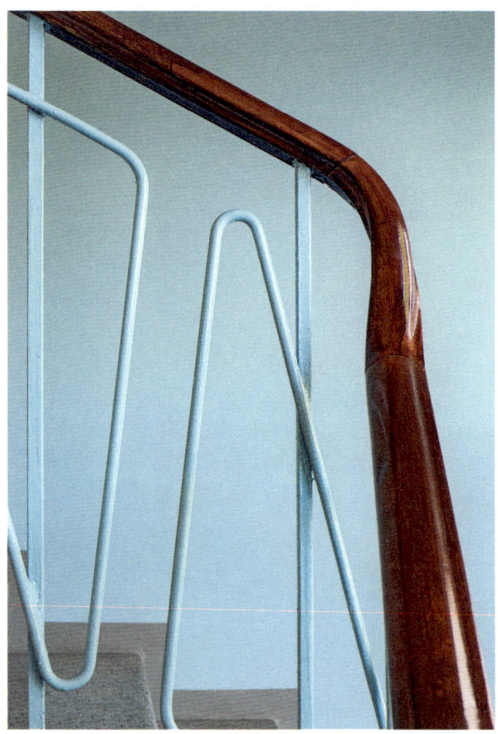

3

2. Staircase with restored original color, after renovation. 3. Staircase railing, after renovation.

4. Stairwell with reconstructed skylight, after renovation.

5. Kitchen with renovated cabinets, after renovation.

6. Exterior view from the courtyard, after renovation.

7

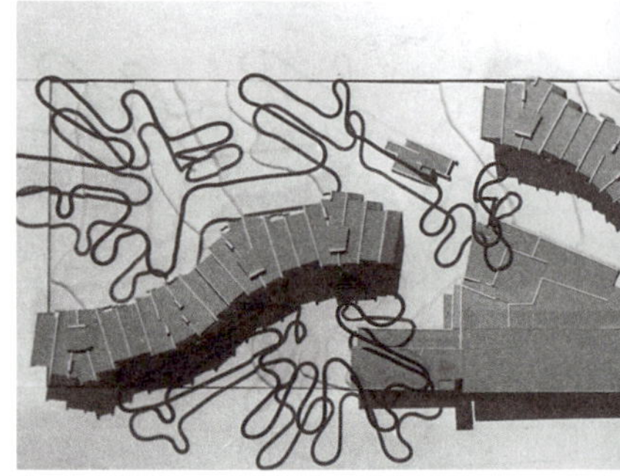

9

8

10

7. Kitchen with cabinets repainted by the tenant, before renovation. 8. Apartment balcony severely deteriorated, before renovation. 9. View of the south block, before renovation. 10. View of the south block, 1950s.

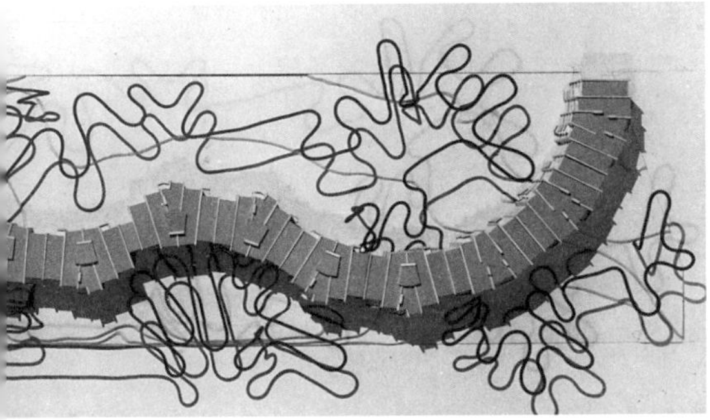

11

12

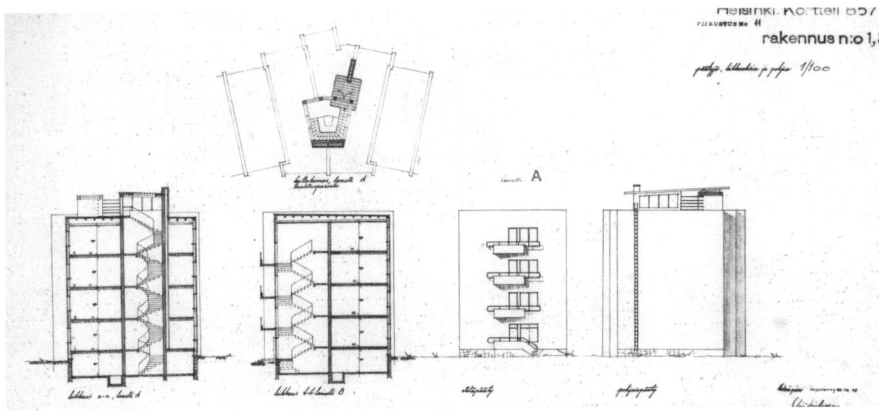

13

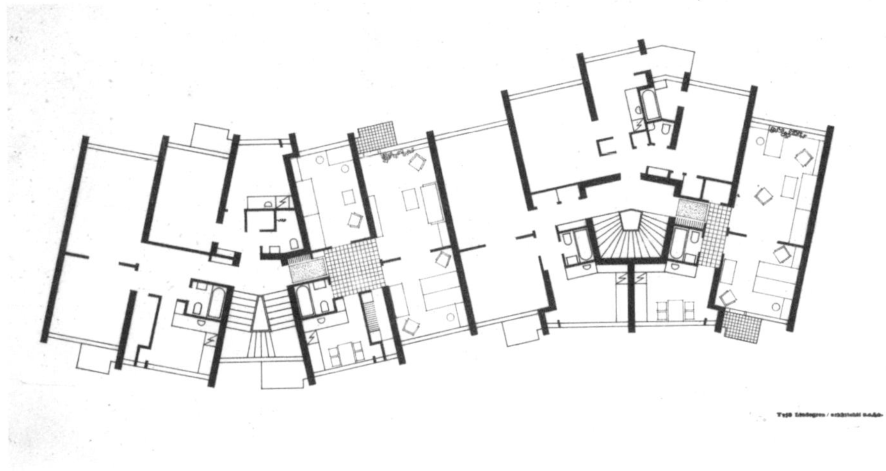

14

11. Photo of the model with housing blocks and service building. 12. Sections, detail of roof plan, north and south elevations, 1949. 13. Floor plan of the two types of units, 1950. 14. View of the north block, 1950s.

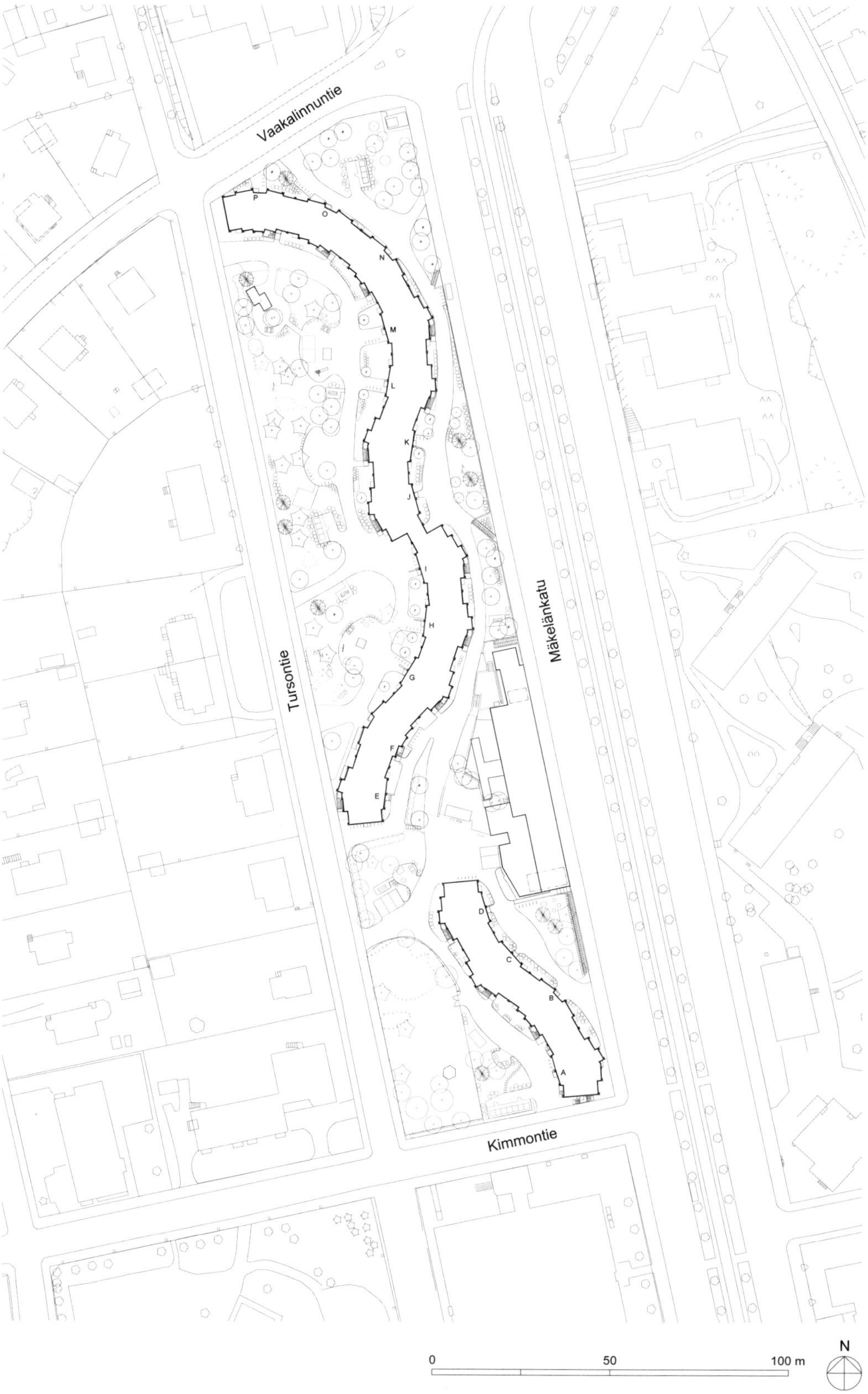

15

 Renovation project: 15. Site plan.

16

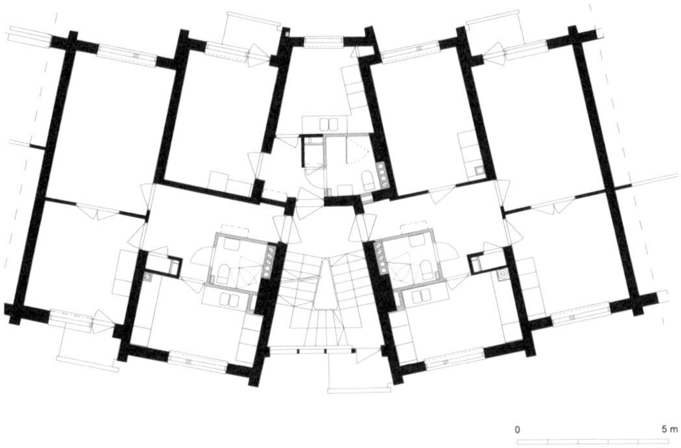

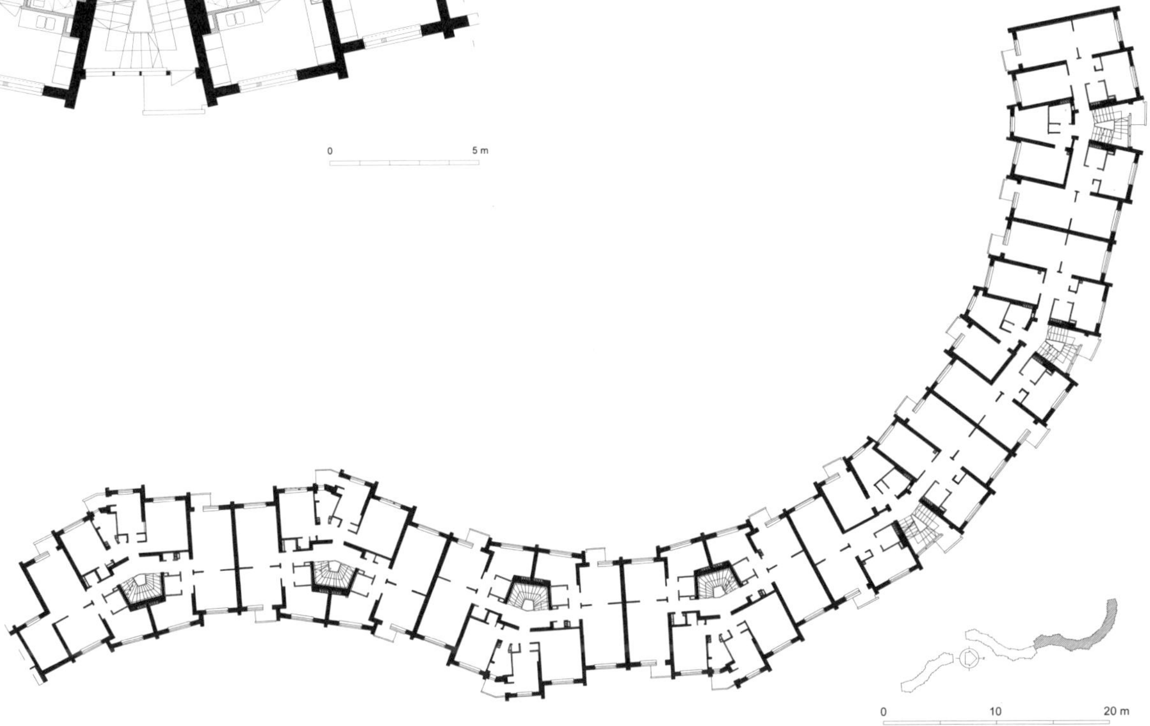

17

18

Renovation project: 16. Floor plan of type "B." 17. Floor plan of the north block. 18. West elevation of the south block.

EXEMPLARY WORKS THAT SAFEGUARD THE DISTINCTIVE IDENTITIES OF MODERN BUILDINGS, WHILE ALLOWING THEM TO BE ADAPTED, IN USE AND FORM, TO CONTEMPORARY NEEDS.

MUNICIPAL ORPHANAGE AMSTERDAM

WDJArchitecten's project for the former Municipal Orphanage of Amsterdam is a fine illustration of an adaptive reuse project that also respects the building's original identity. Forced to metamorphose over time in order to survive, and now used as offices, it was renovated to evoke the original essence of the building, not only through the reinstatement of distinctive lost features, but also through the ingenious manipulation of Aldo van Eyck's original design principles.

YAMANASHI PRESS AND BROADCASTING CENTER

Tange Associates' complex and surgical intervention in the Yamanashi Press and Broadcasting Center provides an essential model for the preservation of modern buildings, in the way it resolved the challenges of a seismic retrofit. This high-tech solution was devised such that it skillfully introduced seismic safety measure without requiring visible reinforcement that would have compromised the buildings' aesthetic.

METAMORPHOSED FUNCTIONS

MUNICIPAL ORPHANAGE AMSTERDAM

METAMORPHOSED FUNCTIONS

Aldo van Eyck's (1918–1999) Municipal Orphanage in Amsterdam dates from 1960 and is internationally celebrated as a key work of post-war Modern Movement architecture. It is generally "recognized as an epitome of the ideas of Team X and the cradle of Structuralism."[1] Originally, the building complex accommodated approximately 125 children in eight pavilions with further service facilities, such as kitchens and offices. Like individual houses, the pavilions are connected to an internal street, which lends the building its particular layout. It has a characteristic repetitive load-bearing structure of fair-faced concrete elements with infills of masonry, glass block, and glazing, covered by eight large and 328 small domes. Both the infills and the fixed furnishings, e.g., built-in play elements, give a very specific signature to each space, designed for a certain age of the children and differentiated for boys and girls. "All efforts have been made to build this house like a small city, recognizing that the city should be like a large house."[2] In Van Eyck's own words, this is "a small world in a large world, a large world in a small world, a house like a city, a city like a house, a home for children, a place where they can live rather than survive."[3]

After being used as a children's home, the building was partly converted into an academy building in the early 1990s, involving various interventions designed by Aldo van Eyck himself. Further refurbishment of the other part to accommodate rental offices had been carried out by others a few years later but within a bit more than a decade the building was eventually abandoned. When it was declared a National Monument in 2014 it had been vacant for a long time and fallen into disrepair. The building was acquired by private investors with the ambition to revitalize it as an up-to-date office environment while doing justice to its original qualities wherever possible. The project was commissioned to WDJArchitecten in 2015. In 2017, this inspiring structure was finally completely renovated according to the architects' design, adapting it to contemporary standards for sustainable office buildings. In early 2018, the building was leased by area developer BPD.

In the past, the fair-faced concrete facades had been treated with a rubbery coating to prevent further carbonation. These sections were stripped, carefully restored, and impregnated with an unobtrusive agent. The masonry facades were repaired and cleaned. The window frames, as replaced by Van Eyck around 1993, were painted according to his original choice of color. The glass was replaced by a slightly sun-repellent double glazing in order to avoid large air conditioning systems and ducts in the interior. The outdoor areas were newly laid out, in close collaboration with landscape designers Atelier Quadrat, based on the original design and current requirements.

The poor thermal and acoustic performance and inadequate building service systems were a major design challenge. As part of the renovation, the work areas have been equipped with underfloor heating and convectors while, in the internal street, column radiators were reinstated. By providing the domes with 35 millimeters of spray plaster to improve room acoustics, the electrical wiring could also be concealed within this thin layer while maintaining the original details. With such a chirurgical approach, comfortable workspaces were created while respecting the original architectural concept.

Later partitions have been removed. Original finishes like the quartzite flooring of the internal street, the concrete architraves and the exposed masonry walls

1. Wessel de Jonge, "Myth and Metamorphosis: Aldo van Eyck's Orphanage (1960) in Amsterdam Restored," in Ana Tostões and Nataša Koselj (eds.), *Metamorphosis – The Continuity of Change. Proceedings of the 15th international Docomomo Conference*, Lisbon/Ljubljana, Docomomo International/Docomomo Slovenia, 2018, 585–591.

2. Vincent Ligtelijn (ed.), *Aldo van Eyck: Works*, Bussum, Toth Publishers, 1999, 89.

3. Aldo van Eyck in *Forum*, 1961, quoted in Vincent Ligtelijn and Francis Strauven (eds.), *Aldo van Eyck: Writings, Vol. 2, Collected Articles and Other Writings*, Amsterdam, SUN Publishers, 2008, 317–320. See also: Francis Strauven, *Aldo van Eyck: The Shape of Relativity*, Amsterdam, Meulenhoff, 1994 (Dutch)/1998 (English); and Christoph Grafe, *Orphanage Amsterdam: Building and Playgrounds by Aldo van Eyck*, Amsterdam, Architectura & Natura Press, 2017.

2015–2017
WDJARCHITECTEN

1955–1960
ALDO VAN EYCK

AMSTERDAM, THE NETHERLANDS

1. Exterior view of the former children pavilions, now office spaces, after renovation.

have been restored, including the concrete light fixtures. The many additional door openings between the pavilions and the internal street were again filled up with the same clinker brick, which fortunately was found to be still available. The original cabinetry and countertops, which remained in three of the pavilions, were carefully restored, including their original finishes and colors. Within this characteristic context, a future-proof office space has been created with beautiful daylit areas, good artificial lighting and room acoustics, and views of the green outdoor spaces. The project was granted Amsterdam's annual heritage award in 2018.

2

2. Former living room under large dome, after renovation. Interior furnishing for the tenant by EX Interiors.

3. Pa[illegible] pavili[illegible] the office, now both office spaces, after renovation.

4. Former celebration hall, after renovation.

5

6

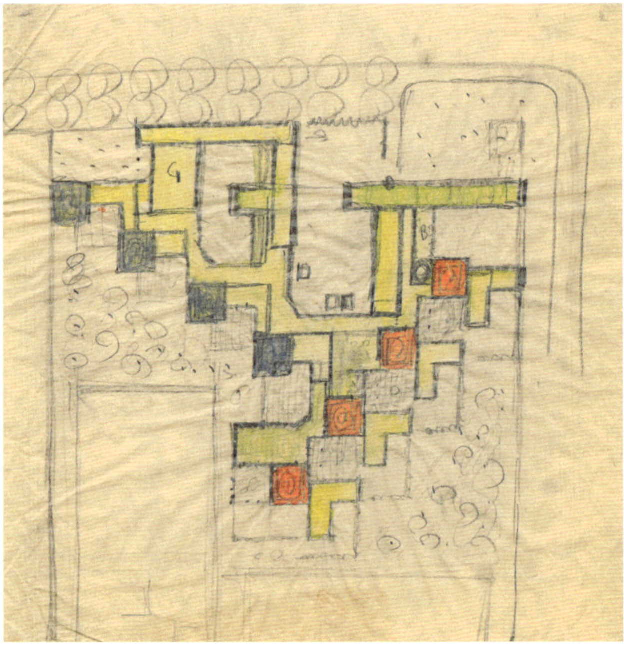

7

8

5. Former celebration hall before renovation. 6. Exterior view of the building with a coating on the concrete facades, before renovation. 7. Schematic plan: in blue the dormitories of the older children, in red the dormitories for the babies and children under ten, and in yellow the circulation and common areas. 8. Water feature.

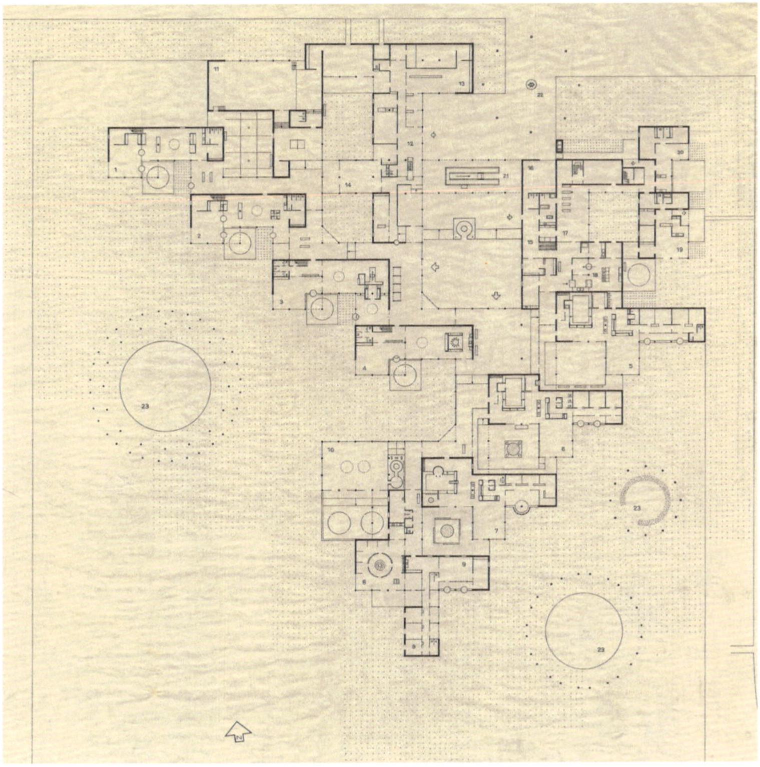

9

10

11

12

9. Ground floor plan. 10. Aerial view, 1960. 11. Girl playing with a ball in the celebration hall. 12. Forecourt, shortly after completion in 1960.

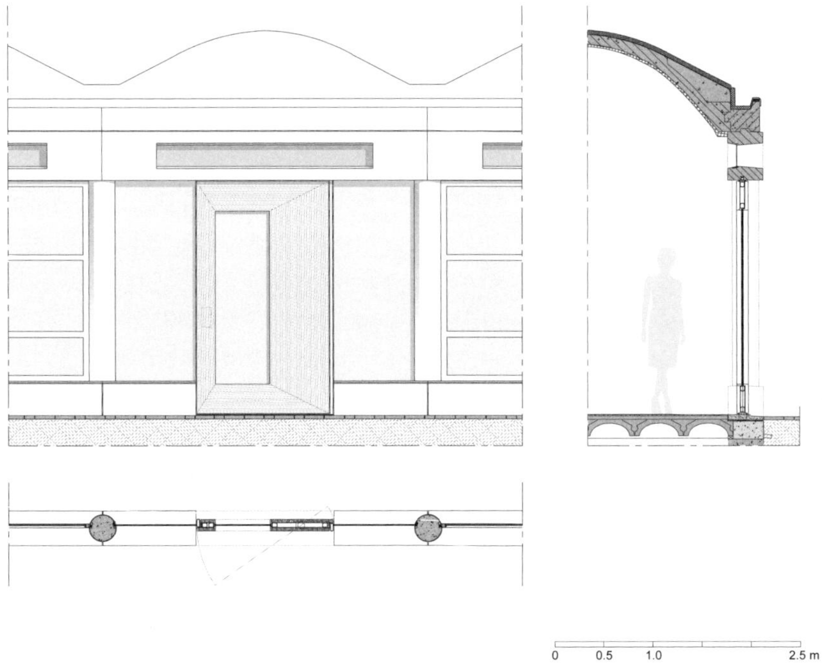

13

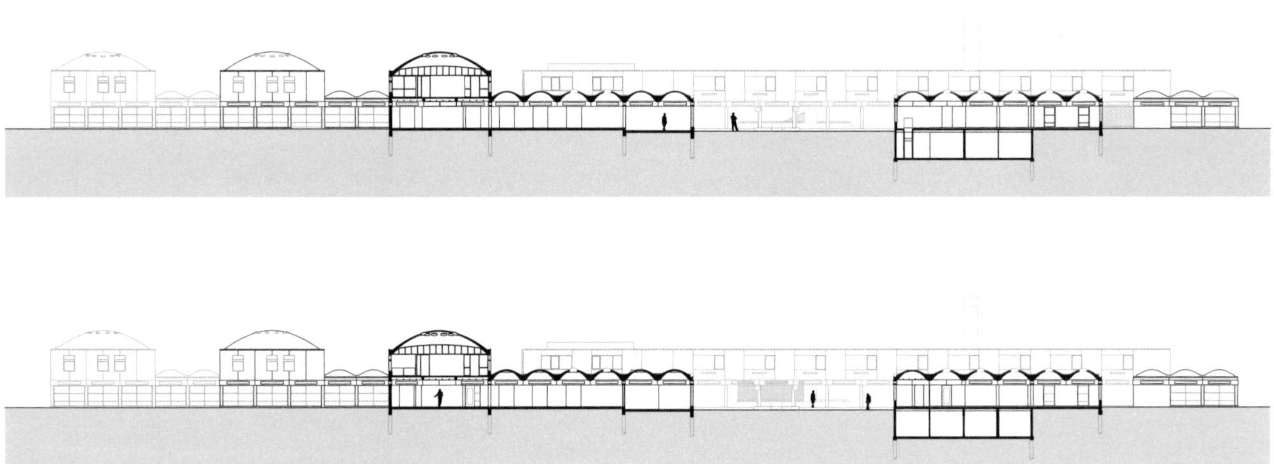

14

Renovation project: 13. Detail plan, section, and elevation of the new entrance door. 14. Section A-A, before and after the intervention.

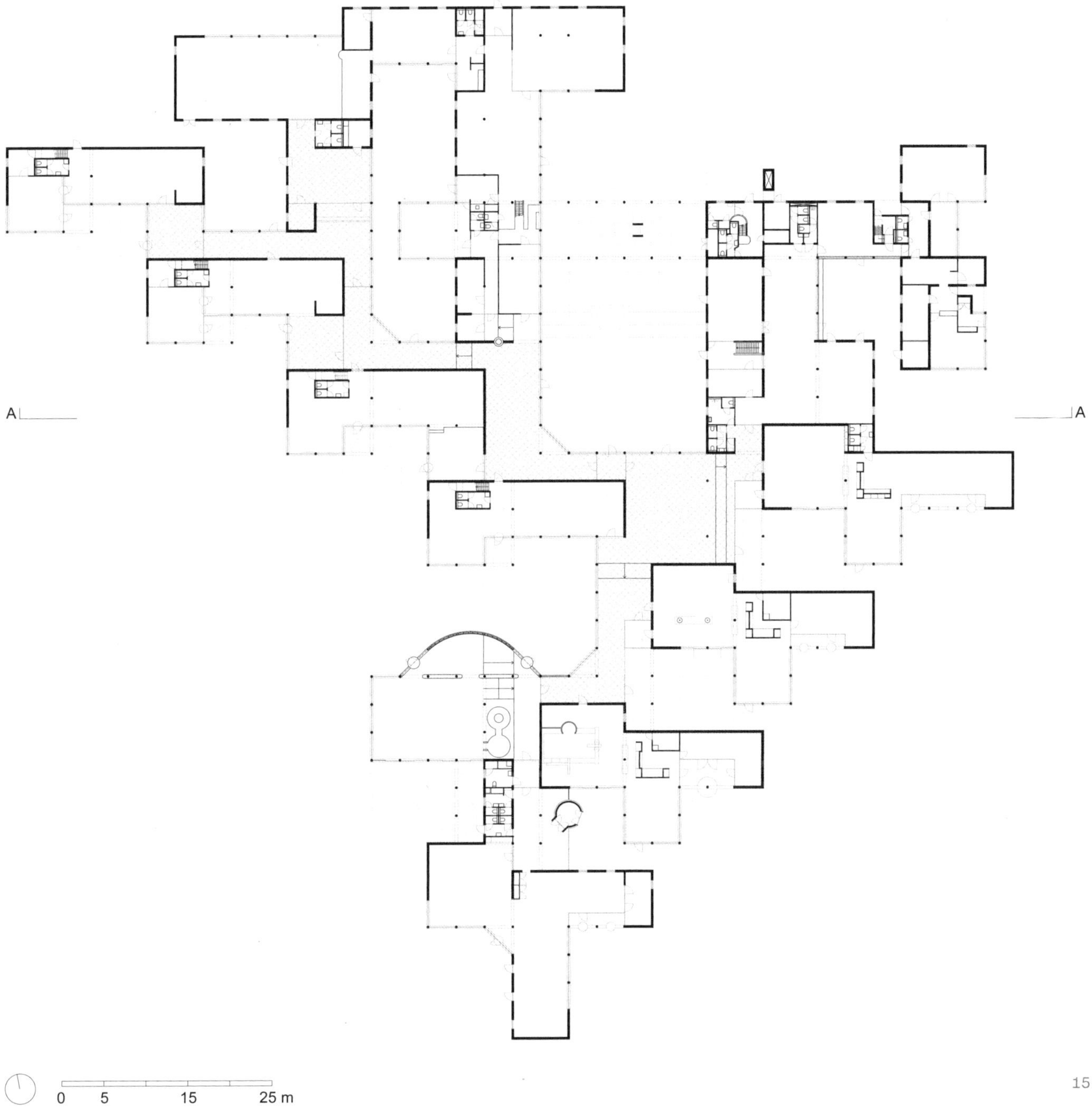

15

16

Renovation project: 15. Ground floor plan. 16. East elevation.

YAMANASHI PRESS AND BROADCASTING CENTER

METAMORPHOSED FUNCTIONS

The Yamanashi Press and Broadcasting Center is a complex building, in which three companies – press, broadcasting, and printing – were integrated under the same roof. To this end, Kenzo Tange's concept for the building enabled its major four independent activities – offices, newspaper printing plant, publication space, and broadcasting studio – to organically relate and it also allowed for future expansion. The different premises were separated as little as possible and similar functions such as office space, production area, or studio space were combined as complexes in the building. Contact between the activities was provided for by several communication shafts, which housed different functions (e.g., stairs, elevators, plumbing), built vertically within a 15 × 17 meter lattice grid. This spatial organization, with a three-dimensional communication grid, was one of the architectural devices allowing adaptability to change and growth. Due to its remarkable architectural solution, the Yamanashi Press and Broadcasting Center became a core symbol of the local information industry.[1] The reinforced concrete construction rises with its two lower and eight upper floors between the sculptural columns on a site of 4000 square meters. Its characteristic appearance is derived from its outer walls of rammed concrete.[2] While Metabolist designs can be in danger of "degenerating into an arid technological fetishism," Tange succeeded in achieving "a dignified and monumental form" with the Yamanashi Press and Broadcasting Center. In particular in plan, the building gives the distinct impression of total flexibility within a fixed framework.[3]

Since the building's completion, seven renovations have been undertaken, in line with the original concept of a changeable and growable building. Worthy of mention among these are: the first renovation, in 1974, in which floors were extended on the north-east side, from the 6th to the 8th floor, and on the south-east side, on the 5th, 6th, and 8th floors; the fourth renovation, in 2000, where, to improve durability and reduce weight, exterior pre-cast panels and handrails were replaced by cast aluminum ones; the fifth renovation, in 2005, in which a broadcasting studio was created by extending floors in a three-story space formerly occupied by a rotary press; and finally, in 2013, the sixth renovation, which was as substantial as the first one, and involved interventions in several areas of the building.

In 2015, to celebrate the 50th anniversary of the building, its owner – the Yamanashi Culture Hall – established what was called the "100-year plan for Yamanashi Press and Broadcasting Center," a refurbishment meant to enable the use of the building for at least another 50 years. Designed by Tange Associates, the main goal of this seventh renovation was to undertake an adequate seismic isolation retrofit. The requirements for this renovation were to retain the exterior design, to maintain the building's function as a facility for transmitting emergency information in the event of a large earthquake, and to keep a 24-hour workplace operating, even during the renovation work. To meet these stringent requirements, mid-story isolation was installed at the second basement level. Four isolation devices were fitted to each of the 16 shafts. The basic isolation clearances for building services pipework were ensured and the flexibility of connections was improved.

The facility's functions have now been updated, while preserving its original design, because the owner values its original concept. The Yamanashi Press and Broadcasting Center will retain its place, for at least another 50 years, in the hearts of the local residents as the landmark that stands in front of Kofu Station.

1. See: "Yamanashi Press and Broadcasting Center," *a+u, Drawings from the Kenzo Tange Archive – National Gymnasiums for Tokyo Olympics*, No. 589, October 2019.

2. Udo Kultermann, *Kenzo Tange 1946–1969. Architecture and Urban Design*, Zurich, Verlag für Architektur – Artemis, 1970, 246.

3. William J.R. Curtis, *Modern Architecture Since 1900. Third edition*, London, Phaidon, 1996, 510.

2015–2016
TANGE ASSOCIATES

1964–1966
KENZO TANGE & URTEC

KOFU CITY, JAPAN

1. Exterior view from south, after renovation.

2

3

4

2. Exterior spiral stair, after renovation. 3. Main entrance, after renovation. 4. Entrance hall, after renovation.

5

6

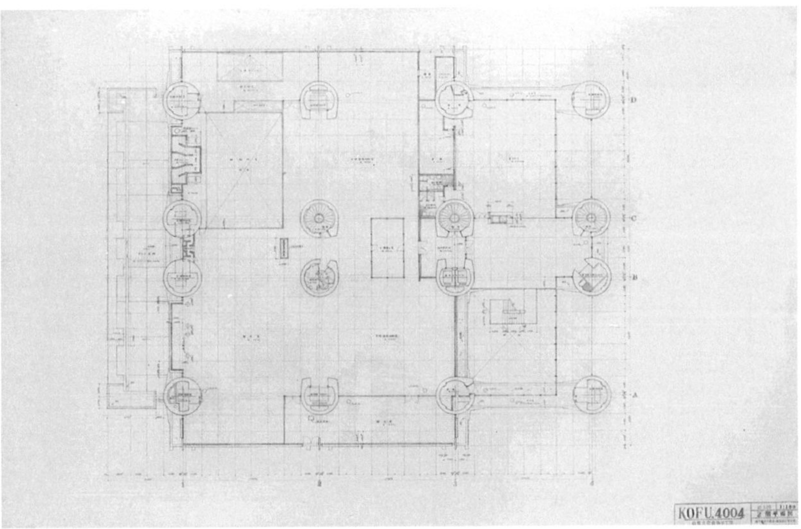

7

8

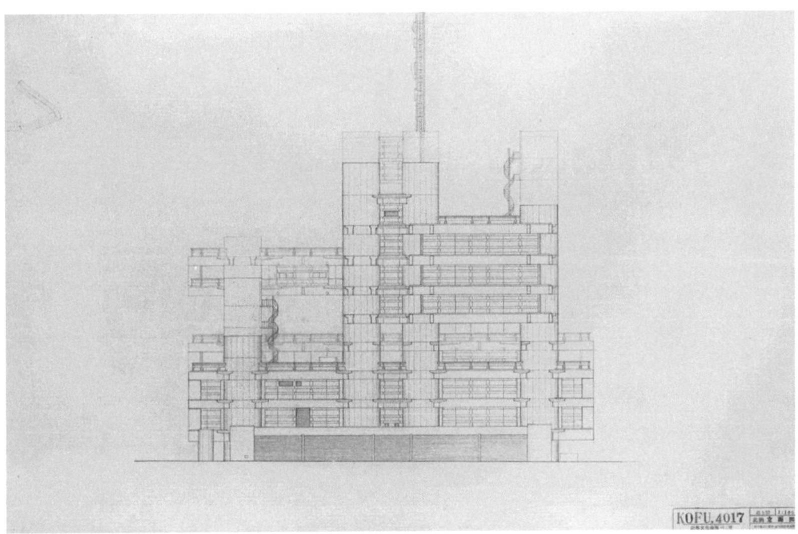

5. Exterior view from west, 1966. 6. Exterior view from east, 1966. 7. First floor plan. 8. North elevation.

9

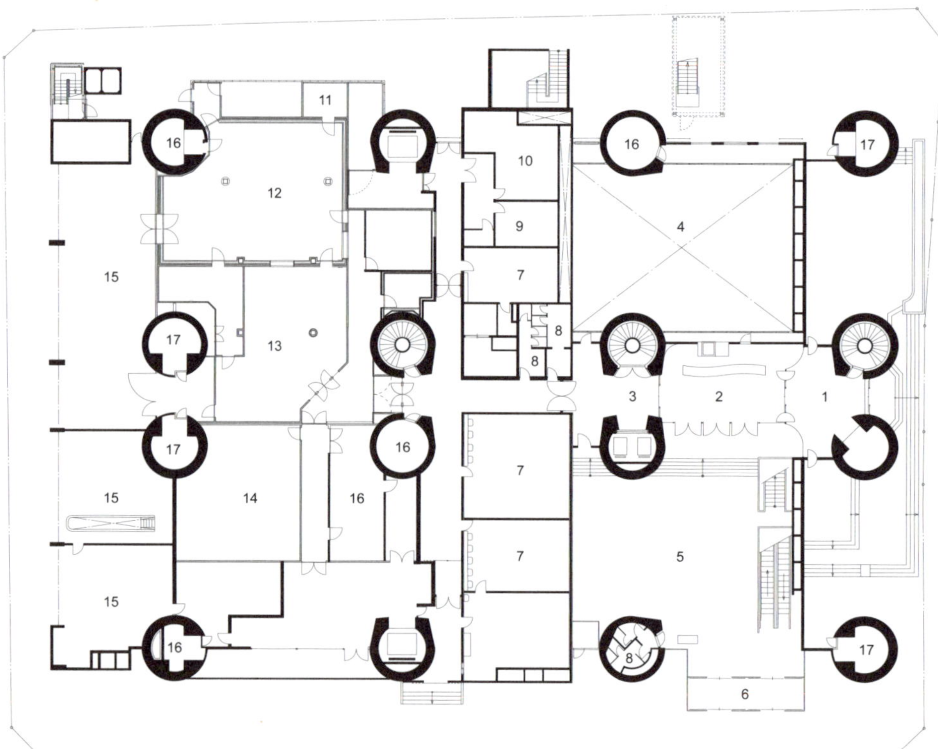

10

9. Seismic retrofit of a shaft at the second basement level, after renovation. Renovation project: 10. Ground floor plan. 1 – main entrance, 2 – reception, 3 – elevator hall, 4 – hall, 5 – lobby, 6 – west entrance, 7 – locker room, 8 – WCs. 9 – massage room, 10 – medical office, 11 – makeup room, 12 – Broadcasting Studio, 13 – studio control room, 14 – YBS technical department, 15 – garage, 16 – storehouse, 17 – air conditioning room.

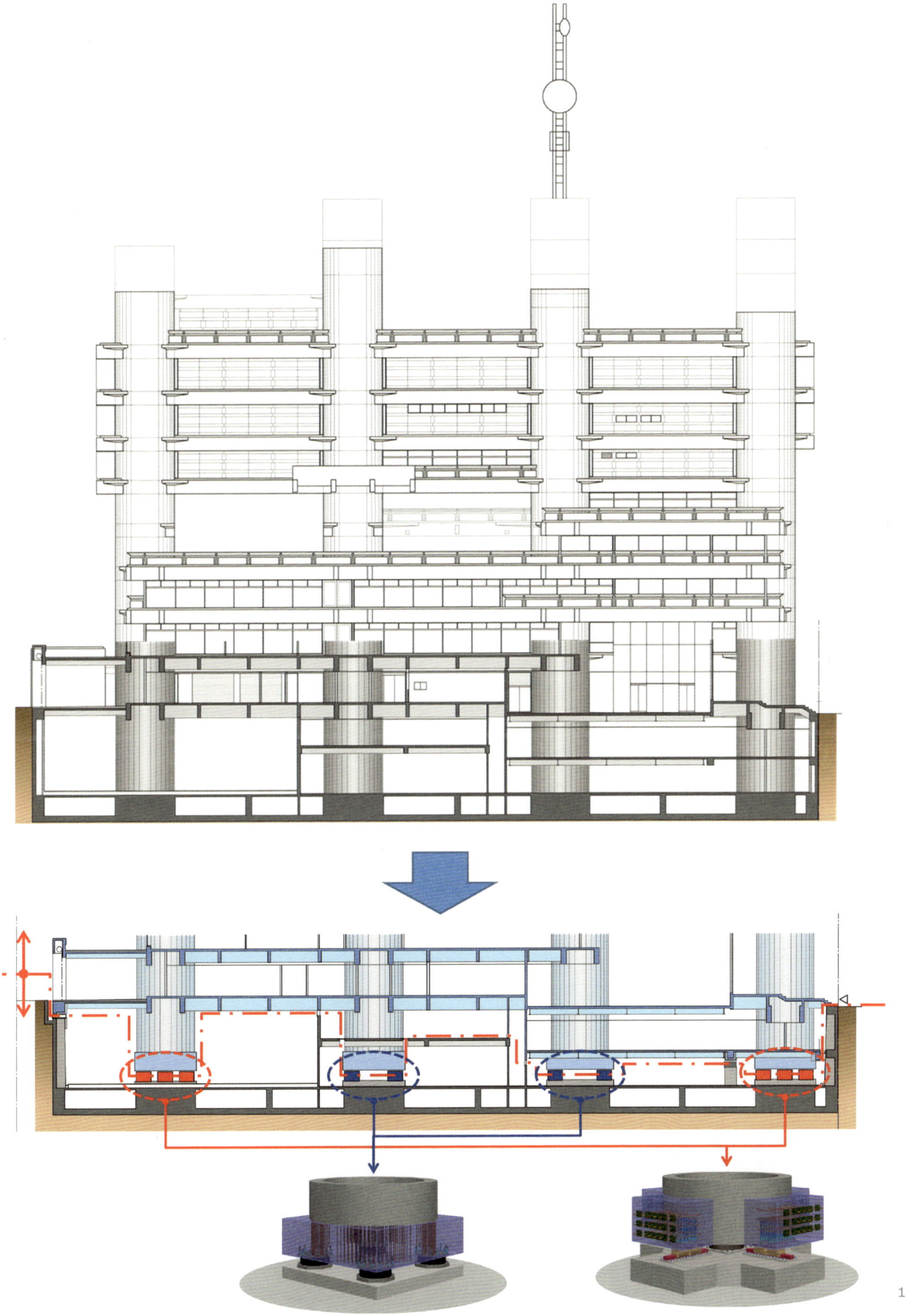

Renovation project: 11. Schematic drawing of the seismic retrofit of the shafts.

PIONEERING STUDIES AND LOW-BUDGET INTERVENTIONS THAT CONTRIBUTE TO RAISING AWARENESS OF THE IMPORTANCE OF PRESERVING THE MODERNIST LEGACY IN ADVERSE LOCATIONS AND CONDITIONS.

AITON COURT

Given the severe deterioration with which it was faced, Aiton Court's restoration has set a valuable benchmark for private maintenance using very limited funding in Africa. Based on the extensive social and architectural documentation of the building undertaken by students from the University of the Witwatersrand, Mayat Hart Architects' project was cleverly developed, enabling an affordable solution to be reached that finely balanced responsibilities to heritage, living conditions and commercial needs.

CASA ESTUDIO PARA ARTISTAS

The restoration of the facades of the Casa Estudio para Artistas sheds new light on public initiatives to preserve built legacies. Realizing the importance of preserving the building's facades, the Buenos Aires city authorities included them in their urban regeneration program. Thus, this public initiative serves as an example of how 20th century architecture can be acknowledged and protected, while including it in a much wider urban program.

EDUCATING PRACTICES

Hillbrow, the originally suburban area where the Aiton Court building is located, would later develop into Johannesburg's infamous Modernist flatland,[1] home to the mid-century "Hillbrow Modern" architectural style[2] as well as post-apartheid inner city slums. Designed by South African architects Angus Stewart (1910–1976) and Bernard Cooke (1910–2011) in the mid-1930s, the Aiton Court is an iconic and early modern apartment building, in which is reflected "their exposure to the formal language of the CIAM architects through Cooke's lecturer Rex Martienssen, the leader of what Le Corbusier termed the Groupe Transvaal."[3]

Built on a 15 × 30 meter lot, the building is formed by two parallel blocks, one four-storied and one seven-storied, orientated northward, toward the sun. It was composed of 25 studio apartments with a bathroom and a kitchen area, located on the lower floors, and, on the upper floors, 18 single rooms with shared sanitary facilities. The lower street-facing block is raised on *pilotis,* creating an entrance foyer and accommodating a caretaker's flat; its roof is occupied by a Corbusian *solarium*. It is separated from the taller rear block by a courtyard, which is overlooked by a sculptural glazed stair and lift tower and two of the access galleries. Thus, the building typology can be considered as a transition between the early 20th century rooming houses with courtyards, and the gallery blocks that were mostly built after 1945. Built cost effectively, the architects opted for a construction based on a relatively light structure and repetitive elements, such as modular steel windows and projecting balconies with steel balustrades, and selected simple finishes, mainly crisp plaster. Aiton Court therefore is recognized as an example of Modernism in its choice of simple, available, and inexpensive materials.[4] The small, simple, and thus visually and spatially rich and welcoming rooms and apartments were occupied mainly by young single tenants and artists at the time.

In the 1980s, Aiton Court, then owned by the Rawat Family, was one of the first buildings to break apartheid segregation laws by welcoming black residents into the area, with the building becoming a base for political activities, as well as offering a hiding place for political operatives from the police. It was during this period that a mosque opened in two of the courtyard-facing apartments on the ground floor, a feature of the building which has been retained by the current owners. The building's fortunes however declined and by the 2000s it was in a crumbling state of disrepair after having been "hijacked" from the owner. Along with the deterioration of the infrastructure, due to the general lack of maintenance the waterproofing of the courtyard and the solarium had failed. On several areas the exposure of the steel bars of the reinforced concrete to the air led them to corrode causing the spalling of the concrete, and electrical installations had reached their end of life.

In 2012, the building was purchased by Trafalgar Property Management as a commercial rental property. Mayat Hart Architects were commissioned for Aiton Court's renovation. Before repair and restoration started, the building was used as a tool for teaching architectural conservation, with full social and architectural documentation of the building being undertaken by architecture students from the University of the Witwatersrand. This documentation looked not only at the building's original forms, condition, and systemic failures (and successes), but also at how the users had adapted and reused the spaces within the building.[5]

1. This area was perceived locally as both the home of a cosmopolitan pan-African diaspora, as well as the site of severe urban decay and known crime zone.

2. Known as a local derivate of the International Style Modernism, the "Hillbrow Modern" architectural style is characterized by the predominance of high-rise apartment buildings built between the 1930s and the 1960s, combining the use of local materials with concrete framing and expressive face brick. See: Clive Chipkin, *Johannesburg Style*, Cape Town, David Phillip, 1993; and Brendan Hart, "The Place of Modernism – Architecture, Politics and Society in Johannesburg," in Ana Tostões and Nataša Koselj (eds.), *Metamorphosis – The Continuity of Change. Proceedings of the 15th International Docomomo Conference*, Lisbon/Ljubljana, Docomomo International/Docomomo Slovenia, 2018, 504–510.

3. Hannah Le Roux, Brendan Hart, and Yasmin Mayat, "Aiton Court: Relocating Conservation between Poverty and Modern Idealism," *Docomomo Journal*, No. 48 – "Modern Africa Tropical Architecture," Barcelona, Docomomo International, 2013, 56–61.

4. Ray Kantorowich, "Aiton Court, Johannesburg," *South African Architectural Review*, April 1938, 105–112

5. Since Aiton Court was built more than 60 years ago, the rules of South Africa's National Heritage Resources Act had to be taken into account..

2012–2014
MAYAT HART ARCHITECTS

1936–1937
BERNARD COOKE
AND ANGUS STEWART

JOHANNESBURG,
SOUTH AFRICA

1. Central courtyard and water feature viewed from above, after restoration

The building functions as affordable rental housing for lower income inner-city residents. As such the budget for restoration and renovation was low with conservation needs having to be balanced with commercial realities. The resulting process can best be described as sitting somewhere between repair and restoration. The approach can possibly be seen as a model for how inner-city regeneration can be balanced with heritage responsibilities and commercial needs.

The limited budget was used to work in the interest of conservation with the repair, restoration, and reuse of original fabric favored over replacement, with skilled and semi-skilled local contractors used for the labor-intensive work. Steel work was repaired and remade where necessary, later additions were reused and recycled (such as the security bars) and damaged timber work patched and repaired. While less visually pristine, this served both the interest of the authentic material conservation of the building as well as the owners' tight budget. After urgent structural repair and the replacement of severely deteriorated services – plumbing, hot water, electrical supply, and waterproofing – the reinstatement of the building's public realm was prioritized as having the highest impact in relation to its investment. Paint colors, through a process of archival research and on-site investigations, were returned to the original scheme of white with accents including cerulean blue, chocolate brown, *eau de nil*, and emerald green. The internal courtyard was restored to its 1930s layout, including its water feature, now doubling as a gathering space outside the building's mosque, which was retained as an important part of the complex hybrid social and architectural history of the building. Further adaptations were removed unless they were considered important for the functioning of the building, being however, when maintained, marked as additions through a different color. "This allows the building to exist in two worlds – both the historic and the adapted present. The restoration is as much an accumulation and layering of history as it is a snapshot of the building as originally designed."[6]

6. Brendan Hart, *op. cit.*, 509.

2

3

2. Aerial view of the building from north, after restoration. 3. Inside view of the stair tower, after restoration.

4. Courtyard facade of the southern block and stair tower, after restoration.

5

6

5. Central courtyard space looking toward the entrance lobby and street, after restoration. 6. View of the courtyard from the entrance lobby, 1937.

7

8

9

7. Central courtyard space at the beginning of the restoration works. 8. View of the internal courtyard and south block, before restoration. 9. South block as viewed from the solarium, before restoration.

10

11

13

12

14

10. Stair tower viewed from below, 1937. 11. Detail of north-facing cantilever balconies, 1937. 12. Internal courtyard design perspective. 13. General view from the north-east, 1937. 14. Aerial view of Aiton Court in its city context, 1937.

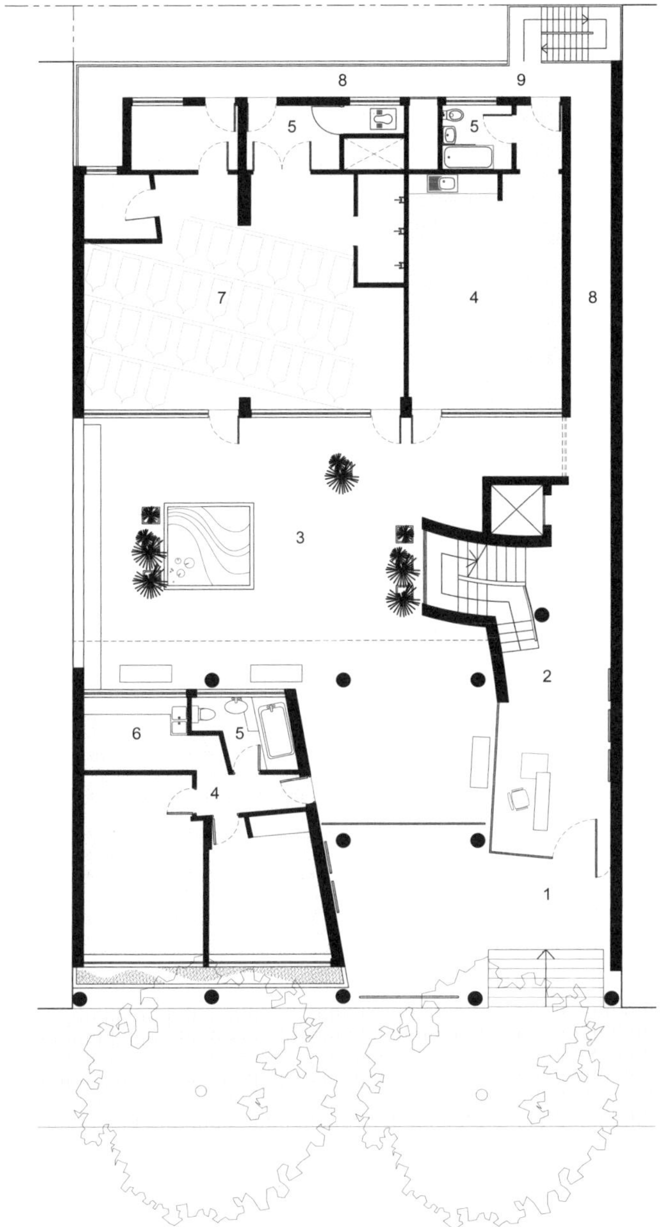

15

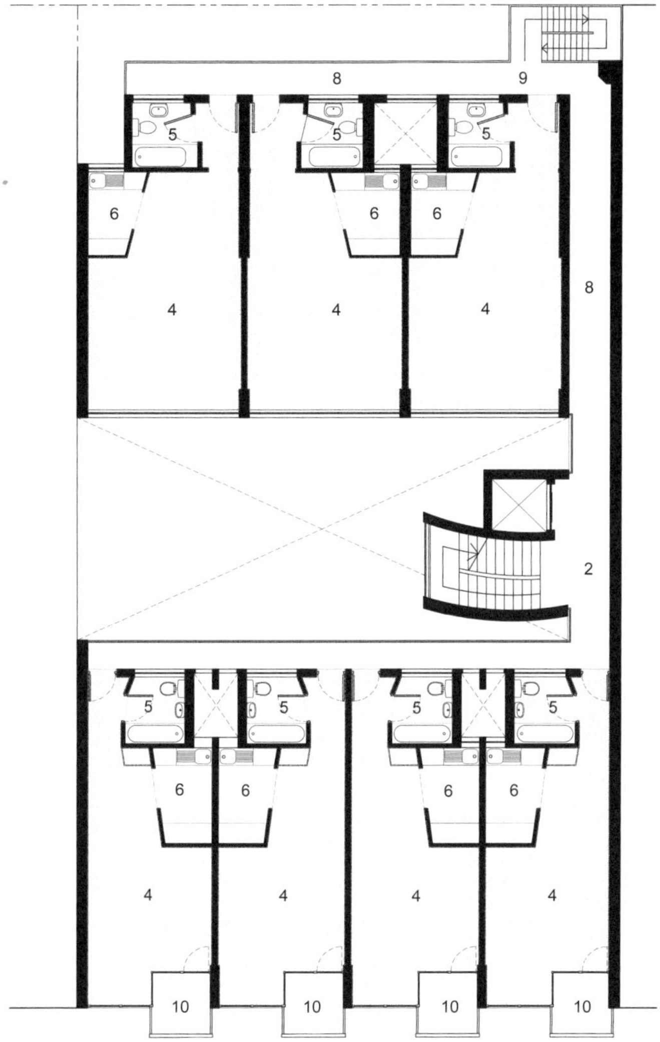

16

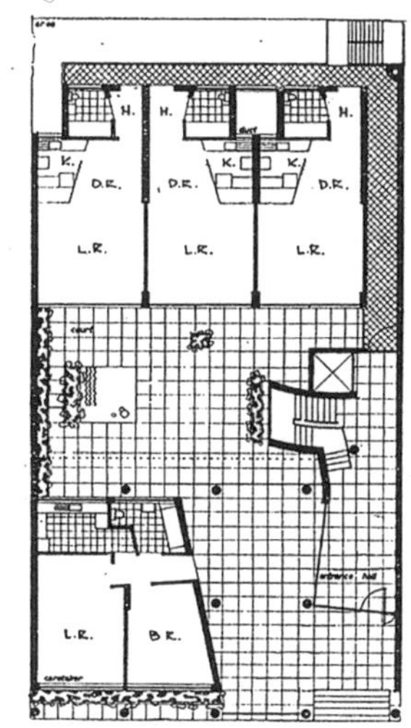

17

GROUND FLOOR

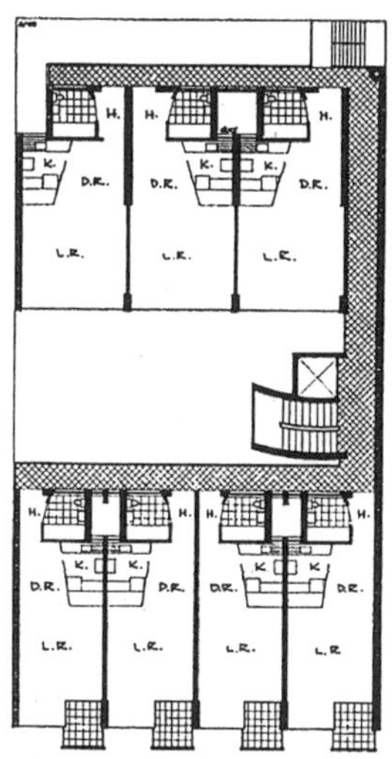

18

TYPICAL FLOOR : FLATS

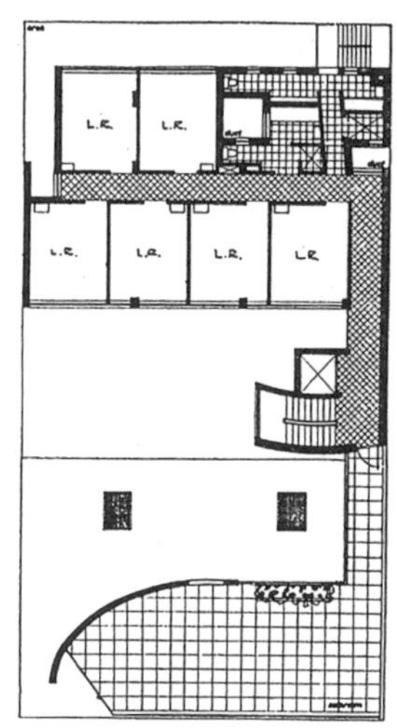

19

TYPICAL FLOOR : ROOMS

Restoration project: 15. Ground floor plan with reinstated courtyard and retained (but renovated) mosque. 1 – entrance, 2 – foyer and staircase, 3 – courtyard, 4 – unit bedroom/living, 5 – bathroom, 6 – kitchen, 7 – mosque, 8 – passage, 9 – fire escape. 16. Typical floor plan. 2 – foyer and staircase, 4 – unit bedroom/living, 5 – bathroom, 6 – kitchen, 8 – passage, 9 – fire escape, 10 – balcony. Original project: 17. Ground floor plan, apartments. B.R. – bedroom, D.R. – dining area, H – hall, K – kitchen, L.R. – living area. 18. Typical first to third floor plan, apartments. D.R. – dining area, H – hall, K – kitchen, L.R. – living area. 19. Typical fourth to sixth floor plan, rooms with shared ablutions. L.R. – living area.

CASA ESTUDIO PARA ARTISTAS

EDUCATING PRACTICES

The Casa Estudio para Artistas is located at the corner of Suipacha and Paraguay Streets, in downtown Buenos Aires. It was designed in 1938 by Antonio Bonet (1913–1989), Horacio Vera Barros, and Abel López Chas, three young architects who had met years before at Le Corbusier's studio, while developing a Master Plan for Buenos Aires, among other projects. All three were active figures in the *avant-garde Grupo Austral* that published the manifesto "Voluntad y acción" and that propagated the thoughts of Modernity. The activity of this pioneering local group brought together intellectuals from various cultural fields and, during its short existence (1937–1941) produced publications, manifestos, urban projects, architecture, and furniture designs. This building is one of the few works they managed to realize and is considered by the history of local architecture as a built manifesto of the group.[1] This view is supported by the work's high degree of technical, spatial, and expressive experimentation, as well as the fact that the Casa Estudio para Artistas was not only designed, but also financed by the architects.[2]

The project was innovative for its time, and the proposed function was unusual for Buenos Aires' architecture of the late 1930s. Seven artists' studios were distributed on the two upper floors, characterized by double-height ceilings, internal courtyards, roof gardens and terraces, while the ground floor was occupied by four independent stores. The innovative decision to introduce studios for artists in the center of the city reflected the group's ideals in terms of the union between urbanism, architecture, and the visual arts. In this building, the artist becomes part of the city's hustle, generating two effects: the shocked reaction of passers-by at the unexpected exhibition of the artists, and in the opposite direction, the irruption of urban life into the artists' spaces.[3] The access to the apartments is located on the first floor and leads to a middle level inside, conceived as a rest space, prior to entering the studios. As singular as the interior with the double-height ceiling apartments with a mezzanine as a resting space (bedroom) and bathroom which is accessed by a spiral staircase, or the domed ceiling on the upper studios, is the design of the building's facade: the recessed window and entrance to stores on the ground floor forms a free and curved glazed volume toward the sidewalk. The pedestrian is offered a different dynamic and a clear separation between the two occupations of the building is created; the height of the floors is as well manifested in the facade by the projection of the slab that generates the eaves, with a marked curve in the corner, framing the building. The use of different materials – bent sheet metal, perforated sheet metal, woven wire, transparent and translucent, flat and curved glass, circular and square glass bricks – provides different textures, shines, shadows, and transparencies that also bring a new conception of the relation between architecture and the city of Buenos Aires.[4] Thus, the materiality of the building represents an important and innovative proposal in respect to the industrialization movement and is an exercise in construction components: the facade seems to be a catalog of new materials, such as iron in different forms and functions and glass of several types and colors, a departure from some of Le Corbusier's previous considerations; dynamic lines, orthogonal and curves are central composition elements that compose all of the building.[5] It is worth mentioning that Bonet, Kurchan, and Ferrari Hardoy designed the BKF armchair especially for these studios. Thus, it is one of the most emblematic buildings of the Modern Movement in Argentina.

1. Jorge Francisco Liernur, "La construcción de una vanguardia. El caso del Grupo Austral (1937–1941)," in *5tas. Jornadas de Teoría e Historia de las Artes: Arte y Poder*, Buenos Aires, CAIA, 1993, 59–68.
2. Ricardo Vera Barros' parents owned the plot where the building is located, and financed its construction, as stated in Gonzalo Fuzs, *Austral 1938–1944. Lo individual y lo colectivo*, PhD thesis, Barcelona, Universidad Politécnica de Catalunya, 2012, 216.
3. Jorge Francisco Liernur and Pablo Pschepiurca, "Arte y vida: una casa en la ciudad, una silla en el mundo," in *La red Austral, Obras y proyectos de Le Corbusier y sus discípulos en la Argentina (1924–1965)*, Bernal/Buenos Aires, Universidad Nacional de Quilmes/Prometeo Libros, 2012, 242.
4. Antonio Bonet et al., "Austral – Casa de Estudios en Buenos Aires," *Nuestra Arquitectura*, No. 12, December 1939.
5. https://www.modernabuenosaires.org/obras/20s-a-70s/ateliers-para-artistas

2017–2018
DIRECCIÓN GENERAL DE REGENERACIÓN URBANA, MINISTERIO DE AMBIENTE Y ESPACIO PÚBLICO, GOBIERNO DE LA CIUDAD AUTÓNOMA DE BUENOS AIRES

1938
ANTONIO BONET, HORACIO VERA BARROS, AND ABEL LÓPEZ CHAS

BUENOS AIRES, ARGENTINA

1. Illumination of the *escaparates* at night, after restoration.

Interestingly, the Casa Estudio para Artistas survived the process of replacing buildings that took place around it (old five-story buildings were replaced by 15-story high-rise constructions). Nonetheless, despite being highly regarded among the local architectural community, and safeguarded by a heritage protection law in 2002, the building's facades were poorly maintained in recent decades and had undergone non-structural modifications of various types that significantly altered its original morphology.

After realizing the pressing need to restore the building's facades, the Buenos Aires city authorities, namely the *Dirección General de Regeneración Urbana, Ministerio de Ambiente y Espacio Público* included the restoration of Casa Estudio para Artistas in their urban regeneration program. Carried out by a team from the *Dirección General de Regeneración Urbana, Ministerio de Ambiente y Espacio Público*, the restoration project attempted to reconcile the idea of reinstating the building's original image with the logical modifications that the inhabitants had had to make for reasons of comfort or safety. Based on existing documentation and *in situ* surveys, research on materiality and colors was crucial for the decisions taken during the intervention. The external illumination of the building and the public space around it were also renovated, improving the quality of urban life.

The project consisted specifically of the restoration of the facade and did not involve interiors. Being a private building, interventions are allowed on interfaces between public and private property, being the owners responsible for the conservation of the interiors. Thus, this government program fomented the contribution of private owners to raise awareness on the monuments they own.

Works consisted in the recuperation of the iron perforated plates that have been hidden during the last years. Glass works were a challenge, as on the inside of the two original plates of glass, the architects used a cotton cloth that provided a particular color and protection. As nowadays this material is not sold anymore, a chemical analysis was needed to collect enough information so that the contractor could fabricate it once again for this project. The Paris stone (or stone simile, a specific plaster) that covered the walls was also chemically analyzed to determine the correct composition and balance to obtain the right formula for the restoration. Parasols were made in metal sheets but filled with cork, and incredibly the inside was in a perfect state of conservation so only the exterior covering was treated. An additional analysis of the color scheme was carried out by comparing the original versus the actual, so that the original concept could be restored. Fortunately, the curved glass of the stores on the ground floor was in perfect condition of conservation and cleaning it was enough.

A further task was the relocation of electricity connections and air conditioning installations that were attached on the facades to the inside patio of the building. This turned out to be a very demanding chore as it also involved the maintenance of many of these installations and the correct reconnection on the new location as, on the one hand, their normal functioning had to be assured and, on the other hand, they had to be located such that they did not compromise the heritage value of the building. The restoration of the Casa Estudio para Artistas' facades was the first opportunity for Buenos Aires City Government to participate directly in the conservation and restoration of modern architecture with its own funds. Herewith both the built heritage and its inevitable evolution over time were consciously valued.

2. Facade to Suipacha Street, after restoration.

3

4

5

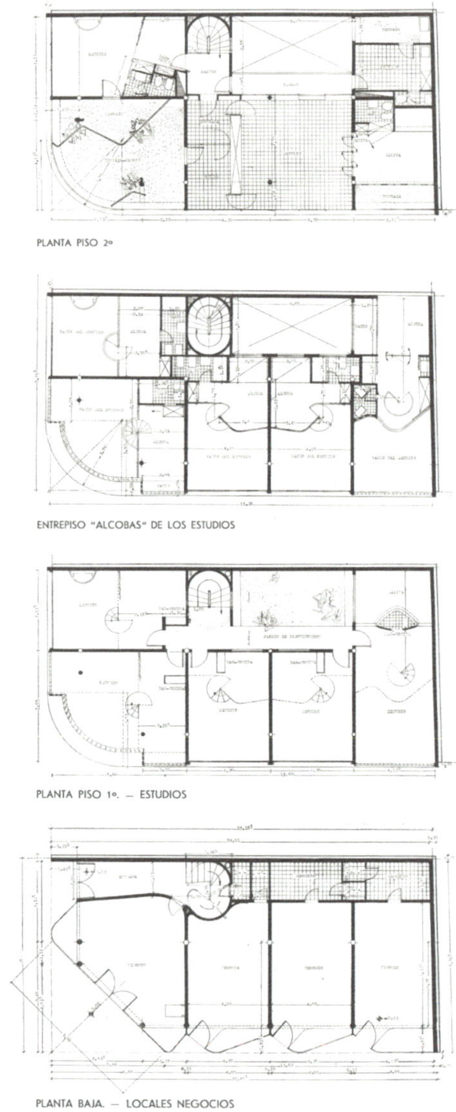

6

7

3. *Escaparates*, before restoration. 4. Facade under ongoing restoration. 5. Facade to Paraguay Street, before restoration. 6. Ground, first, mezzanine, and second floor plans. 7. General view of the facade, 1939.

8

10

9

11

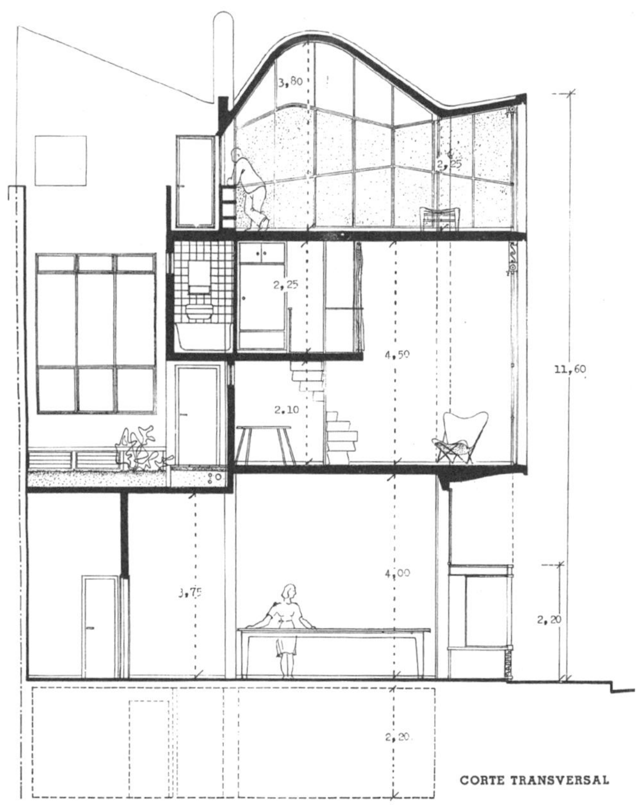

8. Facade to Suipacha Street, 1939. 9. *Escaparates* of the stores, 1939. 10. Interior of a second-floor apartment, 1939. 11. Cross section.

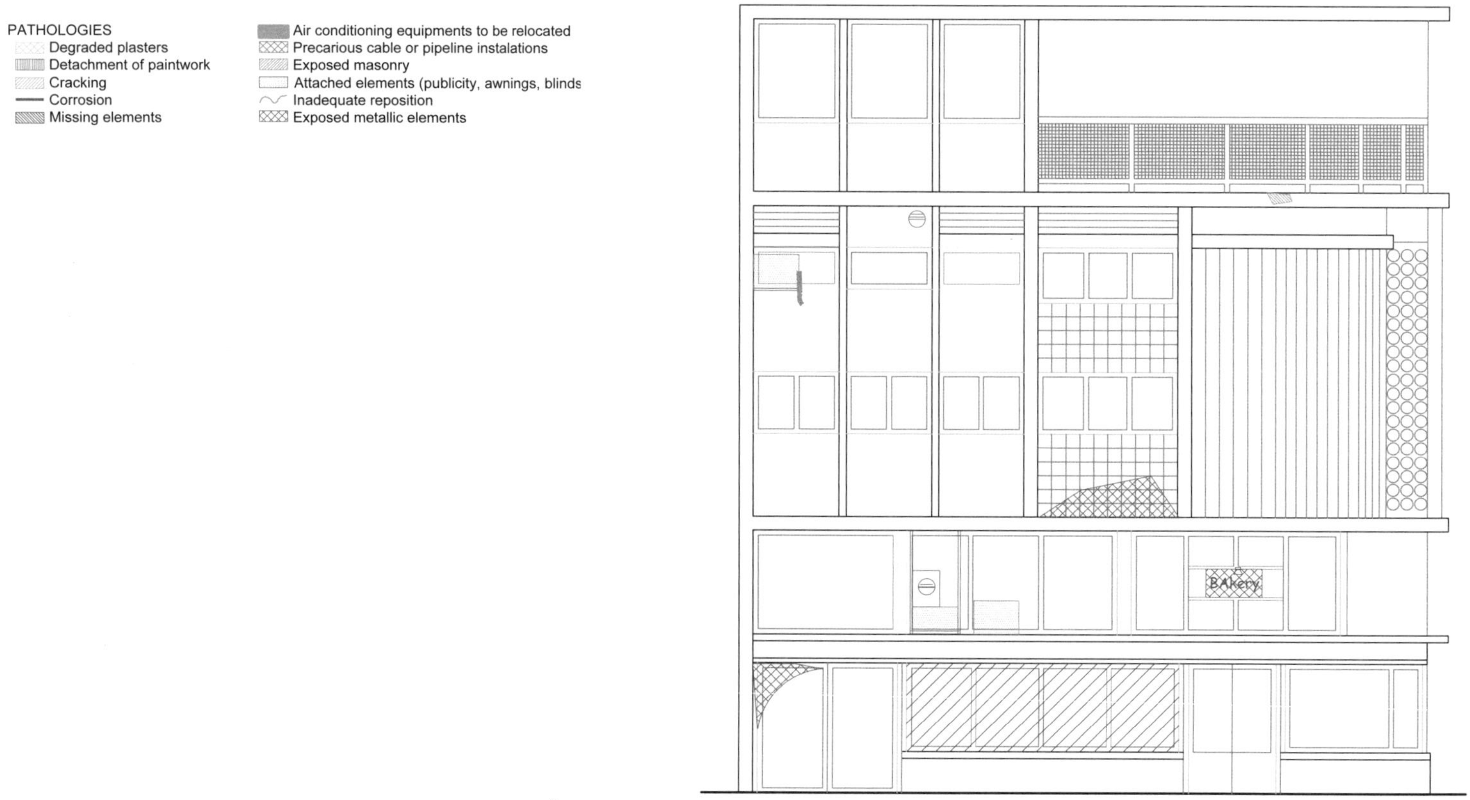

12

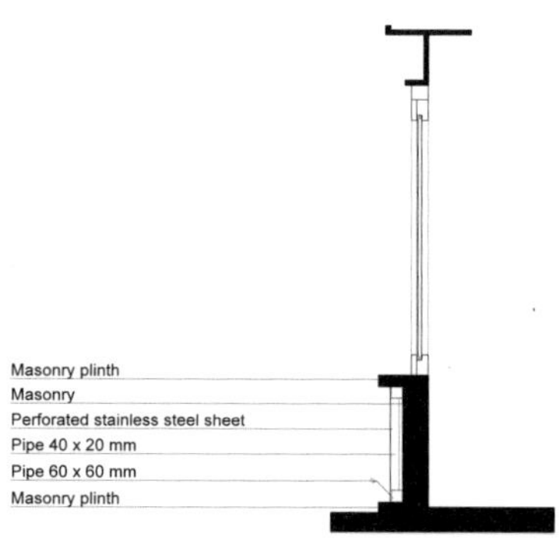

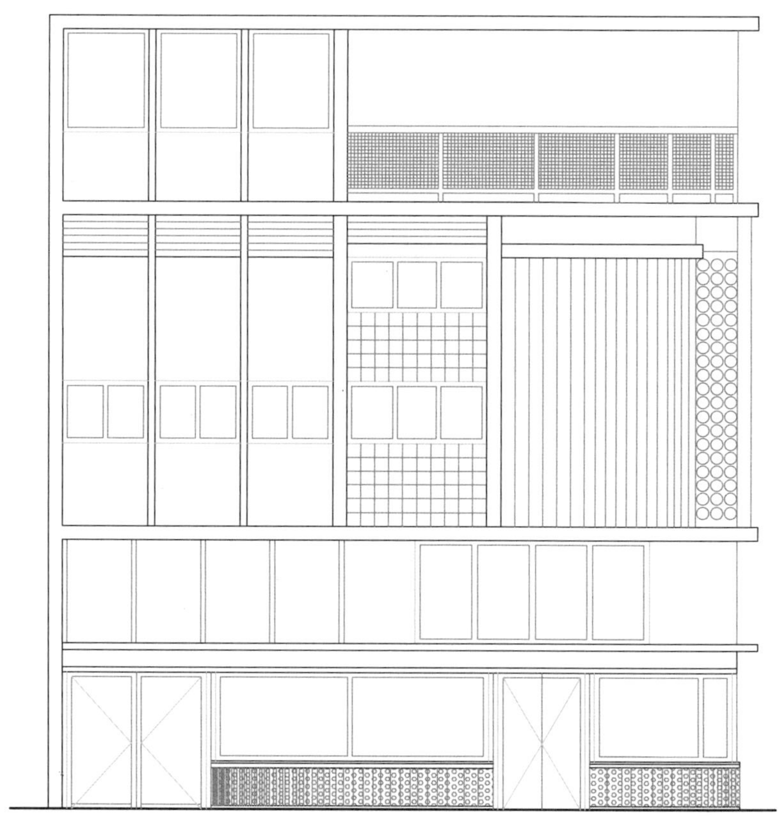

Restoration project: 12. Detail elevation and section of an *escaparate*.

13

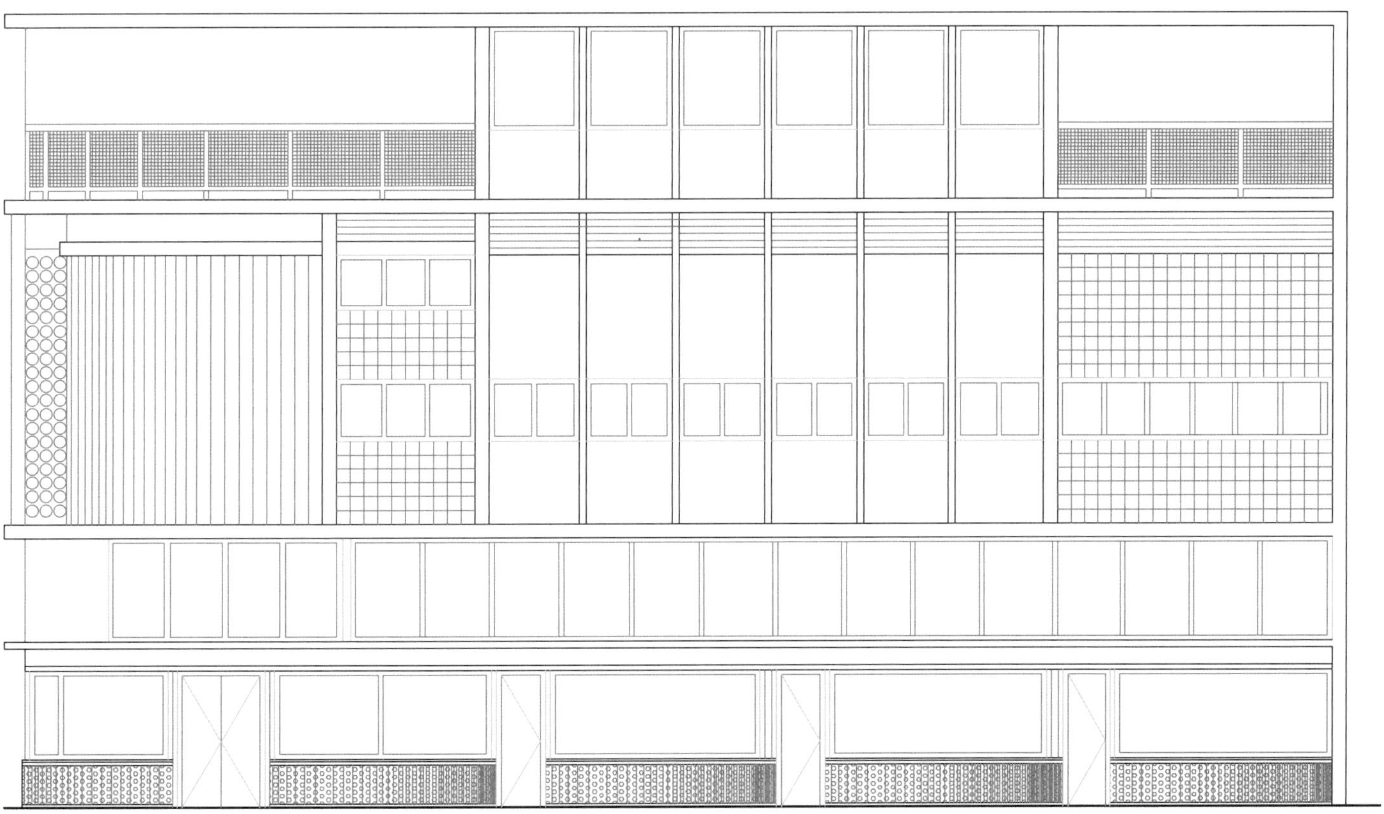

14

Restoration project: 13. Survey of pathologies on the facade. 14. Elevation of the facade.

RESTORATIONS ABLE TO BRING BACK THE LOST INNOVATIVE FEATURES OF FRAGILE AND EXPERIMENTAL VANGUARD CREATIONS, WHILE IMPROVING THEM TO RESIST THE WEAR AND TEAR OF TIME.

CASA O'GORMAN

Victor Jimenez's respectful restoration of the Casa O'Gorman is a noble lesson on how to reinstate and perpetuate the vanguardist characteristics of a unique home and, thereby, reestablish the experimental creativity of the original building. Both reinforcing its structure and reintroducing original features of the architectural Mexican *avant-garde* that had been lost, it is now part of the exhibition spaces of the House-Studio Diego Rivera and Frida Kahlo Museum.

HIPÓDROMO DE LA ZARZUELA

The renovation of the Hipódromo de la Zarzuela demonstrates that it is possible to safeguard large experimental structures. Faced not only with severe structural deterioration, but also with substantial disfiguring modifications, Junquera Arquitectos were able to skillfully restore the distinctive identity of the Torroja racecourse, securing both its original use and the longevity of one of the most important buildings of the Spanish *avant-garde*.

PRESERVED VANGUARDS

PRESERVED VANGUARDS

The Mexican elites of the late 19th and early 20th century adopted the old classic cosmopolitanism as a sign of progress and Modernity in architecture. In 1911, with the fall of the regime of the dictator Porfirio Díaz (1830–1915), this orientation lost its prestige. The revolutionary context favored everything alien to the Porfirian *belle époque*, fostering a nationalist renaissance that had its own Modernist character. Both the local *avant-garde* and the nationalists considered the moment propitious for their aspirations, being complementary rather than antagonistic. It is within this context that architect Juan O'Gorman (1905–1982), a close friend of Frida Kahlo (1907–1954), and Diego Rivera (1886–1957), was to play an outstanding role. Influenced by Le Corbusier, he is credited with having introduced the Modern Movement Functionalism to Mexico. Built by the architect between 1929 and 1930 supposedly for his father, Cecil O'Gorman, Casa O'Gorman was born from this context and is considered a "manifesto" of Juan O'Gorman's innovative ideas on building highly efficient houses, with minimum expense and building effort.[1]

Designed as a house and studio, the two-story house is characterized by a cubic volumetry accented by an exterior spiral concrete staircase that juts out and leads to the upper level. While the ground floor, with living room, dining room, kitchen, servant's room, garage, covered terrace, is dedicated to the family daily life, the upper floor accommodates three bedrooms, two bathrooms, and the studio. Concrete *pilotis* define a small patio; the slabs were not plastered and the walls had baked clay panels with plaster as finishes; open floors, exposed drainage and electrical installations, and detached staircases are other characteristic details. In the words of the architect, I "succeed in applying what my teacher Zárraga had taught: to be as faithful as possible to the human need for shelter, to apply modern constructive systems to architecture, and to take advantage of the climatic conditions of the place where construction is carried out, through the correct orientation of the house. The house was not simply an artistic whim, nor was it built according to an abstract theory. It was actually an application of the principles of functional architecture."[2]

Regardless of its historic importance, by the middle of 2012 the Casa O'Gorman was completely unrecognizable: the helical stair had disappeared, along with the largest studio window, among other things; a newly constructed part, as large as the original house, extended south as far as the plot's edge, bordering the houses of Diego Rivera and Frida Kahlo (also designed by Juan O'Gorman in the neighboring plot in 1931); and the piled-stone low retaining walls in the sloping garden and the cactus fences no longer existed.

The first step was to eliminate the additions. Meanwhile, a restoration plan was drawn up, while all the floors and walls were surveyed in search of information about their original state. It was known that O'Gorman himself had altered the original plans in order to incorporate some of the modifications that the first tenants requested which implied a painstaking analysis during the restoration project. These *in-situ* surveys helped to dispel doubts and correct suppositions. Also helpful were some photographs of the house as it was when just finished. Finally, the experience acquired in 1995 and 1996 while restoring the houses of Diego Rivera and Frida Kahlo provided essential orientation for the intervention strategy.

Mexican construction regulations currently require, as they have done for years, that the structure of all houses be significantly reinforced for seismic reasons.

1. As Juan O'Gorman stated later in the 1970s: "The house I built caused sensation because a construction whose form was derived totally from utilitarian functions had never been seen in Mexico. (...) The appearance of the building, to which a system of reinforced concrete construction had been applied, was strange. In Mexico a purely functional house had never been built." In Victor Jimenez, "Juan O'Gorman House of 1929," in Xavier Guzman, Victor Jimenez, and Toyo Ito, *Casa O'Gorman 1929*, Mexico City, Editorial RM, 2014, 59–69.

2. *Idem.*

2012–2013
VICTOR JIMENEZ

1929–1930
JUAN O'GORMAN

MEXICO CITY, MEXICO

1. Reconstructed spiral staircase, after restoration. Behind Diego Rivera's studio (right) and Frida Kahlo's studio (left), both designed also by Juan O'Gorman.

The load-bearing structure of the Casa O'Gorman was particularly deficient and a cause of real concern. As in the previous restorations, the greater part of the budget and time of the 2012–2013 restoration project by architect Victor Jimenez was invested in a highly complex structural reinforcement. New foundations were laid in many places and all of the isolated supports, as well as a large number of reinforced concrete elements built into the walls, were further strengthened with considerable amounts of steel, without altering their original dimensions. Existing interior walls along the walls that had been destroyed, were fully rebuilt with concrete in order to reinforce the structure even more. The original finishes and colors of the walls, floors, and ceilings were restored. The side windows of the studio were removed, repaired, and reinstalled, as were the windows of the east facade. The large studio window, looking west, had disappeared: a new one was built on the basis of photographs and in line with the model of the side windows of the studio still existing.

The restoration of the exterior required that both the fences along the street and alongside the lot with the houses of Diego Rivera and Frida Kahlo were replaced with the original cacti (as well as along the northern edge of the lot). The piled-stone low walls and original landscaping were restored. According to photographs, the exterior floor of the house was originally tamped earth, as were the neighboring houses of Diego Rivera and Frida Kahlo. Therefore, during the restoration process, gravel and sand were used for both properties, as a clean equivalent that would drain off moisture into the subsoil. This measure had a great impact on the vision of the houses as a group. Before the restoration this aspect had been lost, while now one can gain an impression of the houses as the unit they were once.[3]

3. In the original plans there is even a line indicating an exterior stone stairway that connected the two lots.

Further, as done previously in the houses of Diego Rivera and Frida Kahlo, now Diego Rivera and Frida Kahlo House-Studio Museum, the house was left without running water in order to avoid the risk of moisture or humidity and the original electric exposed installations were redone, but only apparently – no power actually runs through the cables, all necessary lighting is provided by freestanding floor lamps. As for the missing helical staircase, its reconstruction was possible thanks to some original drawings and old photographs. It was necessary to build a brick and plaster scaffolding to shape the whole staircase step by step, carefully finishing the resulting surfaces. Needless to say, a geometrical *tour-de-force*.

2

2. Exterior view from north-west, after restoration: the windows on the north facade were restored; the studio window on the west facade was reconstructed; the spiral staircase was reconstructed; and the cactus fence was renewed. Behind it, the studios of Frida Kahlo and Diego Rivera.

3. Studio, after restoration: the open reconstructed window to the west, and the original restored windows to the north.

4. Exterior view from south-east, after restoration: the windows on the east facade were restored; the spiral staircase was reconstructed; and the cactus fence was renewed.

5. Exterior view from the street, after restoration: in the foreground the renewed cactus fence and car access, with the original concrete frame and steel red doors restored. Behind the house, the inner cactus fence, also renewed, and Diego Rivera's studio (right, glazed windows) and Frida Kahlo's studio (center, gray and blue walls).

6

9

7

8

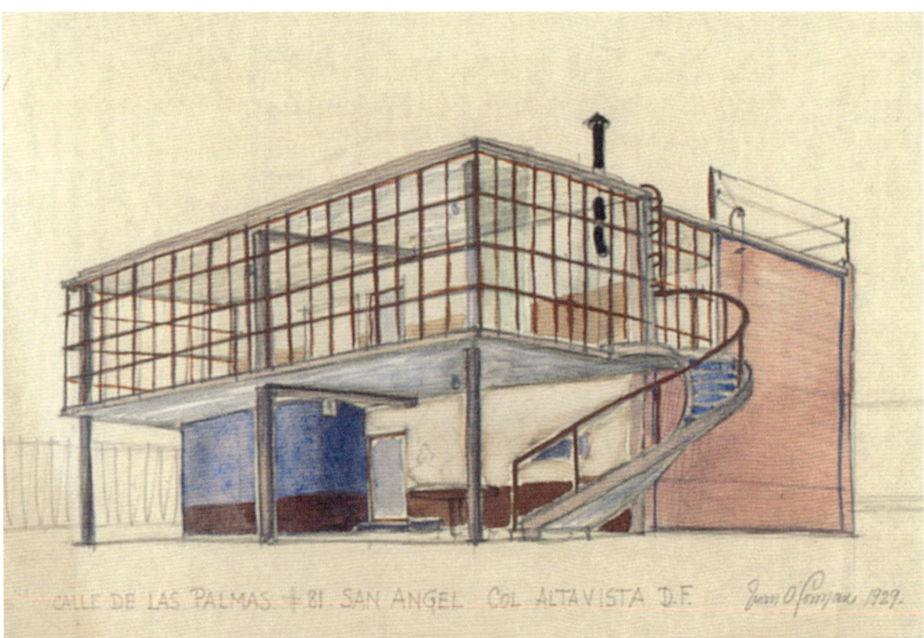

10

6. The house during the restoration: cleaning of the structure and reinforcement of concrete columns with steel; the demolished spiral staircase is still non-existent. 7. View of the east facade, before restoration: it was extended to the left and one window was extended to the floor. 8. Drawing with watercolor: perspective view signed by Juan O'Gorman, 1929. South-west corner, with the spiral staircase, the shade garden, and the glazed studio in the foreground. The colors correspond partly to those actually used. 9. West facade with the completely open studio window and exterior spiral staircase, and cactus fence in the background, c. 1931. 10. The house during the restoration: reconstruction of the spiral staircase with brick scaffolding for vertical elements and a plaster surface for the underside.

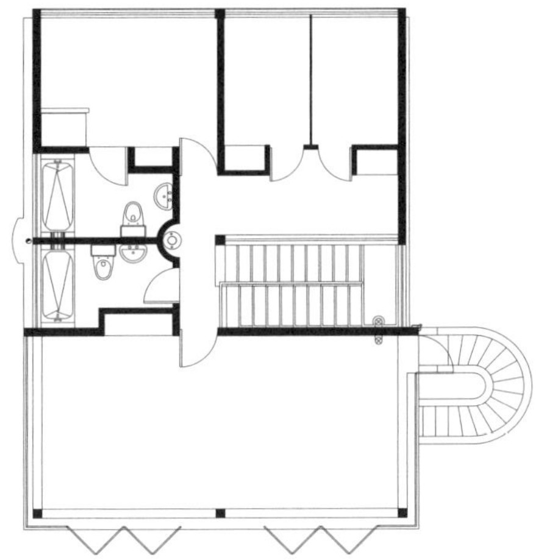

11

12

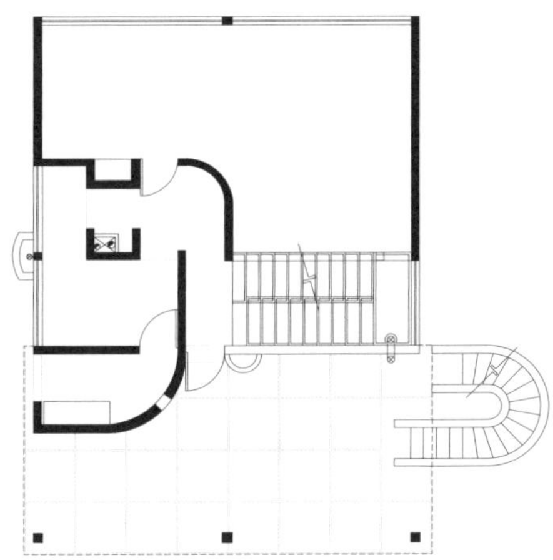

13

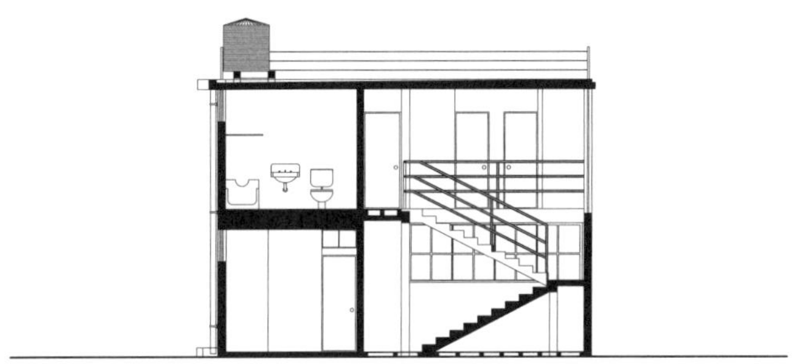

14

Restoration project: 11. First floor plan, with the studio to the west and the bedrooms to the east. 12. Section toward the north. 13. Ground floor plan, with the terrace to the west and the living and dining rooms to the east. 14. Section toward the east, through the interior staircase.

HIPÓDROMO DE LA ZARZUELA

Located in the outskirts of Madrid, the Hipódromo de la Zarzuela (the Zarzuela racecourse) is considered one of the most outstanding works of Spanish modern architecture from the first third of the 20th century. The winning proposal of a competition held for the racecourse's construction in 1934, the Hipódromo de la Zarzuela was designed in 1935 by the two Spanish Modern Movement architects Carlos Arniches (1895–1958) and Martín Domínguez (1897–1971), together with the renowned structural engineer Eduardo Torroja (1899–1961). The construction started a year later, however damages during the Spanish Civil War delayed the completion and it was only inaugurated in 1941.

Perceived as a perfect functional combination between the program requirements of a racecourse and the architectural design of the tribune's roof with its minimized use of material, Hipódromo de la Zarzuela's original structure is characterized by boldly cantilevered, vaulted canopies consisting of reinforced concrete elements – some of them only 6 centimeters thick – jutting out above the tiered seating, while the base is composed of arches that are more traditional.[1] But the cantilevered roof not only covered all three tribunes, it functioned as well as a "counterweight bridge" of more than 12 meters clear span, responding herewith to the necessarily spatial adaptation of the spaces located under the stands. It is considered therefore as an *avant-garde* exponent of technological research on new construction materials and techniques.[2] Furthermore, its design enhanced the integration of the complex into the landscape of Monte de El Pardo, at a time when the La Coruña highway did not yet exist.[3] Chiefly because of its daring structure, Hipódromo de la Zarzuela is seen as one of the great achievements of the century, part of the *racionalismo madrileño*, and is one of the last, if not the last, architectural masterpiece of the Spanish Republic time.[4] As the company operating the racecourse underwent bankruptcy procedures in 1996, Hipódromo de la Zarzuela started deteriorating over time due to lack of maintenance. Specially affected were the canopies, as they also suffered severe damages due to water infiltrations and were altered during previous repair work.

The Zarzuela racecourse complex had already been a historic and artistic monument since 1980, and in 2009, it was declared a monument of cultural interest by the Spanish Ministry of Culture as "it represented in its time and still nowadays an important advancement both from a structural point of view and regarding the type of materials used in its construction."[5] For its renovation an international competition was organized in 2003, in which the renovation proposal by Junquera Arquitectos was selected. The project was then worked out the following years until 2008. The renovation of the building was based on two fundamental premises: research into the historical evolution of the Zarzuela racecourse; and a quest for a balance between the building's core identity and the new requirements demanded by its use.

The first premise – research into the historical evolution of the racecourse – was important in order to identify and rescue the core elements of the 1935 design. This was a difficult task, since the project was only completed in the aftermath of the Civil War, without the presence of its architects, and no reference documents from this period had survived (except for the structural engineering drawings). Nonetheless, the research was undertaken using the original plans from the 1934

1. Ignasi de Solà-Morales, Antón Capitel and Peter Buchanan et al., *Birkhäuser Architectural Guide Spain 1920–1999*, Basel, Birkhäuser, 1998, 239.

2. "El Hipódromo de la Zarzuela, en Madrid," *Revista Nacional de Arquitectura*, No. 81, September 1948, 337–347; Eduardo Torroja, "Hipodromo de la Zarzuela," *Informes de la Construcción*, Vol. 14, No. 137, January–February 1962, 19–38.

3. Julian Peña, "El Hipódromo de la Zarzuela," *Revista Arquitectura*, No. 88, April 1966, 61–64; "El hipódromo de la Zarzuela, monumento histórico-artístico," *El Pais*, 25 November 1980.

4. *El País, op. cit.*

5. *Boletín Oficial del Estado*, No. 266, 4 November 2009, sec. III, 92342.

2003–2015

JUNQUERA ARQUITECTOS

1935–1941

CARLOS ARNICHES, MARTÍN DOMÍNGUEZ, AND EDUARDO TORROJA

MADRID, SPAIN

1. Detail of the canopies, after restoration.

competition and *in situ* surveys. They revealed not only modifications and extensions to the original design, but also significant structural damage, requiring consolidation and repair work. The second premise – the quest for a balance between the building's identity and contemporary requirements – was adopted in order to secure the building's longevity, as only its continuous use would ensure its preservation.

Thus, it was possible to define a renovation project capable of recovering and upgrading the original character of the building. The renovation comprised mainly: the removal of the disfiguring changes that had occurred over time; the restoration of the stands' structure; the adaptation of the topography and circulation of both the public and the horses as laid out in the 1934 project (in particular the public entrances through the patios, and separation from the paddock by a gallery, being so able to follow from here all the horses' movements on the lower level without interfering with it); keeping the original position of the stables, concentrating other racing, jockey and veterinary services in a new building dug into the ground and open to the gardens (providing privacy, natural lighting, and ventilation); and with independent accesses for the horses and a direct connection to the paddock and the central grandstand without crossing paths with the visitors areas. The project also anticipated a possible expansion of an underground convention center in the north yard, without affecting views of the historic buildings and landscape.

Starting with the restoration of the canopies of the tribunes, in 2008, the renovation works lasted until 2015. In parallel to the restoration of the canopies, constructive prospecting works were carried out to discover and analyze the values and original construction systems, distorted and lost due to extensions and modifications carried out in the racecourse. Unfortunately, these made evident that consolidation and repair works of the structure were required, following its restoration afterwards. Thus, the renovation managed to reclaim the racecourse for the city as a facility for equestrian sport, balanced with the use and enjoyment of the monument.

2

2. South tribune hall, after restoration.

3. View of the south tribune from the south patio, after restoration.

4. South grandstand, after restoration.

5

6

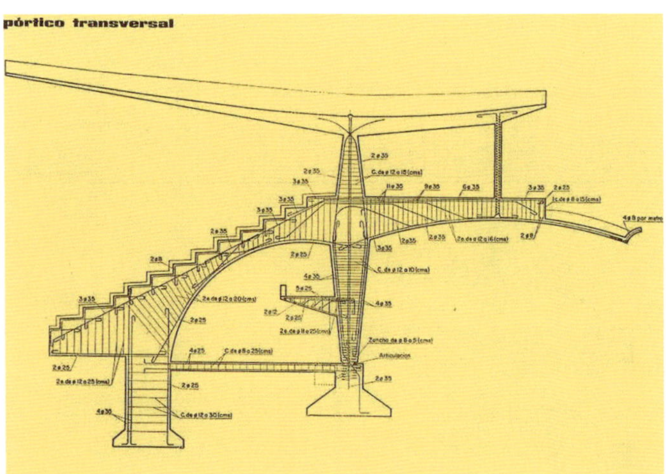

7

8

5. General view from the north, before restoration. 6. Structural section of a transversal portico. 7. The tribunes under construction, 1935. 8. Construction of the tribune canopies, 1935.

9

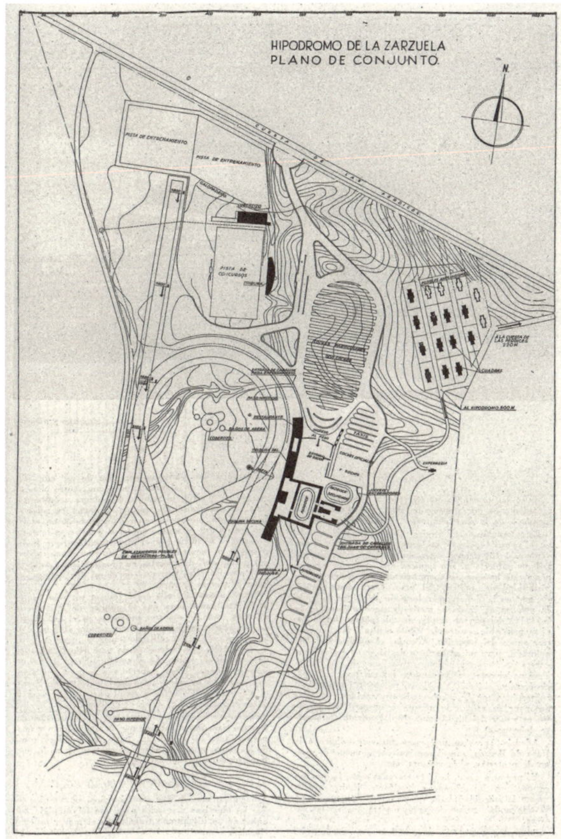

12

10

11

9. Tribunes, before restoration. 10. South tribune hall, before restoration. 11. General view of the complex, 1941. 12. General plan of the complex.

13

14

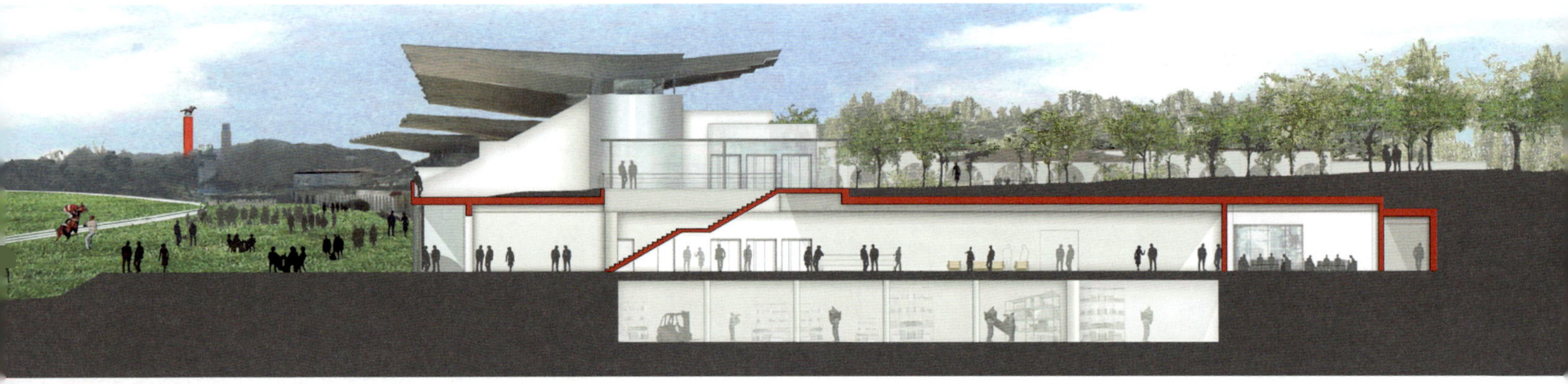

15

Restoration project: 13. Section through the racing club services areas, saddles, paddock, and vaulted room of the central grandstand. 14. Section through the racing club event spaces, saddles, paddock, and central grandstand. 15. Section through the new convention center.

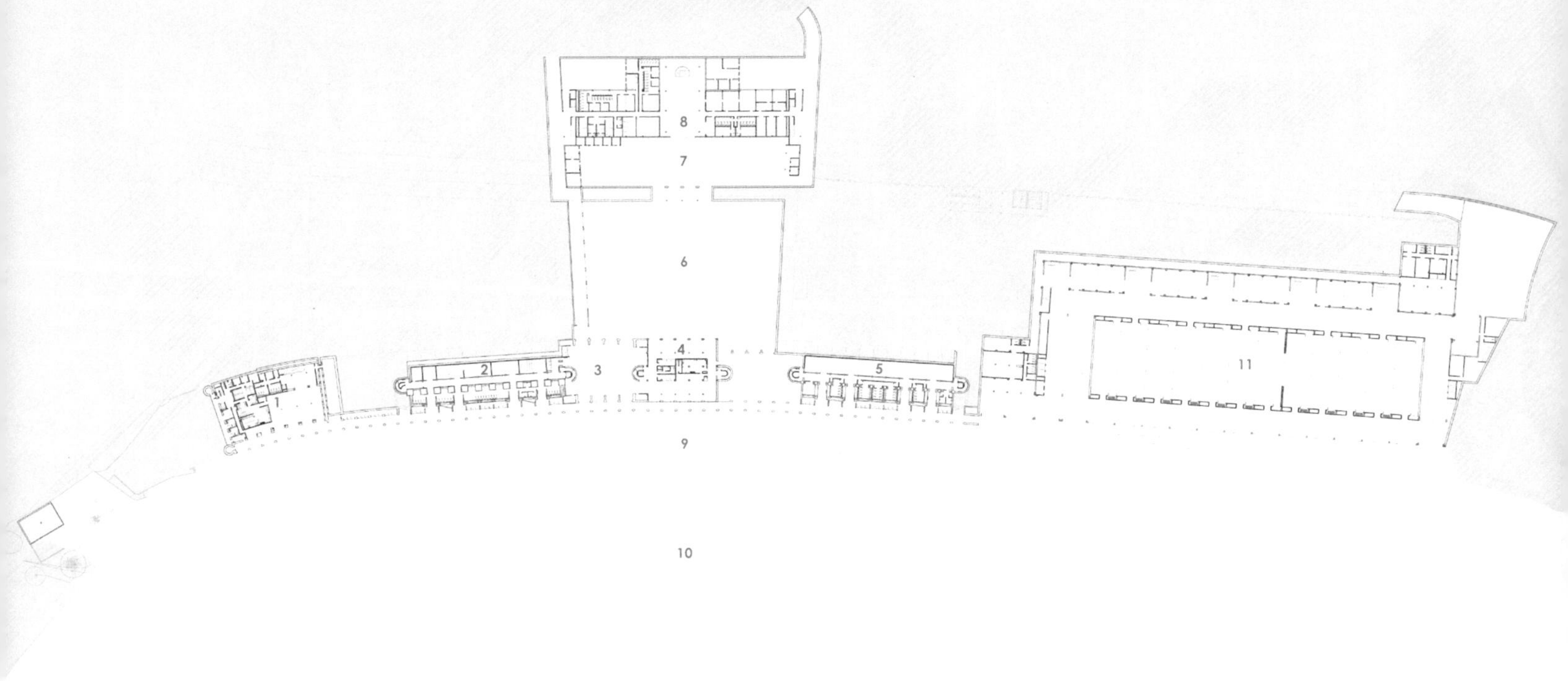

16

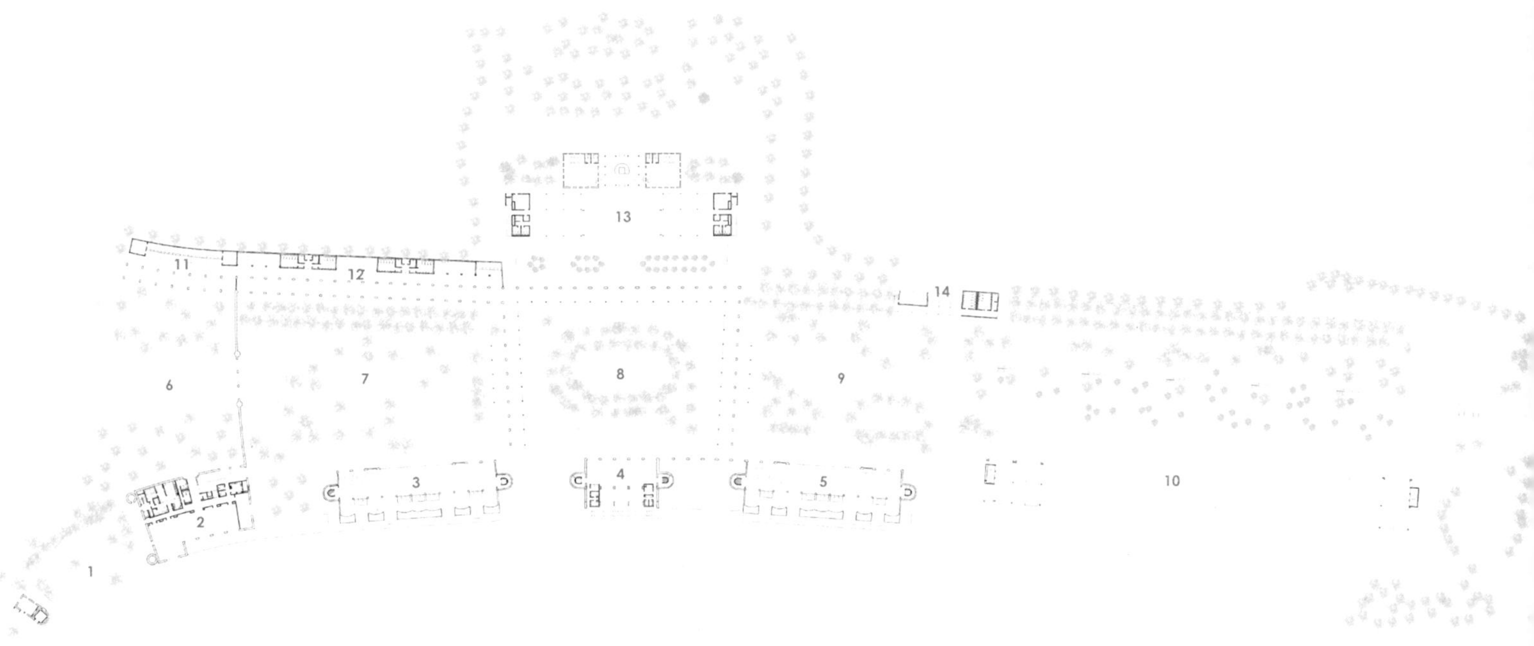

17

Restoration project: 16. Basement (racetrack level) plan. 1 – south restaurant, 2 – south tribune, 3 – carriages space, 4 – central tribune, 5 – north tribune, 6 – paddock, 7 – saddles, 8 – jockey area and administration of the racecourse, 9 – lawn, 10 – racetrack, 11 – congress center. 17. Ground floor plan. 1 – south terrace - commissar tower, 2 – south restaurant, 3 – south tribune, 4 – central tribune, 5 – north tribune, 6 – south access, 7 – south patio, 8 – paddock, 9 – north patio, 10 – roof terrace of the congress center, 11 – new lockers, 12 – services pavilion, 13 – racing club – event spaces, 14 – new north access pavilion.

RENOVATIONS THAT INTRODUCE CONTEMPORARY STANDARDS OF SAFETY AND SUSTAINABILITY, AND IMPROVED TECHNOLOGIES WHILE KEEPING THE BUILDINGS' FUNCTION AND IDENTITY.

GRAND AUDITORIUM OF THE CALOUSTE GULBENKIAN FOUNDATION

The renovation of the Grand Auditorium of the Calouste Gulbenkian Foundation reveals how an "invisible" technical upgrade can be undertaken while leaving the unique character of its embracing interior space untouched. The ingenious approach taken in Teresa Nunes da Ponte's renovation project, has not only enhanced the emblematic *Gesamtkunstwerk* of the Grand Auditorium, but also equipped it with the latest technology and in compliance with current safety standards.

CARTIERA BURGO

Still in operation as an industrial paper mill, the Cartiera Burgo provides an important and commendable lesson on the renovation of a commonly-overlooked functional typology – the industrial complex. The renovation project developed by Massimo Narduzzo and CREA.RE for the Cartiera Burgo, is masterful in both its technical updating and its rescuing of long-lost characteristic features. Now equipped with the latest paper industry technology, the paper mill once again allows Nervi's mystique to be admired.

SUSTAINED USES

GRAND AUDITORIUM OF THE CALOUSTE GULBENKIAN FOUNDATION

SUSTAINED USES

The Grand Auditorium of the Calouste Gulbenkian Foundation, an institution dedicated to the promotion of arts, education, and science through a civic and cultural program, is part of a large complex of three buildings, with the foundation's headquarters and the museum. Together with a garden they form the coherent body of the Buildings and Garden of the Calouste Gulbenkian Foundation.

Opened to the public in 1969, the complex is a distinguished work of the Modern Movement designed by architects Alberto Pessoa (1919–1985), Pedro Cid (1925–1983), and Ruy Jervis d'Athouguia (1917–2006), along with landscape architects António Vianna Barreto (1924–2013) and Gonçalo Ribeiro Telles (1922–2020). It contributed to the emergence of Modernity in the world. As the selected proposal of a limited competition in 1959, the project stood out for its radical and innovative monumentality, where space and light were manipulated based on a rigorous design. Synthesis of the architecture of the Modern Movement between constructed landscape and architectural interiors, it combines the fluidity of space with the composition and expressiveness of the exposed concrete, stone, and glass, and the rigorous detail and sculptural value of the materials, turning it "a pioneering work that brings together architecture, engineering, modern art, design and landscape, achieving the sought after 'synthesis of the arts' that dominated the agenda of post-war architectural culture. The language of architecture becomes abstract and neutral to the point of becoming geometric topography, allowing for a gradual transition between the constructed and natural landscape, thus suggesting spatial continuity. (...) These values are evident in the architectural and landscape design, the structural design and technical innovations, the comfort of the spaces resulting from careful detailing: from the interior design to the integration of works of art."[1]

The buildings are arranged such that they accentuate the highest level of the plot and create a link to the street to the north. With the garden to the south, they form an organically constructed whole with the land: the headquarters and museum's volumes occupy the northern part of the plot, set in the "acropolis" that signals the entrance, to which is added the separate volume of the auditorium facing the garden and overlooking the lake to the south. Thus, the land was modulated as if it were a topographical sculpture and artificial platforms were created.[2]

The complex is a perfect example of interior/exterior interplay and was classified as the first Portuguese Modern National Monument in 2010. The substantial social and cultural impact of the facility has contributed to strengthen the Foundation's reputation of prestige and innovation. Located at the south end of the ensemble and in the center of the garden, shielded from the surrounding noise, the Grand Auditorium is the most emblematic element of the complex. Designed as a compact building with great presence, it has a complex structural solution based on a series of reinforced concrete porticoes. These portico beams had to not only overcome spans of 27 meters, but also support the slab of the technical floor to which the bronze plates that make up the ceiling of the room were attached. The stage area represented an even more complex task since it required suspending the upper part of the beam until the canopy while the last portico suspends a large span of glass across the stage, designed for visual communication with the garden, promoting views toward the tree and lake "and potentially to serve as a stage backdrop, giving the audience a surprising viewpoint."[3] "The lake acts as a surface for

1. Ana Tostões, *Lisboa Moderna*, Lisbon, Docomomo International/Circo de Ideias, 2021, 148–169.
2. *Arquitectura*, No. 111, September–October 1969; *Binário*, No. 134, November 1969; "World Foundation Treat," *The Architectural Review*, No. 889, March 1971, 191–192; Aurora Carapinha and Marc Treib, *O Jardim*, Lisbon, Fundação Calouste Gulbenkian, 2006; Ana Tostões, *Sede e Museu Gulbenkian: A Arquitectura dos anos 60*, Lisbon, Fundação Calouste Gulbenkian, 2006.
3. Ana Tostões, *Fundação Calouste Gulbenkian: Os Edifícios*, Lisbon, Fundação Calouste Gulbenkian, 2006 (Portuguese)/2012 (English); Ana Tostões, Aurora Carapinha, and Paula Corte-Real, *Gulbenkian: Arquitectura e Paisagem*, Lisbon, Fundação Calouste Gulbenkian, 2007.

2013–2014
TERESA NUNES DA PONTE, ARQUITECTURA

1959–1969
ALBERTO PESSOA, PEDRO CID, AND RUY JERVIS D'ATHOUGUIA

LISBON, PORTUGAL

1. Audience seat-rows of the auditorium, after renovation. The wood board cladding of the balcony and control room levels were redesigned with variable depths to improve sound diffusion; the design kept the proportions and used the same wood to ensure a continuity with the original cladding. When seen from the front, the change is only evident in angled views.

reflection and enlargement, which strengthens the *desiderata* of spatial continuity between the interior and exterior."[4]

4. Ana Tostões, 2021, *op. cit.*, 164.

However, despite the quality of both the grand auditorium's design and construction, the passage of time – 45 years – called for a deep restoration and renovation. Taking a very conservative approach to form and materials, only essential modifications were carried out. The project was developed with absolute respect for the guidelines set by the original design and the rules of the existing construction. When design changes were imperative, contemporary solutions inspired by the principles of the original concept were chosen. The main goals were: to comply with current safety standards and provide more modern and reliable facilities in accordance with current regulations; to update performative and stage conditions; and to install new technology capable of meeting the demands of programming versatility and operational efficiency. The spaces were renovated, and public accessibilities were improved, particularly with regard to the accesses for people with reduced mobility.

Energy efficiency and environmental sustainability were a fundamental design principle in a refurbishment that was, in great part, a technical update, with the full replacement of the stage, audio-visual equipment, infrastructure and services networks, including air conditioning. Some changes became necessary to comply with current fire safety standards, including the widening of the stalls' central aisle with the removal of one chair per row. The lost seats were then reinstated by refurbishing unused translation booths into side boxes. A series of marginal gains in acoustic performance, mostly regarding reverb time, led to a significant improvement in the room's acoustics, increasing the reverberation time, which was considered low, most noticeably on the cross aisle in front of the stage, where carpeting was replaced by hardwood flooring. Retractable acoustic banners were installed on the side walls, enabling the reverberation time to be adjusted, which is especially useful for amplified sound.

The new canopy constituted the most visible change of the intervention and offers greater flexibility and operational safety. Using the same ash wood as the original, it is composed of six lightweight, independent modules which improve acoustic diffusion, incorporate base lighting, and allow fly-battens to pass through the gaps between them. The clean contemporary aesthetic was chosen to discreetly and harmoniously blend with the venue. Whenever possible, new stage and services equipment were hidden from view and incorporated in niches and grids on the walls and ceilings. A new orchestra rehearsal room was created in an unused space under the stalls, and the former, outdated rehearsal room was converted into a foyer for the new side boxes. The Grand Auditorium is now adapted to meet the latest programmatic and functional demands, adding value to the monument.[5]

5. Teresa Nunes da Ponte and Aurora Carapinha, *Renovação Edifícios e Jardim*, Lisbon, Fundação Calouste Gulbenkian, 2009; Ana Tostões, *Restauro e renovação do Grande Auditório*, Lisbon, Fundação Calouste Gulbenkian, 2015.

2. View of the stage and the canopy with subtitle panel deployed and opened to the lake, after renovation. Also visible is the hardwood floor installed only in front of the stage to replace the carpet and benefit acoustic performance.

3. View of the stage and the canopy with the concealed base light behind each of the six modules, after renovation.

4

5

6

4. Under-stage lift pit, after renovation. The stage lift structures were inspected and kept, shown in orange, and the original cable system was replaced by a link lift system. The system was designed to keep exactly the same stage geometry and support structural points. 5. Foyer of the auditorium, after renovation. To integrate new emergency exits it was decided to make all doors operable. The original HVAC metal grilles were replaced by wood grilles that integrate these and other equipment such as loudspeakers. 6. New side boxes installed in the original translation booths, after renovation. The original seven individual booths were converted into two boxes connected to the new foyer, created in the former orchestra rehearsal room.

7

8

9

7. Auditorium during the intervention. 8. Aerial view of the Calouste Gulbenkian Foundation complex with garden and buildings of the museum, headquarters, and auditorium, 1969. 9. View of the auditorium toward the audience, balcony, and control rooms, including the translation booths and presidential box, 1970s.

10

11

12

10. View of the stage with the orchestra and pipe organ, before renovation. 11. View of the stage with the upstage window curtains opened to the lake, before renovation. 12. View of the grand auditorium from south-east, with the lake in the foreground, during the final stages of construction, 1969.

13

14

15

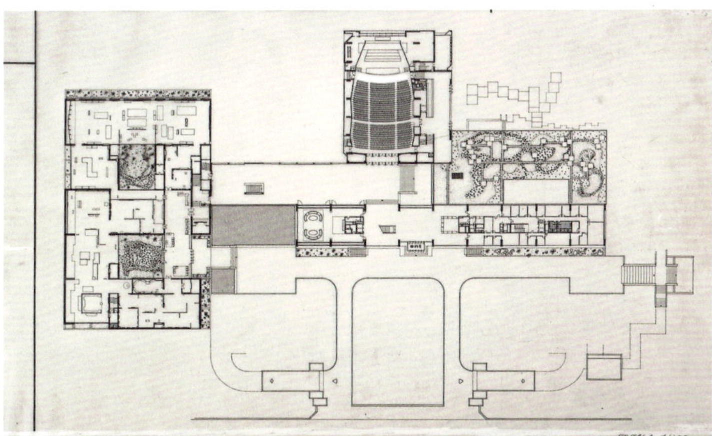

16

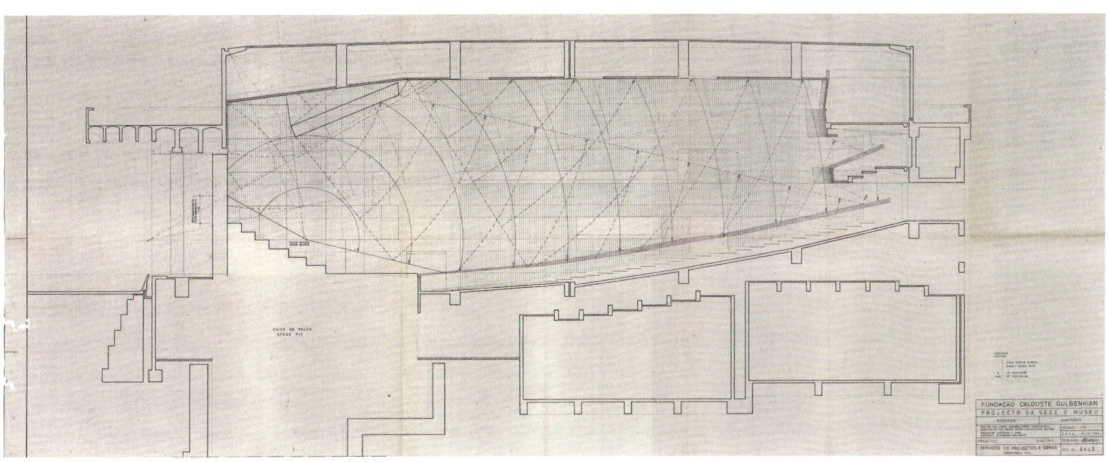

13. Construction of the auditorium's audience level slab and basements, 1966. 14. Placing of the grand auditorium's upstage glass pane, 1968. 15. As-built plans: ground floor plan (third floor on the licensing project) with the grand auditorium at the center. 16. Longitudinal section: acoustic studies, analysis of the sound waves, symphonic orchestra and choir, 1965.

17

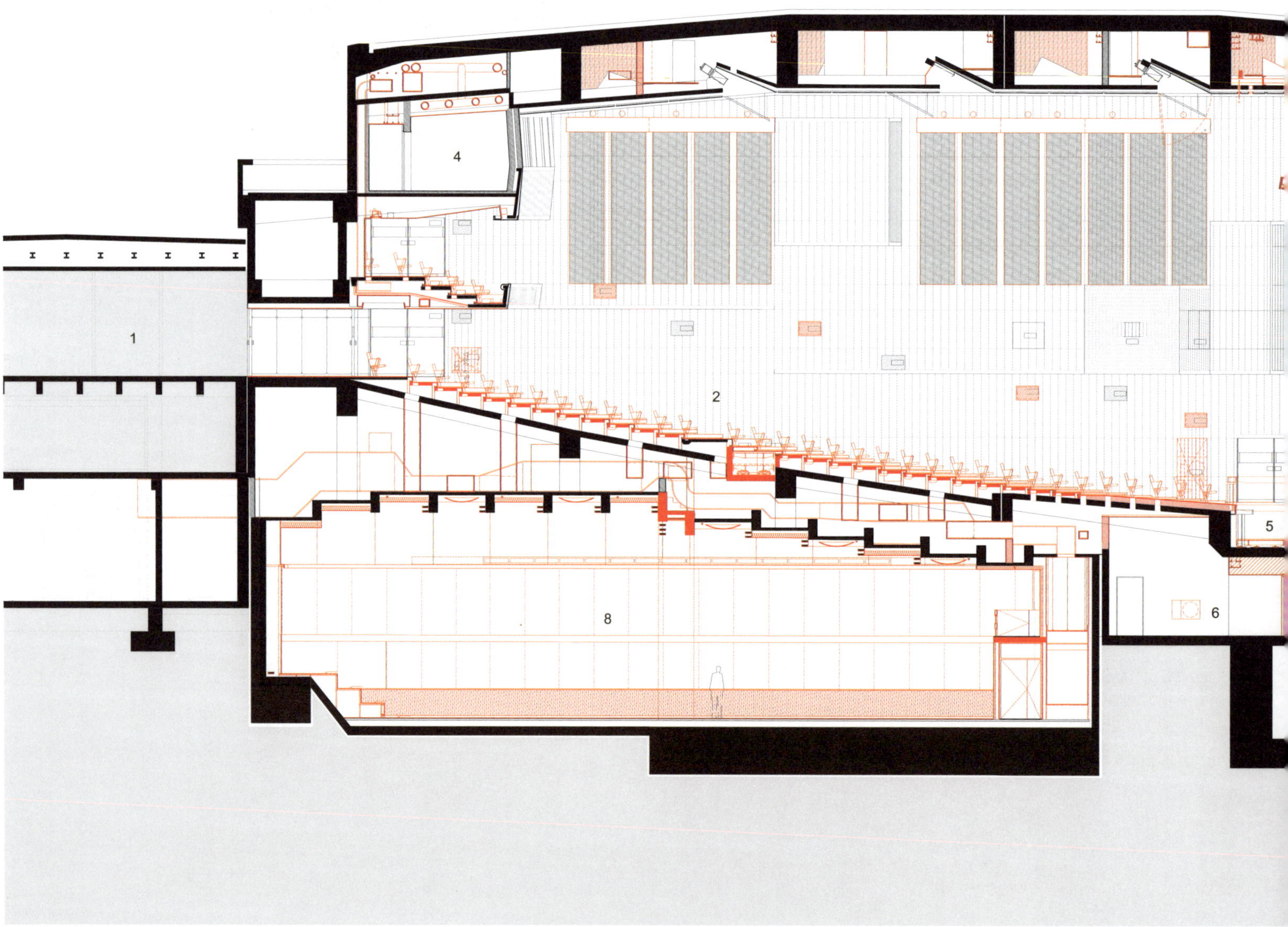

Renovation project: 17. Longitudinal section A–A of the auditorium and new orchestra rehearsal room. In red are marked all new elements. 1 – main hall, 2 – stalls, 3 – stage, 4 – control rooms, 5 – orchestra pit, 6 – understage, 7 – stage lift pit, 8 – orchestra rehearsal room.

18

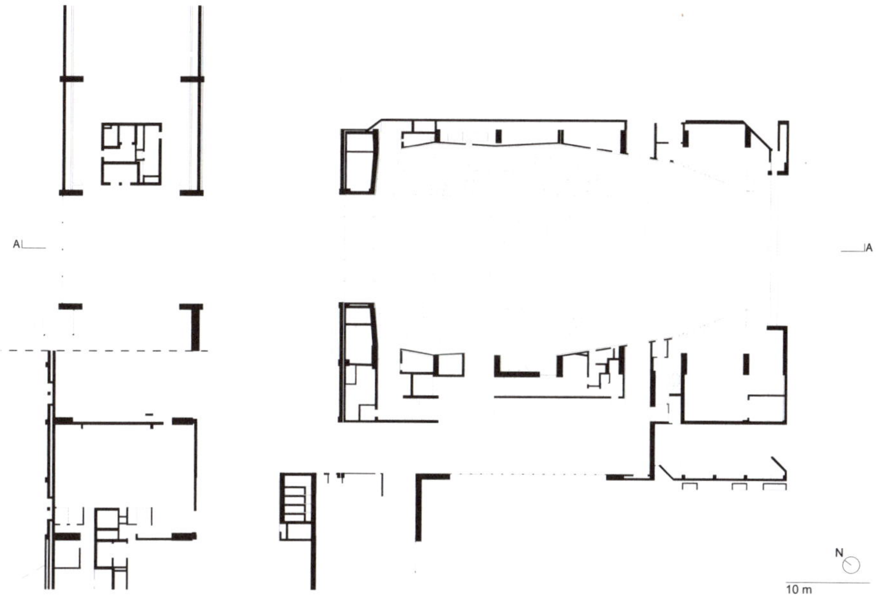

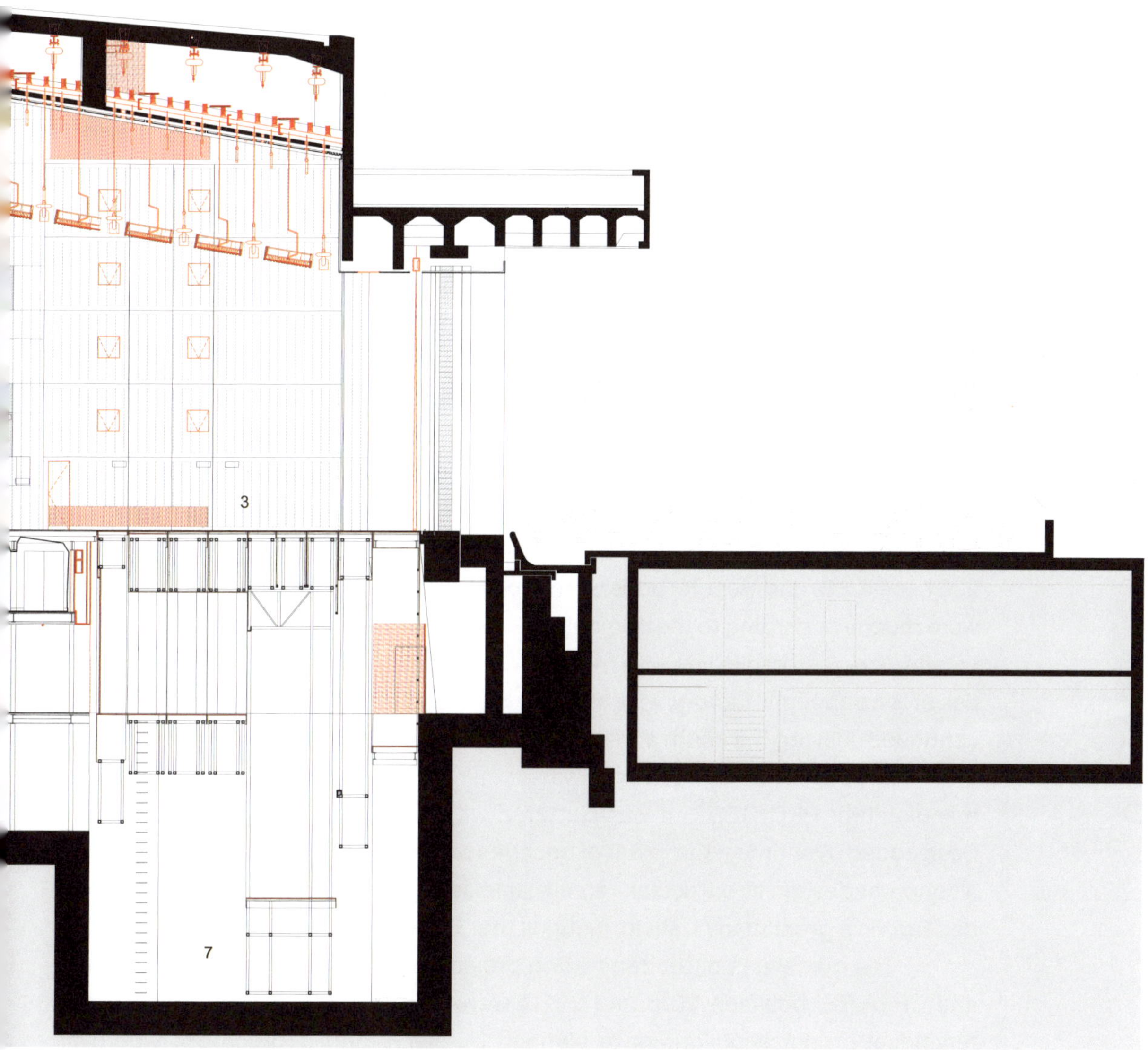

Renovation project: 18. Plan of the auditorium and adjacent areas, levels 0 and -1.

SUSTAINED USES

The Cartiera Burgo was designed by the architect Pier Luigi Nervi, with the structural engineer Gino Covre (1892–1981), for the Piedmont paper manufacturer Burgo, between 1961 and 1964. The program required the creation of a 250-meter long space with a 160-meter long uninterrupted facade to accommodate the paper-producing equipment. Thus, the structure consists of a reinforced concrete basement, that supports the machines and contains various service spaces, covered by an iconic suspended steel roof. With a height of 22 meters, the roof consists of steel lattice beams suspended by four steel cables attached to two reinforced concrete trestles, 47 meters high and 164 meters apart.[1] The inclination and "Y" shape of the two trestles visualizes the stresses transmitted by the cables. Both were constructed by Nervi & Bartoli using the standard system of permanent formwork, prefabricated on site. Herewith, Nervi developed a singular architectural solution that fully responds to the complex functional requirement of the program and simultaneously a building that clearly stands out within the flat landscape of the Po Valley.

1. Alberto Bologna and Cristiana Chiorino, "La fabbrica sospesa. Pier Luigi Nervi, Gino Covre e la cartiera Burgo a Mantova (1961–1964)," in Sergio Pace (ed.), *Pier Luigi Nervi: Torino, la committenza industriale, le culture architettoniche e politecniche italiane*, Torino, Silvana editoriale, 2011.

In addition to the machinery building, the project also included a warehouse for the paper rolls, built with the characteristic orthogonal ribbing system obtained with ferrocemento formwork and mobile scaffolding, patented by Nervi in 1949, as well as offices with continuous aluminum and glass facades, which Nervi already used in the Pirelli skyscraper in Milan and the Palaeur stadium (Palazzo dello Sport) built for the 1960 Olympic Games in Rome. Part of the paper mill are also the Pastalegno [wood pulp] building, entirely in brick, and the two "accelerator" water reservoirs for the decantation of water from the lake, built using a prefabricated system typical of Nervi's architecture,[2] with the same design as the dome of St. Mary's Cathedral, in San Francisco.

2. Pier Luigi Nervi, *Costruire correttamente*, Milan, Hoepli editore, 1965.

A fire occurred in April 1974, irreparably damaging the outer shell of the machinery building. Unfortunately, the glass facades were replaced by cheap metal sheets at the time and its *brise-soleils*, on the south and west facades, were eliminated, stripping the building of these characteristic formal features of Pier Luigi Nervi.

Since then, the acidity of fumes from cellulose processing had rapidly oxidized and seriously deteriorated the infill cladding panels of the facade and the supporting structure. At the end of the 1990s, the facades were in need of repair. In 2001, the north and west facades were replaced. While the mullions and the gutter were redone according to the original drawings, the external and internal infill of the facade were restored in line with the 1974 changes. However, the economic difficulties of the paper mill factory, which closed in 2013, prevented the project from being continued, leaving the south and east facades unrestored.

In 2015, when the complex was acquired by its current owner (the paper manufacturer PRO-GEST), it was cluttered with large technical volumes that had been added over time – the result of decades of purely functional additions without a coherent design. In particular, more than elsewhere, the machinery building had undergone a great many transformations that had distorted its formal appearance.

The guidelines of the renovation project drawn out by Massimo Narduzzo and CREA.RE, between 2015 and 2020, were primarily focused on keeping the functional organization originally planned by Nervi, and upgrading it wherever new production standards demanded so. Secondly, the guidelines focused on the

2015–2020
MASSIMO NARDUZZO AND CREA.RE

1961–1964
PIER LUIGI NERVI AND GINO COVRE

MANTUA, ITALY

1. Detail view of the suspended roof steel structure, after restoration.

restoration of the glass facades and their *brise-soleils*, which, together with the reinforced concrete trestles, are distinctive features of Nervi's design.

The renovation project was, therefore, not a reinterpretation of the buildings designed by Pier Luigi Nervi, but rather a respectful conservation of its identity, recognizing its role as a witness of past values and cultural meanings, that go beyond the pure industrial functionality.[3]

The technical upgrade of the production facilities had to be reconciled with the conservation of as much of the original material as possible. The adaptations required by the new machinery – a new paper machine and its supporting facilities – were subordinated to the design of the existing building, although they were left intentionally readable as contemporary elements.

3. Massimo Narduzzo (ed.), *La Cartiera Burgo, Mantova Pier Luigi Nervi 1961–1964. La ricerca di un equilibrio fra restauro e recupero funzionale 2016–2020*, Treviso, CREA:RE, 2021. See also: Francesco Doglioni, *Nel restauro: Progetti per le architetture del passato*, Venice, Marsilio editore, 2008; Paolo Faccio, *I materiali dell'architettura contemporanea: storia d'uso-degrado-restauro. Il calcestruzzo e il calcestruzzo a facciavista. Caso studio: il restauro della Tomba Brion di Carlo Scarpa organizzato* (masterclass), Treviso, Fondazione Architetti della Provincia di Treviso, September 2016.

2

2. South facade, after restoration.

3. North facade and accelerator tanks, after restoration.

4. Interior of the continuous machine hall, after restoration.

5

6

7

8

5. View of the south facade of the continuous machine building, 1964. 6. Interior of the continuous machine room with the Beloit in operation, 1964. 7. View of the south facade, before restoration. 8. Interior of the machine hall, before restoration.

9

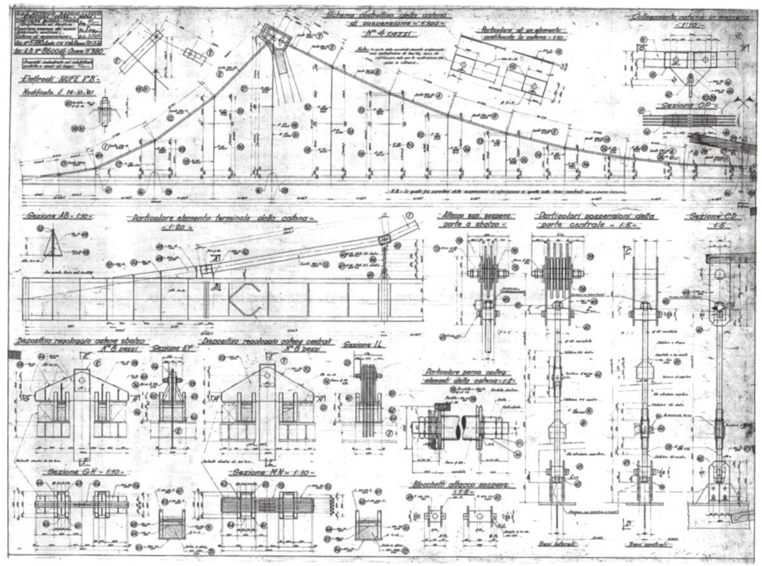

10

11

12

9. Execution project: calculation and design of the catenaries with the definition of nodes. 10. Aerial view of the new Burgo paper mill complex, 1964. 11. Interior of the continuous machine hall after the 1974 fire. 12. The suspended steel deck under construction, 1962.

13

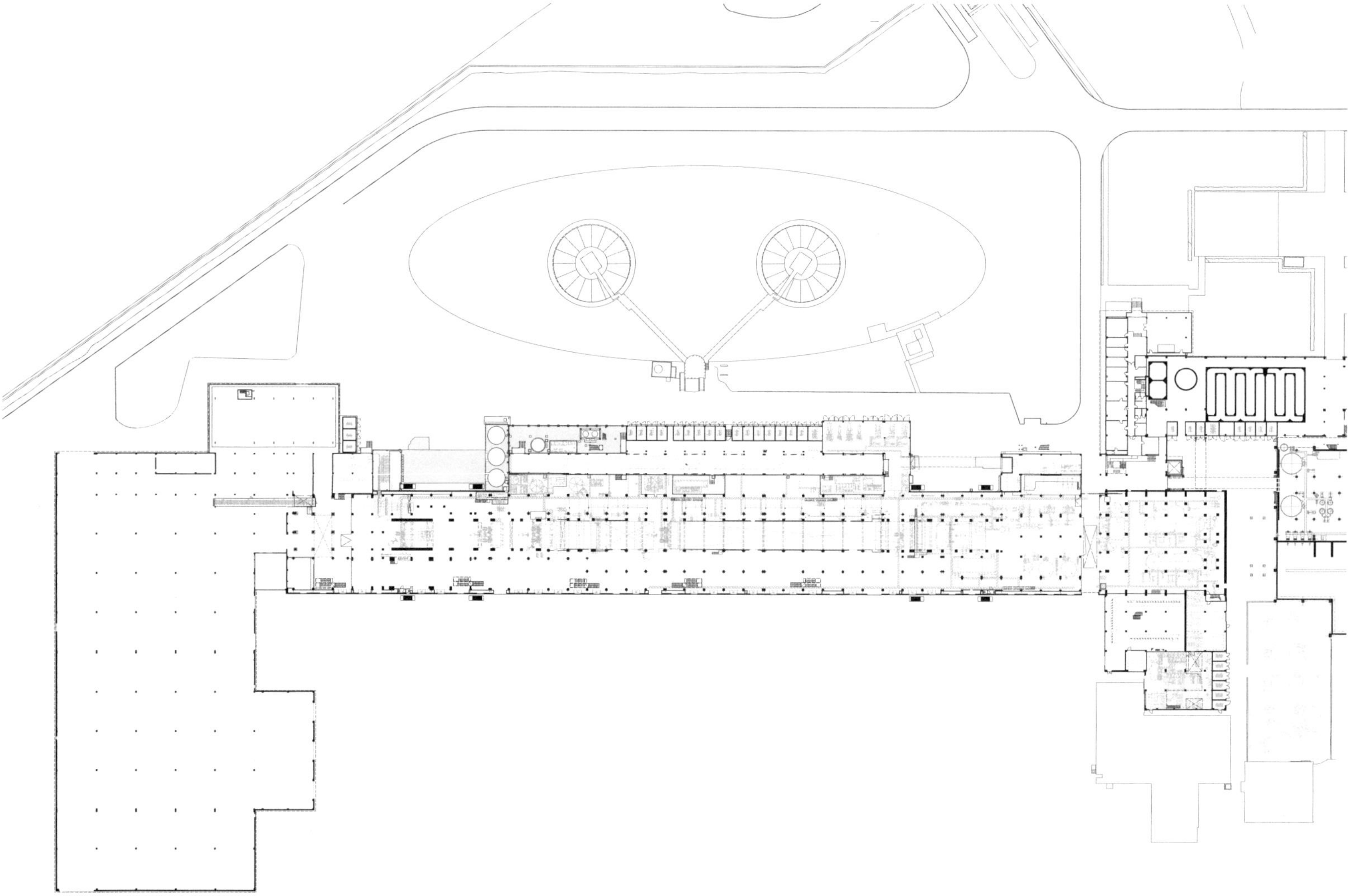

14

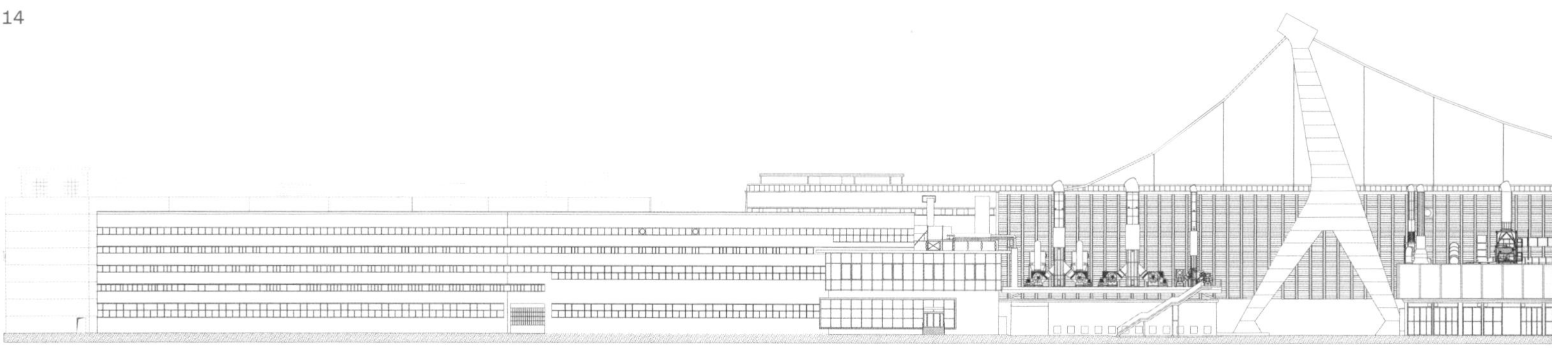

Restoration project: 13. Ground floor plan. 14. North elevation.

15

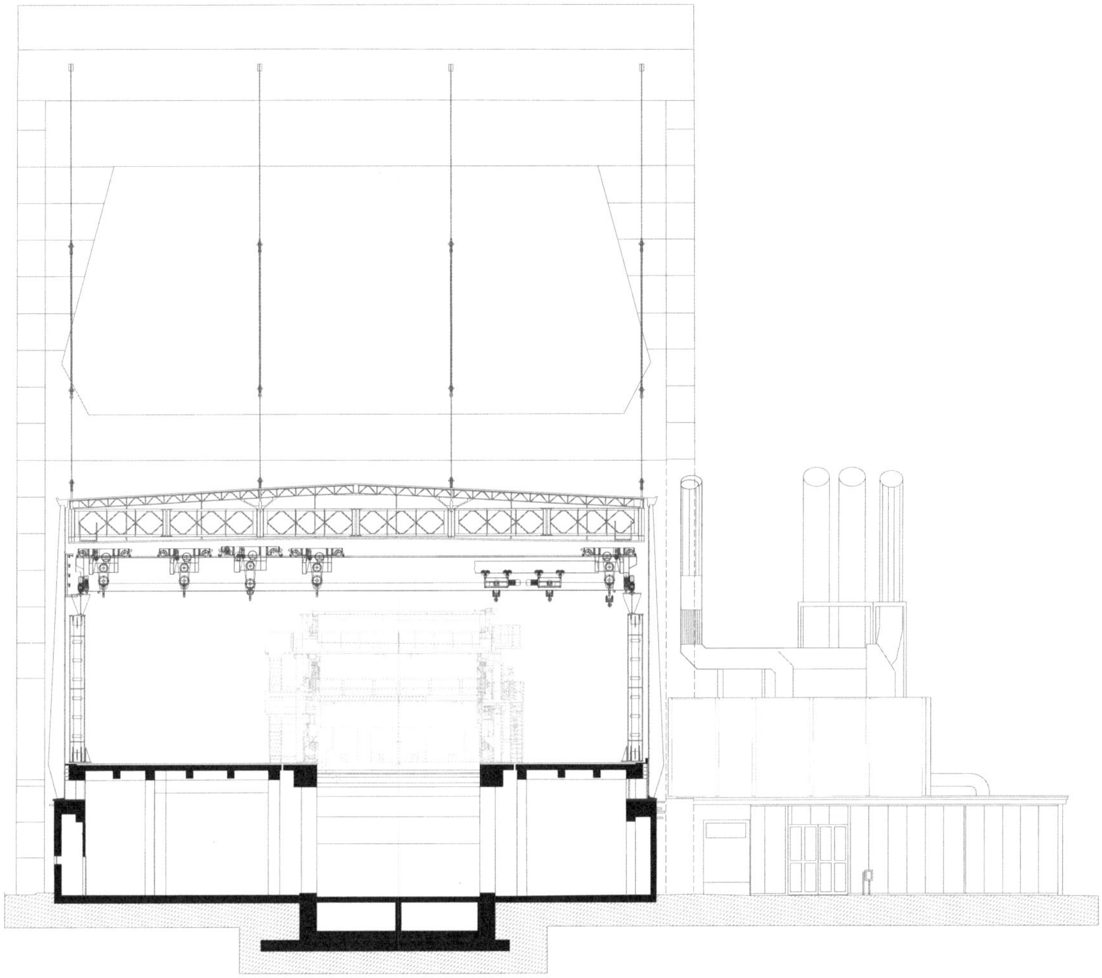

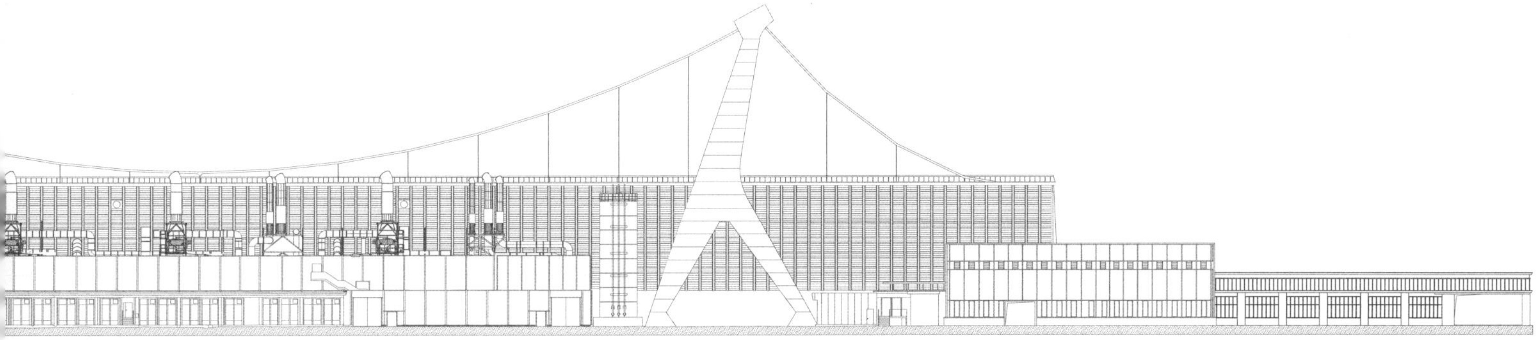

Restoration project: 15. Cross section, showing the suspended roof support system.

INTERVENTIONS THAT RESULT FROM INDIVIDUAL OR GROUP ACTION PROMOTING THE AWARENESS OF MODERN HERITAGE, WHILE SPREADING THE CONCEPT OF RENOVATION FOR THE PUBLIC GOOD.

ISOKON AND ISOKON GALLERY

The Isokon and Isokon Gallery are an impressive example of the activist spirit and determination of the Notting Hill Home Ownership, the Isokon Trust, and Avanti Architects. This spirit led to the acquisition of the then severely deteriorated building and the development of its restoration project by Avanti Architects, which restored the building to its original splendor, while adapting it to current living conditions. To reinforce its value and impact, a small gallery on its history was later created in the building's former garage.

TRENTON BATH HOUSE AND DAY CAMP PAVILIONS

The numerous efforts to promote the safekeeping and restoration of the Trenton Bath House and Day Camp Pavilions, reflect a commendable impulse to preserve small, yet meaningful, built legacies. After years of neglect, several awareness-raising initiatives led to the buying of the building by the public authorities who engaged Mills + Schnoering Architects to implement a comprehensive restoration plan of the building and landscape. Retaining Louis Kahn's original design, the intervention revived the complex's original function and spirit.

CONSERVATION THROUGH ACTIVISM

ISOKON AND ISOKON GALLERY

2003–2004 MAIN BUILDING RESTORATION
2014 CREATION OF ISOKON GALLERY
AVANTI ARCHITECTS

1933–1934
WELLS COATES

LONDON, ENGLAND

CONSERVATION THROUGH ACTIVISM

As one of the first Modern Movement buildings in England, The Isokon building, also known as the Lawn Road Flats, is located in Hampstead, north London. Designed in 1933 by Canadian architect Wells Coates (1895–1958)[1] for Molly (1900–1985), a psychiatrist, and Jack Pritchard (1899–1992), a plywood salesman, the building is a "manifesto of progressive urban living."[2] Influenced by the *Existenzminimum* dwelling experiments, specifically by the Weissenhof Siedlung in Stuttgart, and promoted through the CIAM,[3] client and architect proceeded to develop a reinforced concrete monolithic building (exterior walls only 10 centimeters thick) consisting of 32 flats on four floors with exterior access galleries. Originally, the building comprised three studio flats, 22 "minimum" flats and four double flats, as well as staff quarters, a communal kitchen, and a large garage. Thus, besides the laundry and bed making services, the communal kitchen provided for the preparation and delivery of meals to be sent to the floors above via a dumb waiter. The 22 minimum flats (only 25 square meters in area) were an experiment in minimalist urban living and had a tiny kitchen, a dressing room, and a bathroom alongside the main living/sleeping space. They showed, especially through the dressing room with its compactly designed built-in storage fittings, that *Existenzminimum* could be elegant as well as economical, distinguishing the Isokon units from the average student bedsitter.[4]

The Pritchards lived in a one-bedroom penthouse flat at the rooftop level. Since Jack Pritchard was marketing manager for the Estonian plywood company Venesta, this material was used extensively in the fittings of the apartments.[5] Shortly after its completion in 1934, émigrés fleeing from the dictatorial regimes in Europe began to arrive in England with a number of famous designers becoming residents, including Bauhaus masters Walter Gropius, Marcel Breuer (1902–1981), and László Moholy-Nagy (1895–1946). Later also the novelist Agatha Christie, Soviet spy Arnold Deutsch, archaeologist Max Mallowan, among others, lived in the building. In 1937, the communal kitchen was converted into the Isobar restaurant and bar by Marcel Breuer and F.R.S. Yorke and became a vibrant center for socialist intellectual and artistic life not only for the building residents but the whole Hampstead neighborhood.[6]

The building survived considerable nearby bombing during the war but never quite recovered its pre-war social cachet in the post-war era. In 1969, the building was sold to the *New Statesman* newspaper and the Isobar, which included a porter's flat, was converted to provide three additional flats. In 1972, it was sold again, this time to the local authority, the London Borough of Camden and the building began its years of decline. In 1974 the Isokon was listed Grade II by English Heritage and then raised to Grade I in 1999. However, despite this statutory protection, due to lack of maintenance, the building steadily deteriorated and by 2000 it had reached such an extreme state of dereliction as to become uninhabitable. Had it not been listed the building would certainly have been demolished, and in its dilapidated condition even at Grade I its future was not secure. It was this dire situation that prompted the eventual rescue initiative.

Becoming aware of the risk that the Isokon was facing, a campaign to save the building (in which Docomomo UK was a key participant) was started, ending with the building being sold by LB Camden to the Notting Hill Housing Group, a

1. Sherban Cantacuzino, *Wells Coates: a Monograph*, London, Gordon Fraser Gallery, 1978; Laura Cohn, *The Door to a Secret Room: A Portrait of Wells Coates*, Farnham, Ashgate Publishing, 1999; Elizabeth Darling, *Wells Coates*, London, RIBA Enterprises, 2012.
2. John Allan, "Lawn Road Flats (The Isokon) – A New Vision of Urban Living," *Docomomo Journal*, No. 58 – "Louis I. Kahn – The Permanence," Lisbon, Docomomo International, 2018, 78–81.
3. Leyla Deybelge and Magnus Englund, *Isokon and the Bauhaus in Britain*, Batsford, 2019.
4. John Allan, *op. cit.*, 78.
5. Magnus Englund, "Isokon Furniture – Modernist Dreams in Plywood," *Docomomo Journal*, No. 58 – "Louis I. Kahn – The Permanence," Lisbon, Docomomo International, 2018, 82–85; Jack Pritchard, *View from a Long Chair*, London, Routledge & Kegan Paul, 1984.
6. "Hampstead – Lawn Road Flats, NW3," *The Architectural Review*, London, September 1934; "Apartmenthaus in London," *Detail*, Munich, November 2006, 1254–1256; Catherine Croft, "Isokon," *The Architects' Journal*, London, 30 March 2006, 25–37; Alastair Grieve, "Isokon," in Alan Powers (ed.), *Modern Britain 1929–1939*, London, The Design Museum, 1999; F.R.S. Yorke and Frederick Gibberd, *The Modern Flat*, London, The Architectural Press, 1937, 153–154.

1. Evening view of the building, after restoration.

progressive London-based social landlord who commissioned a team led by Avanti Architects for its restoration project.

Beginning in 2003, the restoration and rehabilitation project sought to re-establish the Isokon as a compact, elegant, and enjoyable place to live – just as envisaged by its original creators. The scheme's tenure model allocated 24 of the 36 flats on a shared equity basis to key-workers, i.e., nurses and teachers, who could normally not hope to live in such an expensive area of London. This greatly appealed to the left-wing Camden Council and has helped to preserve the Pritchards' radical social vision. The remaining units were sold on the open market to support the project budget.

Rescue work entailed every kind of technical intervention including re-roofing, specialist concrete repair, renewal of the non-original windows with authentic replacements, thermal upgrading of the building envelope, and complete re-servicing to current environmental standards, restoration of original colors, and a full scheme of new landscaping. The building's Grade I listed status entailed scrupulous observance of conservation protocols, with the retention or replication of all original interior cabinetry, lighting, and ironmongery details. Specialist restoration was carried out on the surviving plywood paneling and bespoke joinery in the Pritchards' penthouse apartment. The restored building was re-opened in 2004 and in London's current housing crisis has demonstrated that what was once at the cutting edge of modern domestic design has become modern and relevant again.

The goal of the newly established Isokon Gallery, formed within the original garage and opened in 2014, was to present a permanent exhibition of the history and significance of the building and its extraordinary range of residents, thereby re-establishing a communal focus for the building in place of the Isobar, which could not be reinstated within the main project.[7] The display is designed around the existing structural grid and comprises a series of free-standing full-height screens framed in laminated ply, with further wall-mounted panels and glass-topped shelves in a coordinated design format. This allows for presentation of exhibition material in a series of linked themes, which are supplemented by period furniture exhibits, historical memorabilia, a large-scale model of the building itself, two facsimile Isokon rooms created using salvaged 1934 fittings from the building rescue, and a small audio-visual facility showing archival and current films connected with the building. The central screen is demountable to enable the main space to be used for lectures, educational seminars, and small receptions. The doorway presents the venue to the public street, keeping Gallery visitors separate from the residents' private entrance. A small gift shop is included, with all proceeds supporting the upkeep of the Gallery.

The Gallery project, which is run as a charity and stewarded by volunteers, has been funded entirely by donations, sponsorship, and by two Covid support grants, from Historic England and the Heritage Lottery Fund. On 9 July 2018, the 84th anniversary of the original building opening, an English Heritage Blue Plaque was unveiled on the Isokon Gallery wall by Wolf Burchard, the great nephew of Walter Gropius, to mark the residency of the three Bauhaus masters.

7. John Allan et al., *Isokon Gallery: The Story of a New Vision of Urban Living*, London, Isokon Gallery Trust, 2016; www.isokongallery.org. See also: John Allan, *Revaluing Modern Architecture*, London, RIBA Publishing, 2022.

2

3

4

2. Gallery foyer, with a building model (left), Donkeys Mark 2 and 3 (right), and a Breuer Long Chair and original Isokon Donkey exhibit (beyond), after rehabilitation. The far screen is demountable to create a lecture space. 3. Dressing room of a typical studio flat, after restoration. 4. Kitchen of a typical studio flat, after restoration.

5

8

6

7

5. General view of the building, before restoration. 6. View of the rooftop terrace and penthouse, before restoration. 7. Interior condition of a typical flat, before restoration. 8. View of the building from Lawn Road.

9

10

11

12

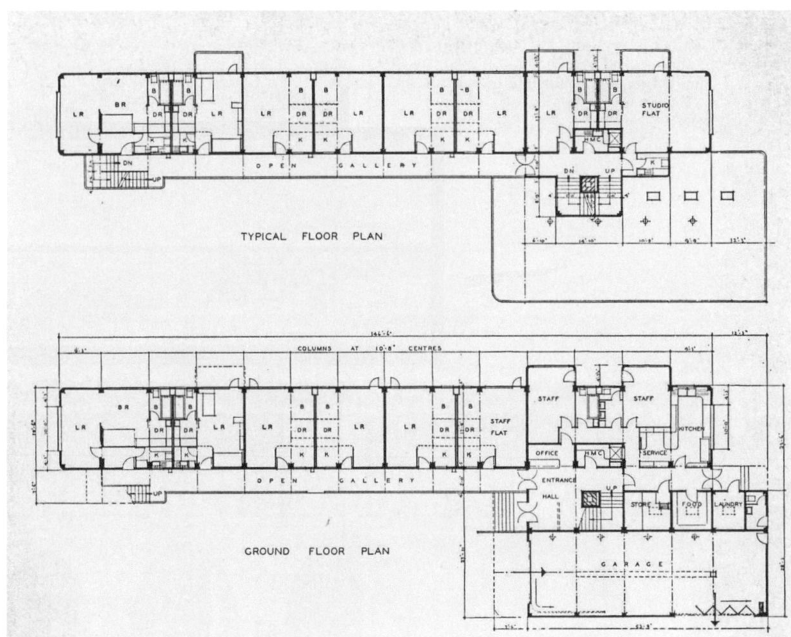

9. Interior of a minimal studio flat. 10. View of the building from Lawn Road, 1934. 11. The Isobar, 1937 (converted into flats in 1970). 12. Ground floor plan and typical floor plan, 1934.

13

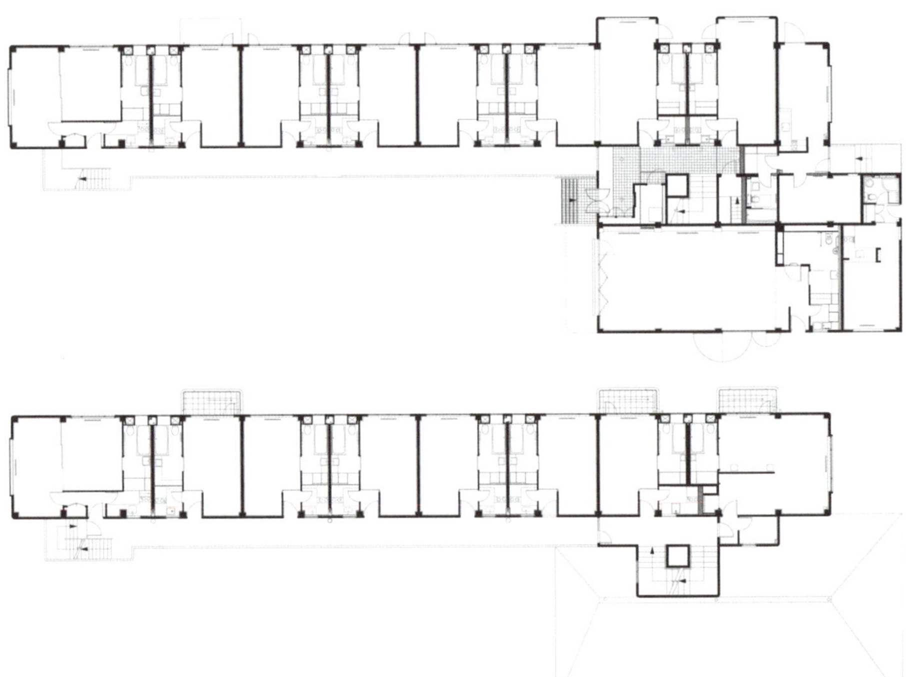

14

13. View of the entrance to the Isokon Gallery, after rehabilitation. Restoration project: 14. Ground floor and typical floor plans.

15

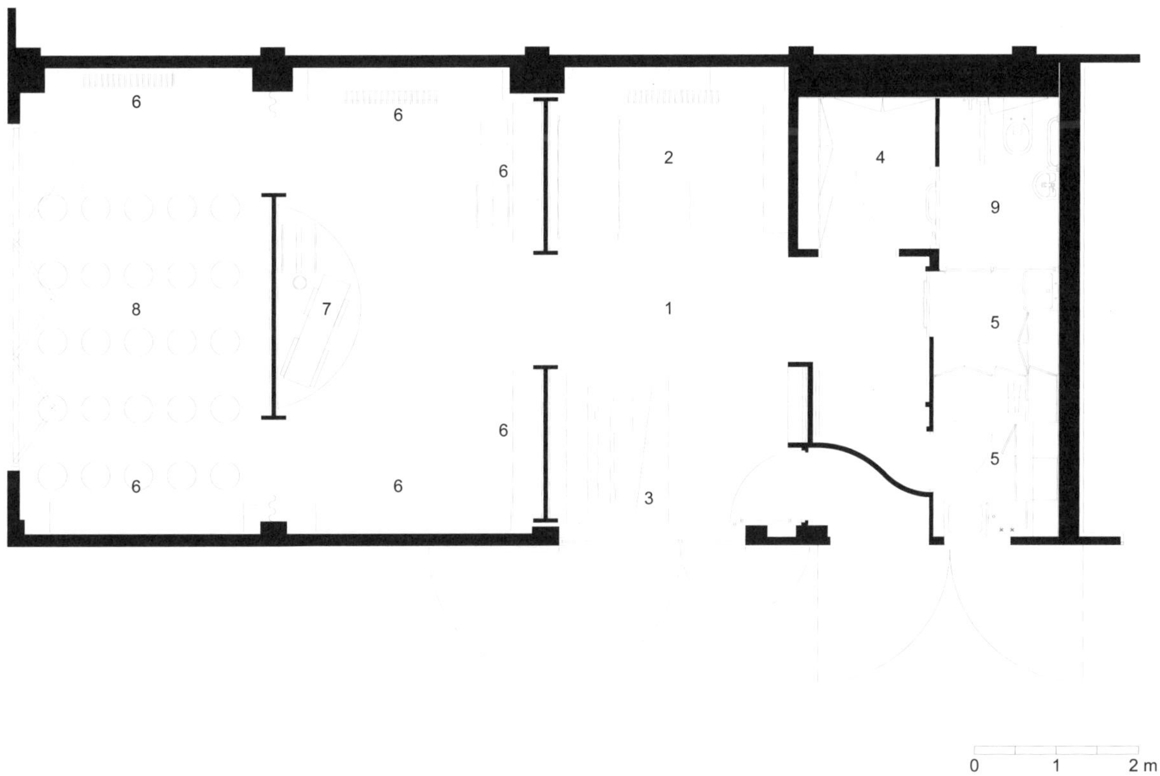

16

Restoration project: 15. Plan of a typical studio flat. 1 – reconfigured window reveal to accommodate new gas boiler, 2 – new double-glazed argon filled windows, 3 – new M&E services and finishes, 4 – new thermal insulation to internal face of all exterior walls, 5 – rebuilt party wall to achieve fire and acoustic compliance, 6 – original party wall upgraded to achieve fire and acoustic compliance, 7 – overhead cupboards conceal new mechanical vents from bathroom, 8 – adjusted position of party wall to accommodate standard refrigerator in kitchen and washing machine in dressing room, 9 – reconfigured kitchen fit-out to provide modern stove, more storage, and refrigerator, 10 – new vertical service ducts. 16. Plan of the Isokon Gallery. 1 – entrance hall, 2 – gift shop, 3 – illuminated model, 4 – A/V facility, 5 – heritage rooms formed from salvaged original fittings, 6 – historical story boards, 7 – original Isokon furniture display, 8 – talks area, 9 – WC.

TRENTON BATH HOUSE AND DAY CAMP PAVILIONS

PROMOTION THROUGH ACTIVISM

In 1954, Louis I. Kahn was hired by the Trenton Jewish Community Center (JCC) to design a new community and recreation complex for the organization in Ewing, operating as a summer day camp program to provide structured recreational activities in its sport and meeting facilities. The Bath House and the adjoining pool were the first portions to be built. Together with Anne Tyng (1920–2011), Kahn designed this small structure in 1955 which opened in the same year. The design and construction of the Day Camp Pavilions followed in 1957. Kahn's Community Center, the largest component of the complex, remained unbuilt and was completed by the firm of Kelly and Gruzen in 1962.[1]

The Bath House consists of five double-axial-symmetrical square concrete block "rooms" arranged in a Greek cross plan. Four of the "rooms" are covered by pyramidal wood-framed roofs with black asphalt shingles, surrounding the fifth which is an open courtyard and the center of the structure. They accommodate changing rooms for men and women with showers and toilets and a place for patrons to store belongings. The roofs, which appear to float, are pyramidal in shape and rest lightly on large concrete block "columns" with concrete caps. These columns generate the narrow servant zones for the primary served zones, a concept that Kahn later implemented in the Richards Labs.[2]

The four Day Camp Pavilions were designed with readily available local materials, including clay chimney tiles and locally manufactured concrete plank. They were meant to recall the relationship of classical structures that Kahn had seen in Corinth, Greece. The two largest pavilions were designed as open structures, one comprising four bays and the other five. The two smaller pavilions were partially enclosed and contained restrooms and storage. The roofs were formed of precast concrete plank spanning between beams above the uprights at the perimeter.[3]

The complex was listed on the New Jersey and National Registers of Historic Places in 1984, only about 30 years after being built, reflecting its high level of significance. However, although routine maintenance works were performed by the JCC and few physical changes had occurred, usage of the complex declined and the pace of its physical deterioration accelerated. There was no full understanding of the vulnerability and ongoing needs of the historic fabric. Both the Bath House and the Day Camp Pavilions had suffered from continual exposure to the rain and snow, magnified by the temporality of the materials and original design features, including: freestanding block walls with no copings, no gutters at the roof edge, and inadequate drainage of both the building and site.[4] Attention was focused on the precarious state of the Bath House property in 1997 with its inclusion on Preservation New Jersey's Ten Most Endangered list, after the JCC had proposed the demolition of two of the Day Camp Pavilions due to their advanced state of deterioration. A series of preservation efforts followed, ranging from a monograph published by Susan G. Solomon in 2000[5] to its inclusion in Nathaniel Kahn's film *My Architect* in 2003.

With the transfer of the property from the JCC to Mercer County in 2007 (and ultimately to Ewing Township with preservation easements), efforts toward its restoration finally became a reality. Mercer County began planning its restoration and future use with assistance from the National Trust for Historic Preservation and with support from the New Jersey Historic and County Open Space Trust Funds. Also in 2007, the County engaged the design team led by Mills + Schnoering Architects[6]

1. Michael Mills and Anne Weber, "The Trenton Bath House Restoration: Challenges in Sustainability," *Docomomo Journal*, No. 58 – "Louis I. Kahn – the Permanence," Lisbon, Docomomo International, 2018, 12–19; Heinz Ronner and Sharad Jhaveri, *Louis I. Kahn Complete Work 1935–1974, Second revised and enlarged edition*, Basel, Birkhäuser, 1987, 82–91.

2. Michael Mills and Anne Weber, *op. cit.*, 15; Klaus-Peter Gast, *Louis I. Kahn – The Idea of Order*, Basel, Birkhäuser, 1998, 29.

3. Michael Mills and Anne Weber, *op. cit.*, 17.

4. *Idem.*, 15.
5. Susan G. Solomon, *Louis I. Kahn's Trenton Jewish Community Center*, Building Studies No. 6, New York, Princeton Architectural Press, 2000.
6. Formerly Farewell Mills Gatsch Architects, LLC.

2007–2013
MILLS + SCHNOERING ARCHITECTS, LLC

1955–1957
LOUIS I. KAHN AND ANNE TYNG

EWING, NEW JERSEY, USA

1. Changing area of the Bath House, after restoration.

and assisted by landscape architects Heritage Landscapes and civil engineers The RBA Group to produce a preservation master plan and historic landscape study to guide the project, updating the 2003 Preservation Plan by Farewell Mills Gatsch Architects. Simultaneously, the County educated the public through a website emphasizing the site's history and significance.[7]

7. http://www.kahntrentonbathhouse.org/

The mission of the project was threefold: 1) implementation of the repair and restoration of the Bath House for ongoing use; 2) reconstruction of two Day Camp Pavilions, based upon Historic American Buildings Survey documentation; and 3) interpretation of the site and improvement of access with a new snack bar and new landscape features intended by Kahn but never realized. The planning and design documents reflected a thorough research-based approach. Archival material was examined at the JCC and within the Louis I. Kahn collection at the Architectural Archives of the University of Pennsylvania; individuals involved in the original project (including architect Anne Tyng and structural engineer Nicholas Gianopulos) were consulted; and a program of detailed materials investigations was undertaken. The restoration of remaining historic fabric, as well as the replacement of features that had been lost over time were the focus of the design. The team sought to recapture the original design intentions; incorporate modern requirements for safety, accessibility, and weatherability; and provide a compatible new design that complemented but did not compete with the original artifact.

At the Bath House, which continues in its original use, the entrance mural and the central, circular atrium floor detail were restored. Structural repairs were made to concrete slabs and the concrete masonry unit (CMU) walls to improve drainage, deteriorated slate partitions were replaced in kind, and exterior and interior materials were restored. Two of the Day Camp Pavilions were reconstructed as they were nearly collapsed and could not be repaired, and two others were restored. A system of terracotta over steel columns without solid fill was used for the columns, as the terracotta could be colored and molded to match the appearance of the original chimney tile. The roof was rebuilt with the Filigree floor system[8] as commercially available concrete plank did not match the width of the original plank. A new roof membrane was installed with no visible change to the edge conditions from the ground. The new pavilions are therefore very close in appearance to the originals. The design of the circular paving that contained the Pavilions was reconstructed with contemporary composite material that not only creates a resilient, accessible, and maintainable surface but also resembles the appearance of the original gravel, contained within a new circular concrete curb. A new, free-standing snack bar of compatible materials was built in one of the locations determined for it in the original drawings. The landscape design and parking areas derive from an interpretation of Kahn's master plan, featuring a community green, as originally intended, with perimeter parking and groves of trees that create outdoor rooms. Further, to achieve barrier-free access to the complex, a new concrete ramp leading from the Bath House level to the pool level was created.

8. The Filigree floor system consisting of a precast base panel with concrete poured on top, interconnected by reinforcing. Thus, the use of this system allowed the existence of false joints similar in appearance to the original planks, while providing a more monolithic slab and reducing significantly the risk of leakage between panels.

The Trenton Bath House and Day Camp Pavilions are of international importance and renown, holding an important place in Kahn's *oeuvre*.[9] Thus, with the restoration and new interventions achieved through 15-years of long-term advocacy, teamwork, and public support, the buildings and landscape are better understood and continue to be beloved.

9. As Kahn stated: "The world discovered me after I designed the Richards Laboratories building, but I discovered myself after designing that little concrete bath house in Trenton." Quoted in Susan Braudy, "The Architectural Metaphysic of Louis Kahn," *New York Times Magazine*, 15 November 1970, 86.

2. Bath House with new fencing and snack bar, looking west, after restoration.

3. Bath House looking north to the pool through the central atrium with the restored circular pavement feature, after restoration.

4. Restored mural at the entry.

5. Restored and reconstructed Day Camp Pavilions looking east.

6. Restored and reconstructed Day Camp Pavilions looking north-east.

7

8

9

7. Bath House central atrium looking north to the pool, before restoration. The circular pavement feature was missing. 8. Day Camp Pavilions soon after completion with the original terracotta columns, c. 1957. 9. Close view of a failing open Day Camp Pavilion, before restoration.

11

12

10

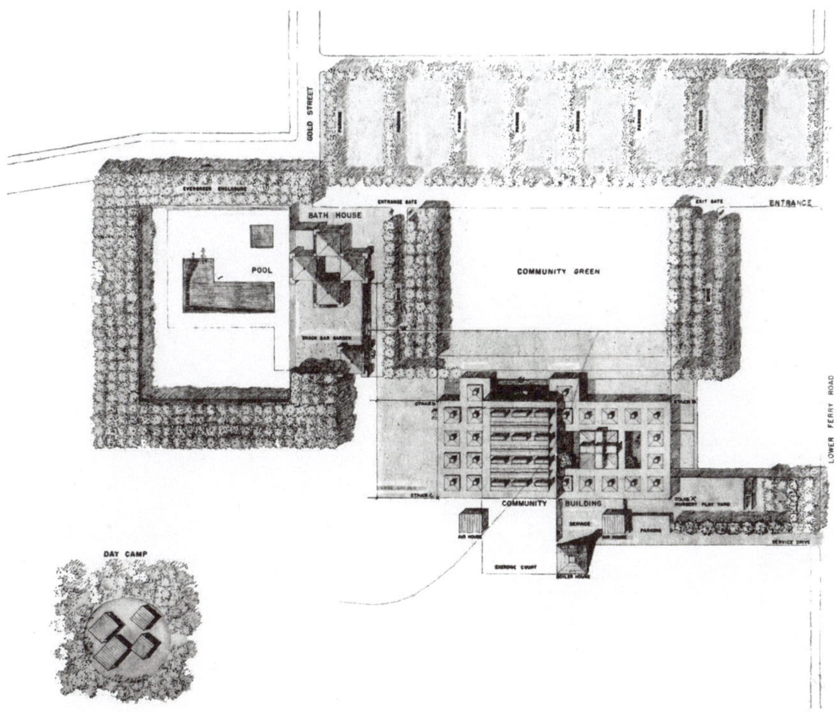

13

10. Bath House soon after completion, central atrium looking south-east, with the circular pavement feature in its original condition, c. 1955. 11. Bath House soon after completion, looking west at east elevation, c. 1955. 12. Bath House central atrium looking north to the pool, with the circular pavement feature filled with grass, c. 1955. 13. Site plan for Bath House, Day Camp Pavilions, Community Center, and green. Only the Bath House and the Day Camp Pavilions were built according to Kahn's plans.

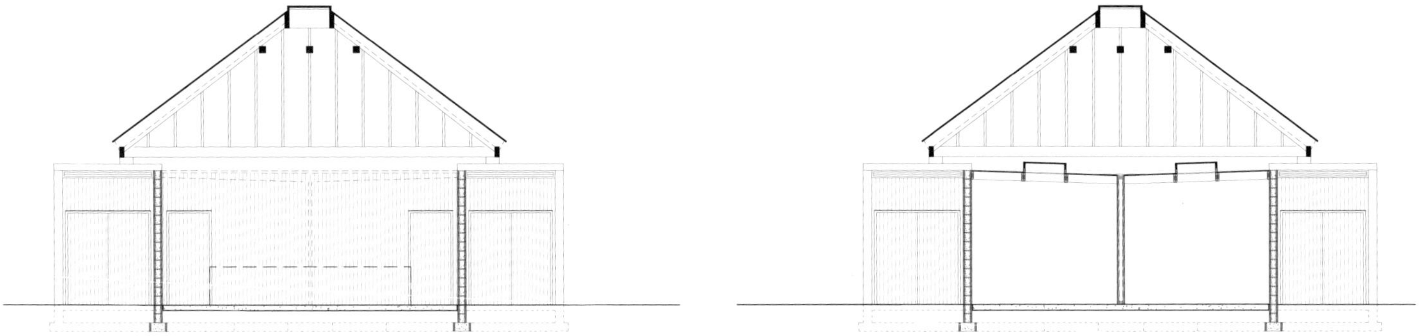

14

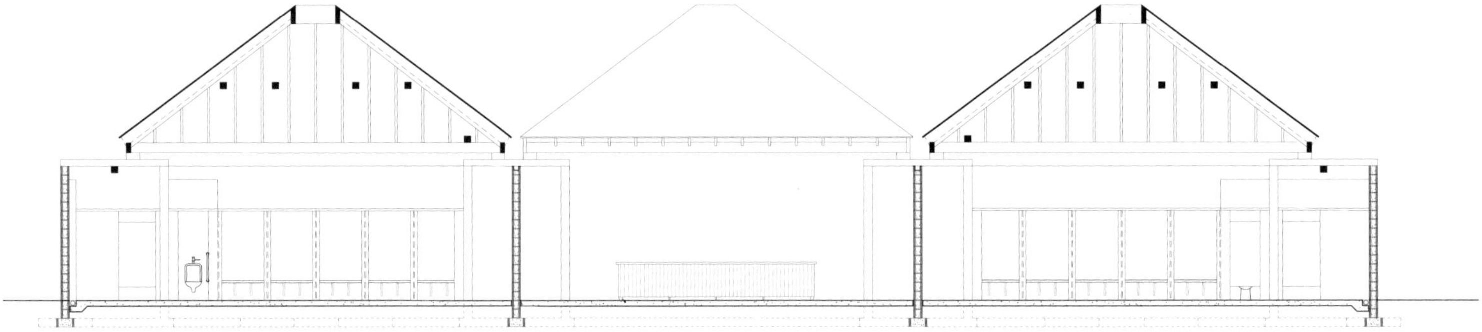

15

Restoration project: 14. Bath House, section through the registration (left), looking south, and section through the offices (right), looking south. 15. Bath House, section through the changing areas and central atrium, looking south.

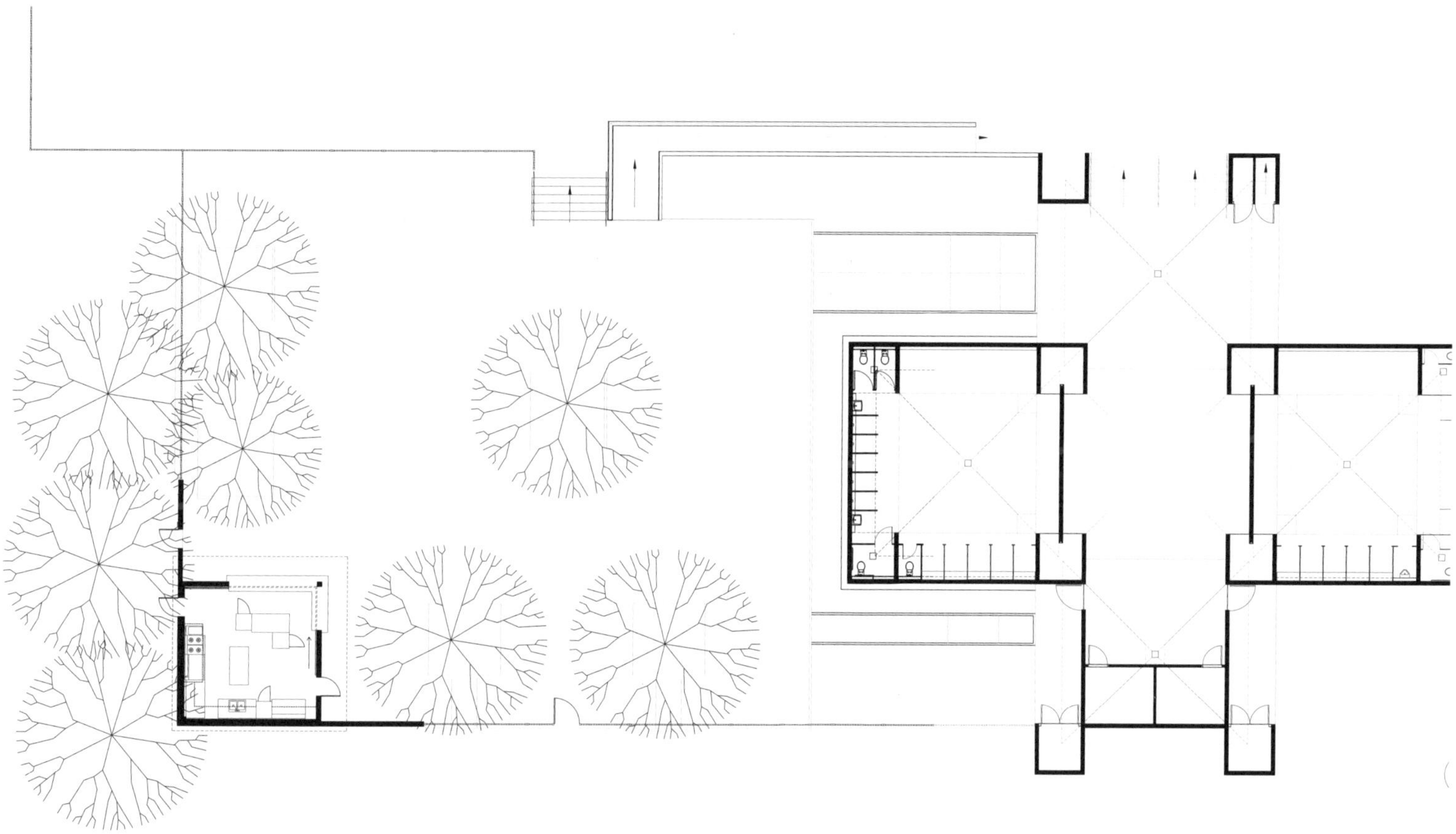

16

Restoration project: 16. Plan of the Bath House and new snack bar at the south-west corner.

PRACTICES IN THE RESTORATION OF REMARKABLE MODERN HOUSES THAT ARE NOW OPEN TO PUBLIC.

LE CORBUSIER'S APARTMENT-STUDIO

The restoration of Le Corbusier's apartment-studio is proof of the importance of documental research for reaching an understanding on which an intervention strategy can then be based. The Foundation Le Corbusier took a cautious approach to the restoration of this exceptional and evolving domestic space, with thorough research, followed by a conservation project by Chatillon Architectes. Conscious of the many transformations that it had undergone throughout the lives of Le Corbusier and his wife, the design team intelligently restored it to represent its final stage, leaving "open scars" to document earlier layers of experiment within the apartment-studio, which was then re-opened to the public.

VILLA TUGENDHAT

Villa Tugendhat's immaculate restoration to its original state – removing adulterations added after the family's departure – shows how the preservation of a world-renowned *Gesamtkunstwerk* can be respectfully addressed. Based on a detailed investigation of documents and the remaining original fabric, the restoration project was able to recover rigorous essence of Mies' design. The restoration team's accuracy and commitment to reinstating every thorough detail – from the technical equipment to the furniture and the door handles – has finally allowed its visitors to truly experience, and be inspired by Mies' genius.

OPEN HOUSE

LE CORBUSIER'S APARTMENT-STUDIO

OPEN HOUSE

When in 1931 Le Corbusier and Pierre Jeanneret (1896–1967) designed the apartment building Immeuble Molitor in Rue Nungesser-et-Coli, at the border between Paris and Boulogne, Le Corbusier kept the top two floors for his own use, creating a split-level apartment. The design of the apartment building was constrained by the narrow and deep configuration of the plot and by strict zoning codes, which specified facade element dimensions.[1] It is built in reinforced concrete, allowing thus an open-plan design and fully glazed facades – of Nevada glass bricks, glass curtain walls, and various other glass products – making this way best use of the exceptional location. Thus "each apartment possesses a wall entirely of glass, running from floor to ceiling. Sun-control devices have been provided. Once the building was inaugurated the tenants spontaneously declared that a new life had started for them, thanks to the glass wall and certain common service facilities."[2] With this building, Le Corbusier returned to the principles of the Ville Radieuse, applying four of his five points of modern architecture – free floor plan, structure supported by *pilotis* rather than walls, free facade, and roof garden – allowing for access to the sky and views of trees.[3] With its entirely glazed facades it became the first glass apartment building in the history of architecture.[4] After its completion in 1934, Le Corbusier lived and worked on his plastic work in the apartment-studio till his death in 1965.

Equipped with all modern comforts, but surprisingly modest, this two-level penthouse of 240 square meters is composed of two wings, using the entire width of the building. On one wing is the studio with a large exposed rough stone wall, where Le Corbusier painted in the morning, while the other wing accommodates the living room, office, bedroom, kitchen, bathroom, and servant areas, arranged such that no corridors were needed and the number of doors was minimized. The walls were painted in pure primary colors. On the upper level, accessed by an interior staircase, there is a guest room and a central roof garden offers panoramic views. The architect frequently intervened in the apartment-studio to experiment with new materials and colors until his death in 1965. It is this last state desired by the architect that the *Fondation Le Corbusier* (FLC) wanted to preserve and show to the public.

Listed as UNESCO World Heritage Site in 2016, Immeuble Molitor is part of the list *The Architectural Work of Le Corbusier, an Outstanding Contribution to the Modern Movement* of 17 works in seven countries and on three continents, being recognized so as it reflects "new architectural concepts, principles, and technical features,"[5] and to demonstrate the influence of Le Corbusier throughout the world over half a century. However, despite its status as an icon of 20th century architecture, this building had been little studied.[6] The FLC therefore decided that this restoration should be an opportunity to increase the historical and material knowledge of the place. It commissioned the Laboratory of Techniques and Preservation of Modern Architecture at the Lausanne Polytechnic (TSAM) to carry out an in-depth heritage study,[7] entrusted the engineering firm A-Bime with the technical studies (structural, thermal, etc.), and Marie-Odile Hubert, a restorer of paintings, with a survey of the polychromy. The office of François Chatillon, chief architect of historical monuments, was chosen to carry out the project and restoration work based on all of these studies.

The main goal of the FLC was to stop infiltrations from the concrete barrel vaults and the roof, and to improve the thermal efficiency of the building.[8] Thanks to

1. Fondation Le Corbusier, *Dossier enseignant Appartement-Atelier de Le Corbusier*, Paris, 4–5; Deborah Gans, *The Le Corbusier Guide*, New York, Princeton Architectural Press, 1987, 47.

2. Le Corbusier, *Oeuvre complète*, volume 2, 1929–1934, Zurich, Boesiger; Bertrand Lemoine, *Birkhäuser Architectural Guide France 20th century*, Basel, Birkhäuser, 2000, 175.

3. Willy Boesiger and Hans Girsberger, *Le Corbusier 1910–65*, Basel, Birkhäuser, 1999, 64.
4. Fondation Le Corbusier, *op. cit.*, 5.

5. https://lecorbusier-worldheritage.org and https://whc.unesco.org/en/list/1321
6. Jacques Sbriglio, *Immeuble 24 N.C. et appartement Le Corbusier/Apartment Block 24 N.C.*, Basel, Birkhäuser/Fondation Le Corbusier, 1996.
7. Franz Graf and Giulia Marino, *Les multiples vies de l'appartement-atelier de Le Corbusier*, Lausanne, EPFL Press, 2017.
8. Christine Mengin and Bénédicte Gandini, "L'appartement de Le Corbusier, au 24 NC," *Monumental* – "Dossier Le patrimoine des années 1925–1935," No. 2, 2018, 16–19.

2016–2018
CHATILLON ARCHITECTES

1931–1934
LE CORBUSIER

PARIS, FRANCE

1. Living room, after restoration: the furniture was subject of particular attention. The cowhide carpet was restored and the restored polychromy includes the gray of the rods.

simulations with different materials and thicknesses, as well as prototypes, the chosen solution combines two insulators. They are associated with a bituminous waterproofing evoking the color of the concrete. The cement tile paving of the roof has been redone, and the terrace was replanted as it was in 1965, taking into account its ease of maintenance.

Whenever possible, a simple cleaning was undertaken, such as for the white ceramic floor tiles. The original glass bricks were preserved and when necessary repaired, as in the shower. But when materials had been changed after Le Corbusier's death, and were in bad conditions, they were replaced with more efficient but authentic products. For instance, the original Nevada glass blocks had previously been replaced by blocks with wider joints, hence reducing the original number of rows. The new glass bricks are thus closer to the original, with narrow joints and the initial number of rows.

The most spectacular intervention is the restoration of the interior polychromy, hidden since the place was occupied by André Wogenscky's (1916–2004) office after Le Corbusier's death. The painting of the apartment-studio was done in accordance with the color-palette of 1965, using oil emulsions specially made for the apartment. The FLC, aware that any material intervention would be irreversible, was keen to guarantee the traceability of these gestures that have become invisible. Thus the 300 stratigraphies will remain visible, so as to testify to the evolution over time of Corbusier's choices in terms of color and to show the approach adopted for the restitution of the polychromy of the apartment. The stratification of the layers of paint also constitutes a sensitive testimony of the 30-year occupation of the place.

The *Fondation Le Corbusier* and François Chatillon's office made every effort to ensure the operation was exemplary, relying on a wide range of technical and artisanal skills. Eager to share this experience and the discoveries which occurred with a broader audience, the FLC commissioned the publication of an inexpensive pocket guide[9] and the making of a documentary film.[10]

9. Christine Desmoulins, *Le Corbusier's Apartment-Studio*, Lyon, Carapace Édition, 2018.
10. Olivier Lemaire, *Chez Le Corbusier*, coproduction Imagissime/Fondation Le Corbusier, 2018. Available at: https://www.youtube.com/watch?v=ldBCotxOtY8.

2. Bedroom, after restoration: the cupboard fixed on the rotating door between the bedroom and the dining room was restored and put back in mobility; the black color of the wall was restored.

3. Dining room with passage to the kitchen on the left, after restoration: the large sliding window was removed, asbestos was removed and the glass was replaced by more insulating glass.

4. Bedroom and bathroom, after restoration: the wall behind the bed regained its ultramarine blue hue.

5. Le Corbusier's studio, after restoration: the tiles were simply cleaned, the paint is in conformity with the 1965 state, the metal joineries were restored and repainted.

6. Le Corbusier's bureau, after restoration: the glass paving stone panel was redone.

7

9

8

10

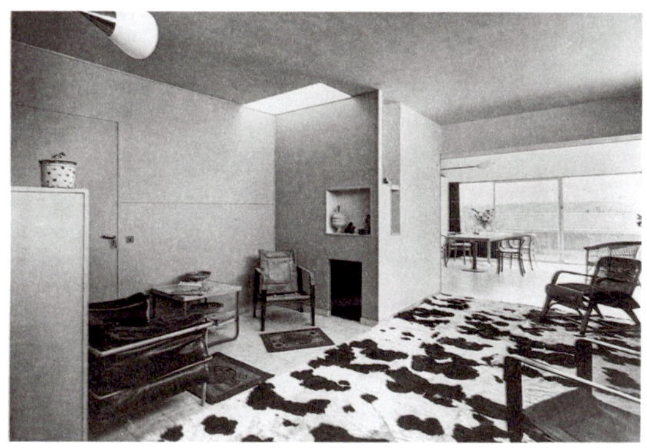

11

7. Analysis of the vault before restoration: the waterproofing had never been completed, therefore the various bituminous layers and numerous stitches over the years did not prevent infiltration. 8. View toward the studio from the entrance/vestibule, before restoration. 9. Kitchen, 1934. 10. View from the living room to the elevator machinery, 1934. 11. Bedroom and, behind, the bathroom, 1934.

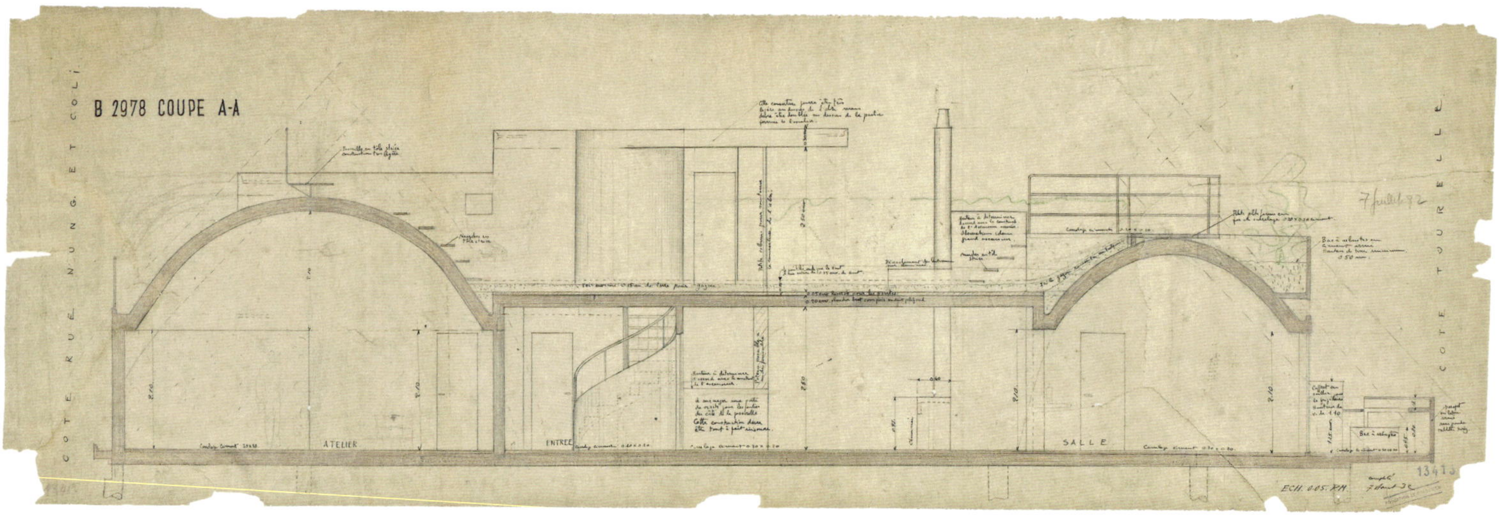

12

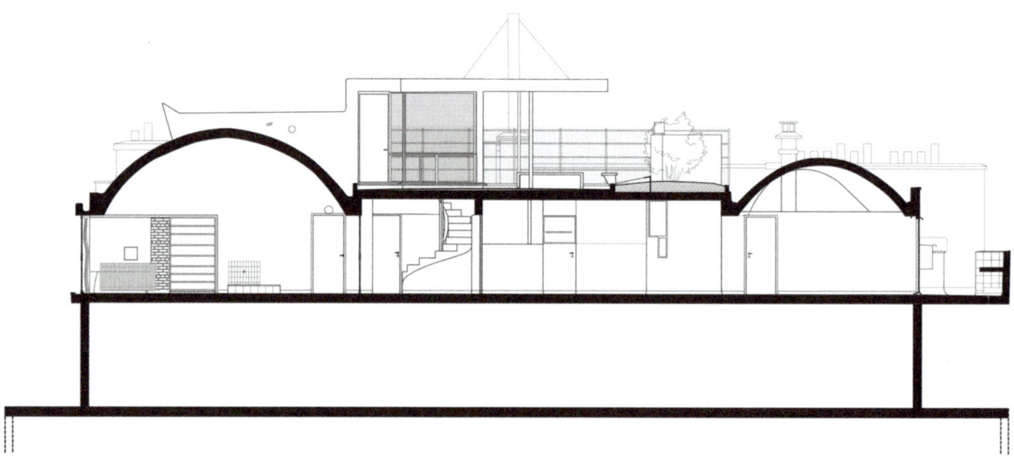

13

Original project: 12. Cross section of the central core, vegetated part of the flat roof, with indication of materials. Restoration project: 13. Section A–A, from left to right, the vault of the studio, the spiral staircase, the living room with the roof-garden above, the vault of the dining room, the balcony overlooking Boulogne.

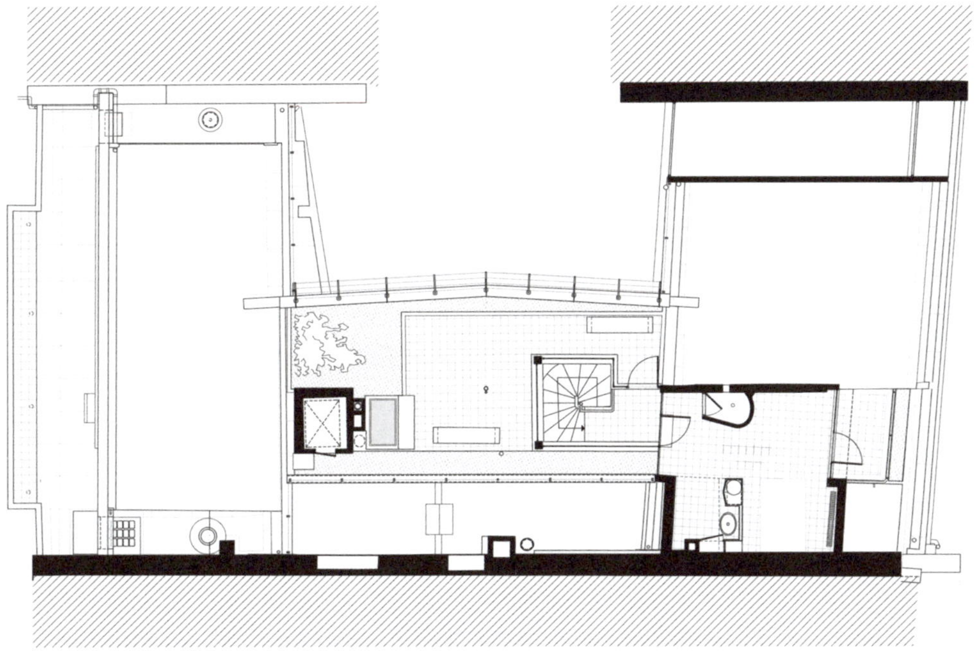

14

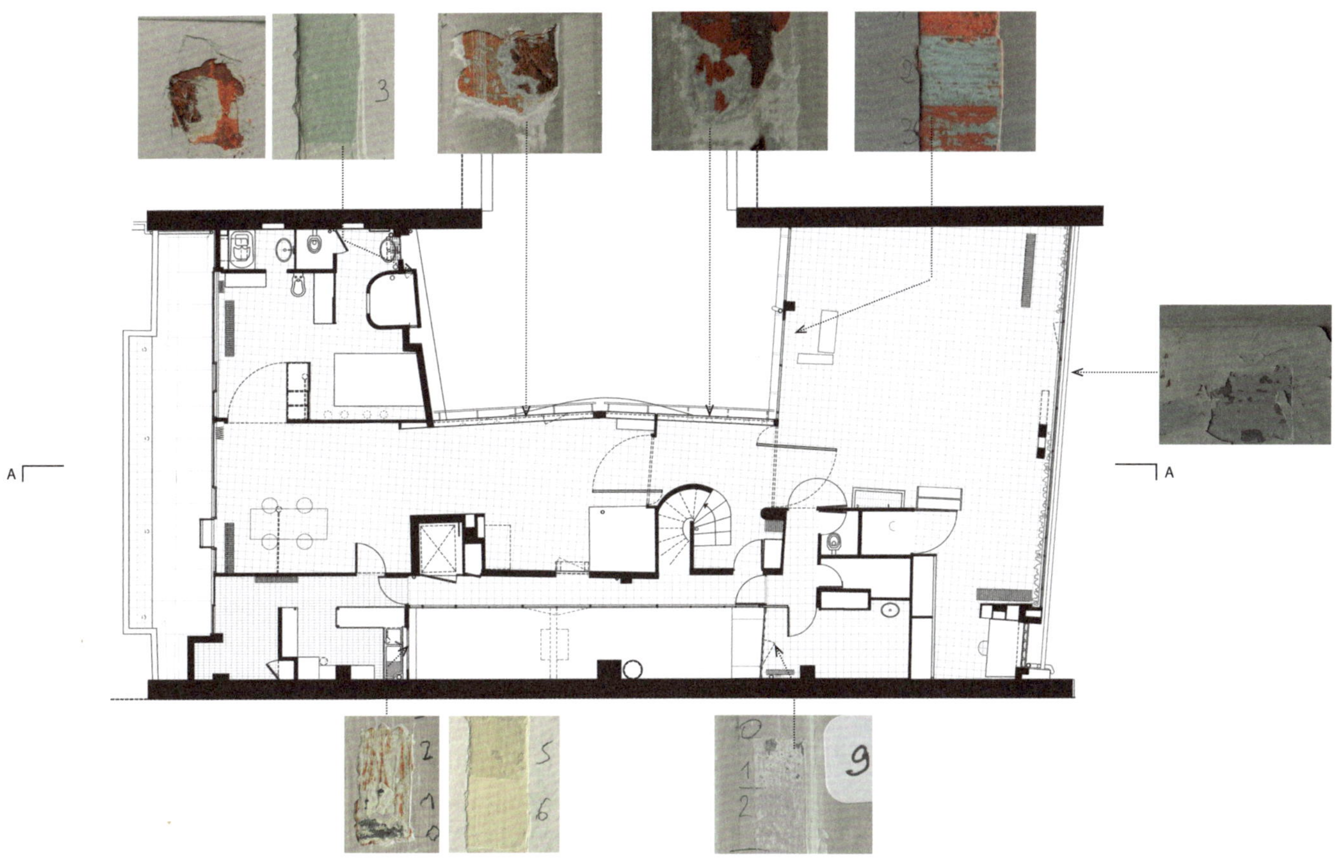

15

Restoration project: 14. Plan of the 8th floor. 15. Study of polychromies on the 7th floor.

OPEN HOUSE

The Villa Tugendhat in Brno, one of Ludwig Mies van der Rohe's major works, was commissioned in 1928 by Grete and Fritz Tugendhat as their family home. The site – a slope with a beautiful view of historic Brno – was determinant in Mies' design, in particular for "the concept of opening up the interior space of the house to its natural surroundings."[1] Together with Lilly Reich (1885–1947), Mies created a house that provided an exceptional way of modern life based on an open plan and advanced technologies. The house is "a unique global work of art – *Gesamtkunstwerk* – in terms of its placement into its natural setting, its spatial organization, construction, technical equipment and interior furnishings."[2]

The three-story residence was adapted to the terrain, oriented toward the garden and, thus, extending the open space out into the landscape. The street entrance leads to the upper level, with the family rooms on the one side and the garage and driver's apartment on the other. From the top level a staircase enclosed by a floor-to-ceiling steel frame window wall with milk glass leads down to the lower level. The steel frame structure in the form of cross-shaped columns – used here for the first time in a residence – enabled open floor plans, thinner walls, and glazed walls of almost 15 square meters, which could be retracted down into the floor using a vertical sliding lift.[3] Different from the upper level with its series of enclosed rooms, the lower floor with its representative living areas is very spacious. It also accommodates the kitchen and servants' area, while the basement comprises Fritz' photo laboratory and rooms for technical equipment, such as central heating water and central air-conditioning, that provided a combination of heating, ventilation and humidifier, and thus filtered and thermally treated air in the main living room.

Materials, furniture, and fittings play an important role. Mies van der Rohe and Lilly Reich designed a number of pieces, including the Brno chair and armchair, specifically for the house and also specified upholstery colors and textile furnishings.[4] The house's fluid spaces, complete with opulent partitions in massive onyx marble and Macassar ebony (used for the semi-circular wall of the dining area), in contrast with the tubular and strip steel of the columns, create "a complete vision of luxurious Modernist living."[5]

The Jewish family lived in the house from late 1930 until 1938, when they fled from Czechoslovakia on the *Anschluss* day. The villa was then confiscated by the Gestapo and in 1942 became illegal property of the German Reich, suffering radical changes.[6] After 1945, the house was used for military purposes, then as a private dancing school, and, until 1979, as a rehabilitation center for children. After being classified as a National Monument in 1963[7] and moving from property of the state to property of the City of Brno, first renovation attempts were undertaken during the 1980s. However, they led to damages to many of the original elements rather than their preservation, while adapting the house to a guesthouse.[8]

Following a declaration by the Tugendhat family in 1993 that the villa should be opened up to the public, the house became a museum in 1994, thereby fulfilling Grete's wish.[9] Herewith efforts toward the restoration of the villa began to be undertaken aiming the preservation of the historic fabric considered as significant while adapting it to the specific requirements of a museum. In this context, in 2001, Villa Tugendhat was listed as a UNESCO World Heritage as "an outstanding example

1. Daniela Hammer-Tugendhat, Ivo Hammer, and Wolf Tegethoff, *Tugendhat House. Ludwig Mies van der Rohe*, Basel, Birkhäuser, 2020, 30.

2. Ana Tostões, Ivo Hammer, and Zara Ferreira, "The Re-birth of the Tugendhat House," *Docomomo Journal*, No. 56 – "The Heritage of Mies," Lisbon, Docomomo International, 2017, 45.

3. *Idem*, 45–46; Ivo Hammer, "The Tugendhat House: Between Craftmanship and Technological Innovation. Preservation as Sustainable Building Policy," in *Docomomo Journal*, No. 44 – "Modern and Sustainable," Barcelona, Docomomo International, 2011, 51.
4. Carsten Krohn, *Mies van der Rohe – The Built Work*, Basel, Birkhäuser, 2014, 82–87.
5. Julia Jamrozik and Coryn Kempster, *Growing up Modern. Childhoods in Iconic Homes*, Basel, Birkhäuser, 2021, 83.
6. "The bombardments smashed all but one of the windows, furniture was stolen or used as firewood, and several modifications were undertaken – inner walls were inserted, the chimney increased height, the boiler was broken, the half cylinder from Macassar ebony went missing." In Ana Tostões, Ivo Hammer, and Zara Ferreira, *op. cit.*, 46.
7. More precisely as a Cultural Monument of Southern Moravia (No. 0098).
8. Ana Tostões, Ivo Hammer, and Zara Ferreira, *op. cit.*, 47–48; Ivo Hammer, "Surface is Interface. History of the Tugendhat House 1938–1997. Criteria for the preservation," in Daniela Hammer-Tugendhat, Ivo Hammer, and Wolf Tegethoff, *op. cit.*, 149.
9. Ivo Hammer, "Materiality. History of the Tugendhat House 1997–2012. Conservation-Science Study and Restoration," in Daniela Hammer-Tugendhat, Ivo Hammer, and Wolf Tegethoff, *op. cit.*, 164.

2010–2012
ASSOCIATION FOR VILLA TUGENDHAT

1929–1930
LUDWIG MIES VAN DER ROHE AND LILLI REICH

BRNO, CZECH REPUBLIC

1. Late evening view from south of the garden facade, after restoration.

of the international style in the Modern Movement of architecture as it developed in Europe in the 1920s,"[10] under the condition of restoration and reconstruction of missing original parts. Therefore, a careful conservation-science research study, coordinated by Ivo Hammer, was undertaken between 2003 and 2010. In parallel the Association for Villa Tugendhat, combining the firms OMNIA Projekt, ARCHTEAM, ARCHATT, and Atelier RAW, was formed, who carried out the rehabilitation project with the guidance of the International Expert Advisory Commission (THICOM).

Then, between 2010 and 2012, based on the conviction that "heritage conservation as a societal practice only makes sense (...) if the material authenticity is preserved,"[11] the Villa Tugendhat underwent restoration work during which both the structure and the adjoining gardens were brought back to their original appearance. The interiors were fitted out with exact replicas of the original furnishings, and the technical equipment in the basement was restored. The wooden furniture was restored preserving original elements and replacing all the missing pieces with exact replicas, recreated through research on surviving original pieces and archive photographs.[12]

The restoration had three goals: the physical preservation of the monument; the presentation of Mies' design in its original form; and the use of the villa as a museum. The first goal involved the reinforcement of the structure, the repair of technical equipment, and the replacement of the insulation systems of both the roof and terraces. The second goal comprised the removal of inappropriate modifications of later periods.[13] All the plasters were preserved after removal of secondary coatings from the surfaces; the pavement of the floor and stairs were replaced with the original material; as before, oil-based paint was applied to all metal coatings. Worth mentioning is the semi-circular Macassar wall as this unique element had been destroyed in the 1940s. It had been impossible to properly restore the wall until several of the original Macassar panels were found in the former headquarters of the Gestapo at the University of Law in Brno in 2011.[14] Finally, the adaptation of the villa for use as a museum comprised public access management and a walking route through the house for groups of visitors. An exhibition on the architect, the owners, and family life in the villa up to 1938, as well as a small bookshop also had to be accommodated. These structures were designed to be legible, but always removable.

10. http://whc.unesco.org/en/list/1052

11. Ivo Hammer, *op. cit.*, 165.

12. *Idem.*, 216.

13. As stated in Daniela Hammer-Tugendhat, Ivo Hammer, and Wolf Tegethoff, *op. cit.*, 12. "The analysis of materials, their surfaces, and the changes they have undergone is a precondition for both the critical assessment of the sources concerning their interpretation with regard to the history of art, as well as for the conservation and restoration of surviving original building fabric and furniture." Whenever additions had to be kept, they were subordinated to the original substance of the building, resorting to reconstructions and replicas where the original design was known. By adhering to this concept, nothing valuable was lost, as the protection of the original was given priority. Thus, the resulting state is extremely authentic.

14. Ana Tostões, Ivo Hammer and Zara Ferreira, *op. cit.*, 51; Ivo Hammer, *op. cit.*, 216.

2. Main living room, suites in front of the onyx marble wall and Macassar wall of the dining area, after restoration.

3. Dining area with the restored curved Macassar ebony wall, view toward south, after restoration.

4. Semi-circular staircase with the reconstructed semi-translucent curved glass wall and the original metal framing painted with cream-white oil paint, after restoration.

5

6

7

8

9

5. Garden staircase, before restoration. Stability problems are evident, as well as facade areas still with the original plaster and others with later coatings; the garden walls were reconstructed in 1970 using carved stones. 6. Exterior view from the north showing the cracking of the basement wall, before restoration. 7. Restoration of the main living room. 8. Reconstruction of the steel-framed window wall with milk glass at the street entrance level corresponding to the stairs volume. 9. Main living room, before restoration. Visible are the PVC-flooring, the distemper paint on the ceiling, the plastic curtains, and commercial copies of the furniture. The Macassar semi-circular wall had been replicated not matching the original.

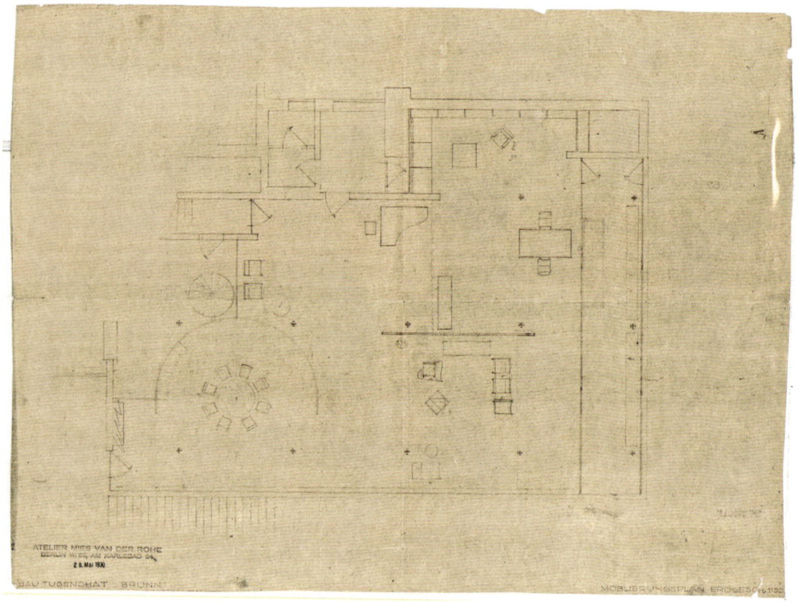

10

11

12

13

15

14

10. Partial floor plan: main living area. 11. Garden facade, view from south-west, 1931. 12. View toward the main living area from the garden terrace. 13. Main living room, view to the library, the onyx marble wall, and the suite, 1931. 14. Living room, semi-circular wall consisting of Macassar ebony veneer of the dining area, 1931. 15. Grete Tugendhat's bedroom, 1931.

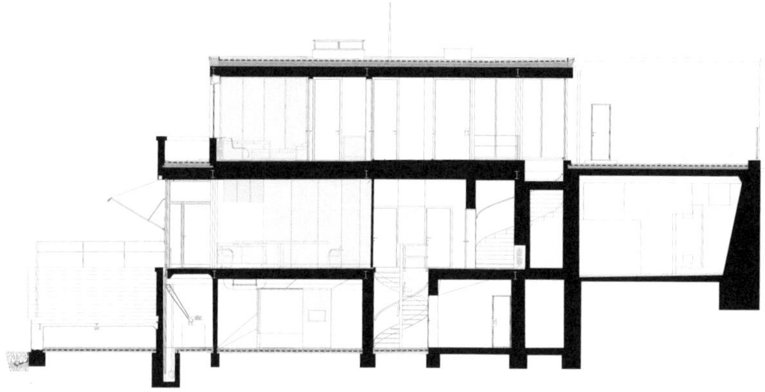

16

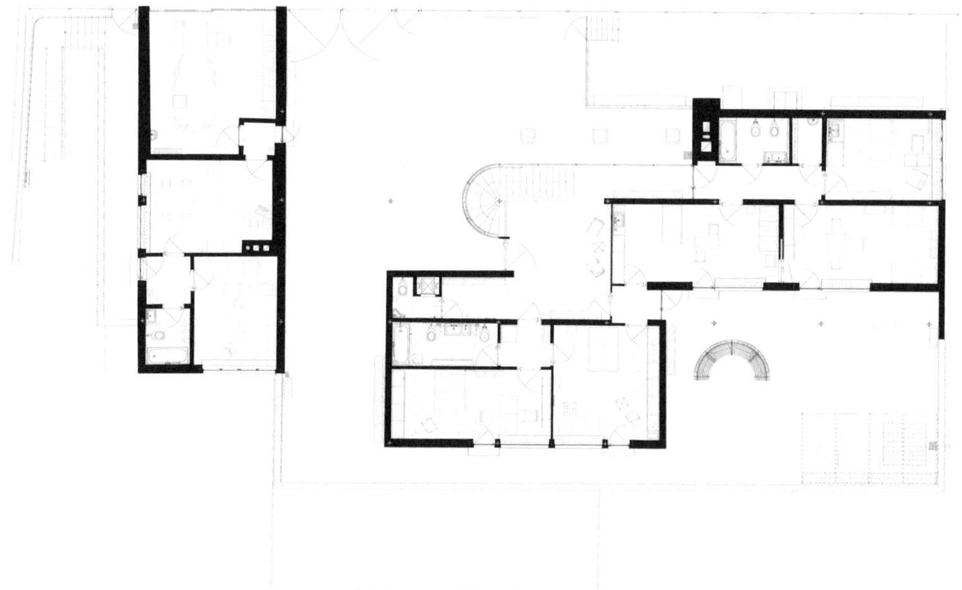

17

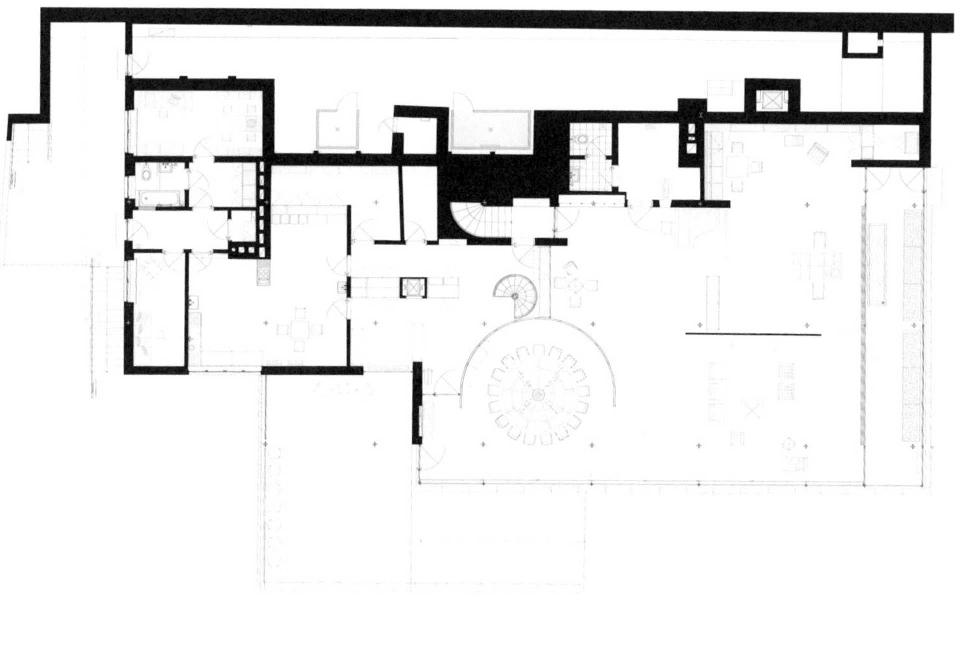

18

Restoration project: 16. Cross section. 17. Second floor plan. 18. First floor plan.

EXEMPLARY LIFETIME ACHIEVEMENT ON THE PROMOTION OF THE MODERN MOVEMENT'S LEGACY.

WINFRIED BRENNE

The achievements of Winfried Brenne, founder of the office Brenne Architekten, over his career, perfectly synthesize, in a single personality, the preservation of the values of Modernity in architecture. Throughout his career, he has worked laudably and continuously, and did not limit himself to on-site intervention. In a rare, all-encompassing attitude, Winfried Brenne, from the outset, combined the pleasure of practice, research and even defense of 20th century architecture, and a commitment to transmit this to future generations. Addressing a large and wide-ranging series of building typologies, his many projects extend from interventions in world renowned icons – such as the Bauhaus Dessau – to more modest housing estates – like the Waldsiedlung Zehlendorf, and even the preparation of conservation and management plans. He had a fundamental role in the listing process of several Berlin *Siedlungen* as part of UNESCO's World Heritage List. In all of his work there is a clear and refined attention to detail and materiality, which manages to perfectly balance the challenging relationship between the needs for technical refurbishment and the safeguarding of original identities.

LIFETIME ACHIEVEMENT

WALDSIEDLUNG ZEHLENDORF

LIFETIME ACHIEVEMENT

On a spacious area on the outskirts of Berlin the Modernist housing estate Waldsiedlung Zehlendorf, also called Onkel-Toms-Hütte, was built between 1926 and 1932 in seven construction phases according to plans by architects Bruno Taut, Hugo Häring (1882–1958), and Otto Rudolf Salvisberg (1888–1940). The client was the social housing association GEHAG. By using the most elementary architectural design, a total of 1915 residential units were built in multi-family or single-family row houses accommodating 15,000 residents – therefore one of the biggest housing estates of the *Weimarer Republik;* because of the relatively high rents, demand came chiefly from middle-class families.[1] The planning of the estate was divided between the architects, Taut being responsible for the planning of the northern section, Salvisberg for the south-western part, and Häring for the south-east. Bruno Taut was inspired by the topography of the site with its pine trees and the sloping Fischtal valley, thus, in his urban planning concept, outside space and architecture were closely linked: singular outdoor spaces, interesting perspectives, staggered housing units, square-like spaces, and the manipulation of the different facade elements created lively streetscapes. Similar to the Hufeisensiedlung, that Bruno Taut and Martin Wagner (1885–1957) had planned a year earlier, serial construction, standardized floor plans, and a limited palette of building materials made the estate economically feasible. Taut used color as the "cheapest means of design,"[2] which resulted in contemporary nicknames such as "parrot estate" or "paint pot." The estate with its Modernist flat roofs also played a role in the so-called "Zehlendorf war of roofs" since it was adjacent to Heinrich Tessenow's (1876–1950) experimental estate "Am Fischtal" (1929) with its more traditional gabled roofs.

House at Riemeisterstraße, before restoration.

By the mid-1970s, the housing estate had lost its original quality: the smooth render had been replaced by rough render, the wooden windows by plastic windows without glazing bars, and the complex color schemes were barely recognizable. To conserve the estate in accordance with listed building standards, it was necessary to examine the existing building fabric and to investigate the historical building techniques used, of which no records existed. After drawing up a building inventory and in-depth material and color surveys, a concept for the conservation measures was developed by Architekturwerkstatt Pitz-Brenne.[3] The importance of the restoration was further enhanced by the listing of the estate as a protected site in 1982.

Beginning in 1977, the restoration of the original form and color of the houses took place step by step, applying a holistic architectural concept.[4] The integration of modern building services and the energetic modernization were required. The original appearance of a large part of the multi-family housing was restored, while the privately owned single-family houses were selectively renovated in accordance with listed buildings standards. Since then, the office has been working closely with the Waldsiedlung Zehlendorf estate administration envisaging the development of heritage protection regulation.[5] This laid the foundations for the monument preservation work by Brenne Architekten for the six Berlin World Heritage housing estates of the 1920s. The nomination of the Waldsiedlung Zehlendorf for the UNESCO World Heritage List is currently being prepared, so it hopefully will be added to the list of the six Berlin *Siedlungen* that became UNESCO World Heritage in 2008.

1. Berlin Bauhaus-Archiv (ed.), *Vier Berliner Siedlungen der Weimarer Republik*, Berlin, 1987.

2. Winfried Brenne, *Bruno Taut – Meister des farbigen Bauens in Berlin*, Berlin, Verlagshaus Braun, 2005.
3. Helge Pitz and Winfried Brenne, *Siedlung Onkel Tom Zehlendorf – Einfamilienreihenhäuser 1929*, Berlin, 1980; Architekturwerkstatt Pitz-Brenne, *Gutachten Waldsiedlung Zehlendorf (Onkel-Toms-Hütte) – Dokumentation und Rekonstruktion des Originalzustandes*, Berlin 1985–1991.
4. Wolfgang Schäche (ed.), *75 Jahre GEHAG. 1924–1999*, Berlin, Gebrüder Mann Verlag, 1999, 60.
5. Winfried Brenne Architekten, *Waldsiedlung Zehlendorf Onkel-Toms-Hütte*, Berlin, Bezirksamt Steglitz-Zehlendorf von Berlin, Untere Denkmalschutzbehörde, 2006.

SINCE 1977
ARCHITEKTURWERKSTATT PITZ-BRENNE (1977–1990) AND BRENNE ARCHITEKTEN (SINCE 1990)

1926–1932
BRUNO TAUT
HUGO HÄRING AND
OTTO RUDOLF SALVISBERG

BERLIN, GERMANY

House at Riemeisterstraße, after restoration.

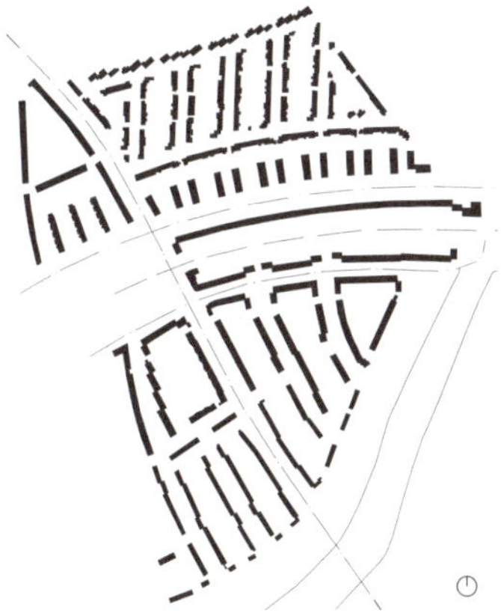

Site plan.

GARTENSTADT FALKENBERG

From 1913 to 1916 Bruno Taut designed the Gartenstadt Falkenberg estate, which was intended to create affordable living space in Berlin-Köpenick. He had been commissioned by the Berliner Bau- und Wohnungsgenossenschaft von 1892 eG, and the cooperative housing project with 1500 housing units, mostly two-storied, for around 7500 residents, was supposed to offer the urban population a more decent life than the city's gray tenement blocks. Together with the landscape architect Ludwig Lesser (1869–1957), Taut designed a garden city based on the English garden city model combining urban and rural life. By 1916, due to World War I, it had only been possible to complete two smaller phases of Taut's visionary plan – Akazienhof and Gartenstadtweg – and merely 127 housing units were built. The house types were lined up in rows or as double houses. Spaces for socializing were created outside and each unit had a garden of up to 600 square meters behind the house, for partial self-sufficiency of the inhabitants.[1] The simple architectural forms with their finely tuned proportions heralded the principles of the new housing development. The coloring was intended not only to express the social ideals of the cooperative, but at the same time, to give the houses individuality. Taut dispensed with traditional decorative shapes and instead opted for intensive coloring of the facades, red roofs, lattice windows, and wooden components that emphasized the rural character of the garden city. In fact, color is such an important part of the design concept that the estate is considered the most colorful among Europe's garden cities, being therefore also called "Tuschkastensiedlung" (paintbox estate), Taut used full, bright colors "in combinations which no one had dared using them to that date for painting the outside of residential buildings."[2]

House at Gartenstadtweg 33, before restoration.

In 1963, the settlement was granted protected status. In 1991, the cooperative commissioned Brenne Architekten to undertake the gradual conservation of the houses according to listed buildings standards.[3] In addition to the repair or replication of windows, roofs, dormers, shutters, doors, chimney heads, trellises, pergolas, house gazebos, and garden fences, special attention was paid to the restoration of the original paintwork.[4] With the insulation of the roofs and the installation of gas heating, the houses were adapted to today's energy standards.

Thus, the Gartenstadt Falkenberg has been preserved as an important testimony to reformed housing estates. Following the world heritage application prepared by the architects, six Berlin housing estates, including the Gartenstadt Falkenberg, were added to the UNESCO World Heritage List in 2008,[5] considering that these "are examples of the paradigm shift in European housing construction, since they are an expression of a broad housing reform movement and, as such, made a decisive contribution to improving housing and living conditions in Berlin." Justifying the selection of the Gartenstadt Falkenberg, the application further stated that it was "developed by a building cooperative as a model for reforming housing estates and living, which emerged as the result of criticism of big city life and the Berlin tenement house system."[6]

1. "According to Taut's understanding the inhabitants of the area should be offered common areas – he called them 'Außenwohnräume' (outdoor living spaces) which would invite them to come outside to enjoy sunlight and fresh air. With these spaces he wanted to enhance the use value of the flats." In: *Housing Estates in the Berlin Modern Style. Nomination for inscription on the UNESCO World Heritage List*, Berlin, 2006, 33–36, 74–76.

2. *Idem.*, 74. See also: Bruno Taut, "Architektonisches zum Siedlungswerk," *Der Siedler*, Vol. 1, 1918, 255.

3. Winfried Brenne, "Zum baulichen Umgang mit dem Erbe von Bruno Taut," in *Genossenschaftliche Wohnanlagen von Messel und Taut. Zur Wiederentdeckung baulicher und kultureller Höhepunkte*, Berlin, Berliner Bau- und Wohnungsgenossenschaft von 1892 eG, 2004, 36–41.

1992–2003
BRENNE ARCHITEKTEN

1913–1916
BRUNO TAUT

BERLIN, GERMANY

House at Gartenstadtweg 33, after restoration.

4. Winfried Brenne, "Wohnbauten von Bruno Taut. Erhaltung und Wiederherstellung farbiger Architektur," in Winfried Nerdinger, Kristiana Hartmann, Matthias Schirren, and Manferd Speidel (eds.), *Bruno Taut 1880–1938. Architekt zwischen Moderne und Avantgarde*, Stuttgart/Munchen, Deutsche Verlags Anstalt, 2001, 275–298.

5. https://whc.unesco.org/en/list/1239/

6. *Housing Estates in the Berlin Modern Style. Nomination for inscription on the UNESCO World Heritage List, op. cit.*, 70, 73.

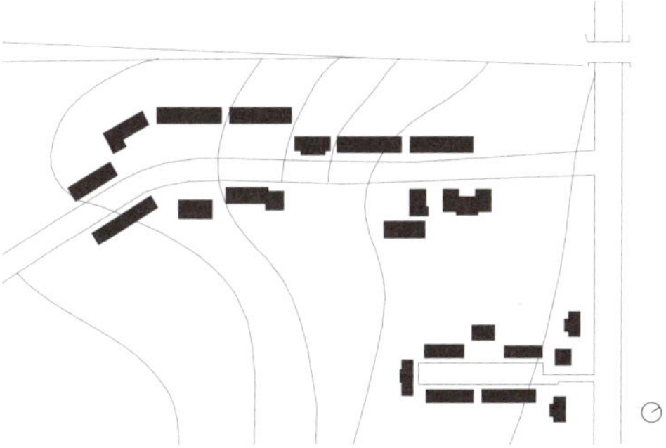

Site plan.

MEISTERHAUS MUCHE-SCHLEMMER

The Meisterhaus Muche-Schlemmer was built in 1925–1926 for the Bauhaus masters Georg Muche (1895–1987) and Oskar Schlemmer (1888–1943), according to plans by Walter Gropius, as one of three semi-detached houses located near the Bauhaus in Dessau (see pp. 246–247). Each Meisterhaus accommodated two senior Bauhaus masters with their families and a single house was intended for the director, in which Gropius moved into. The other two double houses were built for László Moholy-Nagy (1895–1946) and Lyonel Feininger (1871–1956) – destroyed in 1945 – and for Wassily Kandinsky (1866–1944) and Paul Klee (1879–1940). The asymmetrical composition of the volumes results from mirroring and a 90-degree-rotation of the plan of one half of the house. Balconies and roof slabs, as well as the upper story, are cantilevered, thus making the first floor larger than the ground floor. Both on the outside and the inside, the primary colors red, yellow, and blue were used.[1] Thus, the cubic houses with flat roofs, corner balconies, and large studio windows are today regarded as classics of modern architecture.

In 1932, after the Bauhaus was closed, the buildings were changed due to their "alien design" and, among other elements, the studio windows and stairwell glazing were bricked up. During the GDR era, false (suspended) ceilings were introduced, external chimneys were installed, and the facade was covered with sprayed render.

From 1998 to 2001, the Meisterhaus Muche-Schlemmer, which was classified, along with the Bauhaus sites of Dessau and Weimar, as a UNESCO World Heritage Site in 1996,[2] underwent a deep renovation by Brenne Architekten under the auspices of the *Wüstenrot Foundation*. The Foundation recommended reconstructing the condition of the building during the Third Reich to show the "desecration of the Bauhaus" under the Nazi regime, in contrast to the original condition of the preserved neighboring houses, but the city of Dessau wanted to restore the house to its original condition. Finally, a non-reconstructive conservation approach was worked out that made it possible to expose all the layers of time in the Meisterhaus. Thus, around 75 percent of the original exterior render, and the radiators from GDR times are still present after the refurbishment. Traces of alterations have been left on the linoleum floor, dating from the original construction. It was possible to refurbish and preserve the original windowsills and built-in cupboards. The extensive glazing of the staircase and studio windows, removed in 1939, were restored according to historical models. In addition, the electrical and building services were modernized. Thanks to a building inventory and scientific research, it has been possible to verify and reconstruct the color scheme from the original construction in almost half of the rooms. All other rooms were given a neutral color.[3]

North facade before restoration.

The restoration of the Meisterhaus Muche-Schlemmer has enabled a testimony to the modern age to be preserved without concealing the signs of its history of use. The Meisterhaus Muche-Schlemmer has been used by the Bauhaus Dessau Foundation for exhibitions and events since 2002. More recently, between 2017 and 2019, the Meisterhaus Kandinsky-Klee was also refurbished by the office.

1. Carsten Krohn, *Walter Gropius. Buildings and Projects*, Basel, Birkhäuser, 2019, 78–83.

2. https://whc.unesco.org/en/list/729/

1998–2001
BRENNE ARCHITEKTEN

1925–1926
WALTER GROPIUS

DESSAU, GERMANY

North facade, after restoration.

3. Winfried Brenne, "Vom Wohnhaus zum öffentlichen Veranstaltungsort – Die Meisterhäuser Muche/Schlemmer als Teil der Weltkulturerbestätten des Bauhauses," *Das öffentliche Denkmal – Denkmalpflege zwischen Fachdisziplin und gesellschaftlichen Erwartungen,"* Dresden, Arbeitskreis Theorie und Lehre der Denkmalpflege, Vol. 15, 2004, 86–88; Winfried Brenne, "Materialien an Bauten der Moderne," in Stiftung Bauhaus Dessau (ed.), *Umgang mit Bauten der klassischen Moderne – Kolloquium am Bauhaus Dessau, Teil 2 Sanierung von Oberflächen*, Dessau, Stiftung Bauhaus Dessau, 2001, No. 334, 15–23.

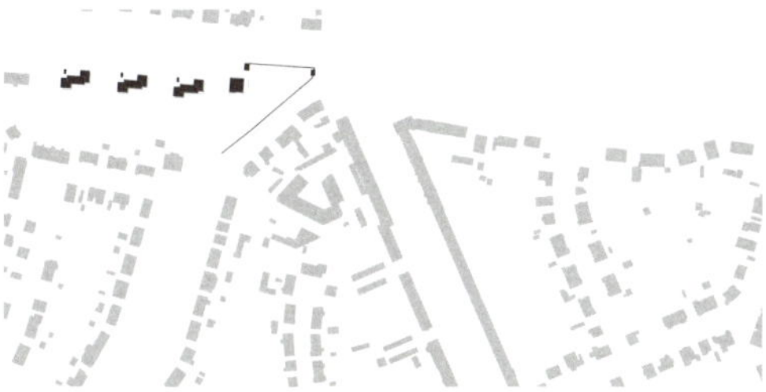

Site plan.

The Bauhaus building in Dessau was built between 1925 and 1926 according to plans by Bauhaus director Walter Gropius, after the forced move of the Bauhaus school from Weimar there. The building complex consists of five parts: the workshop wing, the vocational school wing, the studio building, bridge, and "in-between" building. Despite their height differences, the three main parts – the three-story workshop wing, the three-story vocational school wing, and the five-story studio building –, arranged like a pinwheel, form a coherent whole. The almost completely glazed workshop wing with the main entrance is connected

Site plan.

with the studio building by a one-story volume (the "in-between" building) accommodating the so-called festive area comprising auditorium, stage, and canteen; and with the vocational school wing to the north by a two-story bridge, where the administrative spaces were located. The studio building had 28 studio flats as accommodations for students and junior masters and a roof terrace. It is characterized by clear, modern structures, transparency, and many construction details previously employed in Gropius' industrial buildings, namely in the Fagus Factory.[1] There is no visual amplification of the corners of the building, thus supporting the impression of transparency. Particularly noteworthy is the workshop wing with its filigree curtain wall which provides a clear view of the constructive element. Gropius designed the parts of the complex differently, separating them consistently according to functions, and he positioned the wings asymmetrically, such that there is no central view of the complex. The seven masters' houses near the school (see pp. 244–245) were built by Gropius as well. Closed by the Nazi regime in 1932, the Bauhaus in Dessau was used as a school by the NSDAP, and after the war it served as a vocational school.

1. Carsten Krohn, *Walter Gropius. Buildings and Projects*, Basel, Birkhäuser, 2019, 66–77.

Windows of the workshop wing, before restoration.

Severely damaged during World War II, the Bauhaus building was rebuilt as far as possible at the time, however without taking into account the appearance of the building as it was originally: for example, the damaged facade of the workshop wing was removed and restored with a perforated facade. The architectural value of the building was only recognized in the 1970s, and in 1974 it was listed as a national monument. In 1976, as part of a general renovation, an attempt was made to restore the building to its historical state. The curtain wall, for example, was reconstructed on the basis of a preserved section, however the other windows of the buildings were recreated using reinforced aluminum profiles, rather than steel (the material used in the original profiles).[2]

The Bauhaus sites of Dessau, including the seven masters' houses, and Weimar have been on the UNESCO World Heritage List since 1996, considering that "these buildings stand for an architectural quality that derives from the scientifically-based design methodology and the functional-economic design with social objectives. The Bauhaus itself and the other buildings designed by the masters of the Bauhaus are fundamental representatives of Classical Modernism and as such are essential components, which represent the 20th century. (...) For this reason, they are important monuments not only for art and culture, but also for the historic ideas of the 20th century." [3]

2. Wolfgang Paul, "Renovation 1976," in Bauhaus Dessau Foundation, and Margret Kentgens-Craig (eds.), *The Dessau Bauhaus Building 1926–1999*, Basel, Birkhäuser, 1998, 160–173.
3. Originally comprising only the buildings in Weimar and Dessau, the Bauhaus sites were extended in 2017 including now as well the houses with balcony access in Dessau and the ADGB School in Bernau. https://whc.unesco.org/en/list/729/

2010–2016
BRENNE ARCHITEKTEN

1925–1926
WALTER GROPIUS

DESSAU, GERMANY

Windows of the workshop wing, after restoration.

In 2010, Brenne Architekten were commissioned to undertake an energy and technical renovation and adapt the building to current user requirements. Thermal separation of the window profiles was made possible using the latest technology, which led to a considerable reduction in energy consumption. At the same time, the dimensions of the steel profiles used could be adapted to the profiles from the original construction period.[4] Today, regulating the indoor environment, namely the room humidity, is helped by awareness-raising measures, such as a decentralized heating control system that reminds employees to ventilate spaces regularly. In addition, the winter temperature in the workshop wing – no longer used permanently for workplaces, but only for public events –, which is enclosed by large curtain walls on three sides, was set at 16°C what helped to reduce energy consumption in that wing significantly.[5] A photovoltaic system on the roof of the northern school wing generates a large part of the energy used on site.[6] In order to adapt the Bauhaus building to the needs of an increasing number of visitors, new visitor toilets were installed in the basement of the workshop wing without affecting the fabric of the building. This complex conservation process enabled the overall energy consumption of the Bauhaus building to be reduced by a third, while through a holistic, integral planning, and the incorporation of high-tech and low-tech solutions, it was possible to preserve the authenticity of the building.[7]

4. Winfried Brenne, Ulrich Nickmann, Mark Mathijssen, Bernhard Weller, and Stefan Reich, “Innovative Stahlfensterkonstruktion für das Weltkulturerbe Bauhaus Dessau,” in Silke Tasche and Bernhard Weller (eds.), *Glasbau 2012*, Berlin, Ernst & Sohn, 2012, 348–363.

5. Angel Ayón, Uta Pottgiesser, and Nathaniel Richards, *Reglazing Modernism.* Intervention Strategies *for 20th-Century Icons*, Basel, Birkhäuser, 2019, 199.

6. Winfried Brenne, “Bauhaus energetisch. Klimaschutz im Weltkulturerbe,” in Dietmar Danner (ed.), *xia intelligente architektur*, Leinfelden-Echterdingen, Verlagsanstalt Alexander Koch, 2012, No. 79, 19.

7. Bauhaus Dessau Foundation (ed.), *Archaeology of Modernism. Conservation of the Bauhaus Dessau*, Berlin, Jovis Verlag, 2021.

The School of the *Allgemeiner Deutscher Gewerkschaftsbund* (General German Union Federation, ADGB) in Bernau near Berlin was built between 1928 and 1930 by the second Bauhaus director Hannes Meyer (1889–1954) and his long-time office partner Hans Wittwer (1894–1952) with the participation of the students at the Bauhaus. The school in Bernau was the first of the schools planned by the ADGB to give basic and further training to its members in various regions of Germany. Much of the interior and the furniture was created in the workshops at the Dessau Bauhaus (see pp. 246–247), and modern amenities, such as oil-fired heating and washbasins in the rooms, were included. Designed in harmony with the surrounding landscape, the buildings of the school are organized on the slope site in a rational sequence,

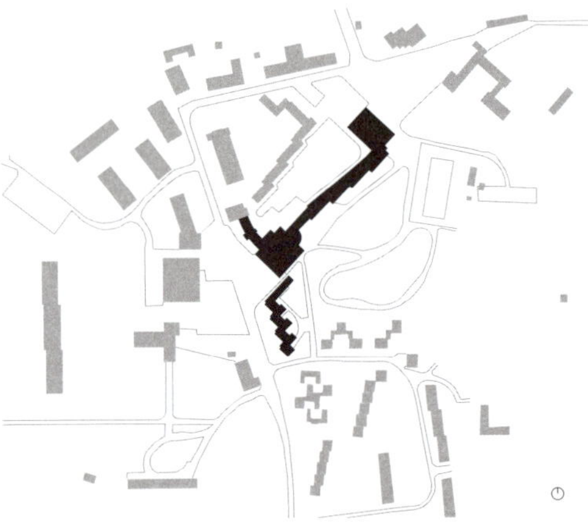

Site plan.

based on usage, thus representing an example of Functionalist architecture. Built in reinforced concrete, with load-bearing masonry block walls, the facades are of yellow exposed brick without plaster along glass and steel.[1] The large windows in the double rooms were unusual and offered views of nature. All living spaces with their large windows are oriented to the surrounding landscape and, in fact, nature is the most important reference for the building and the physical and visual presence of the outside constantly asserts itself.[2] The auditorium and the dining hall, with its glass veranda and unobstructed views of the landscape, are accommodated in the two-story main building. From there, five three-story residential wings descend the hillside to a building with the library, gymnasium, and classrooms. All the individual buildings of the Z-shaped layout are linked by a long glass and red-painted steel corridor. Next to the school building four offset teacher residences were built in a row as well as two semi-detached houses. Since its completion in 1930 until the banning of these unions in 1933, some 4000 trade unionists attended the courses offered at the school.

1. Monika Markgraf (ed.), *Bauhaus World Heritage Site*, Leipzig, Spector Books, 2017.

2. Andreas Vass, "Pädagogik in der Architektur Hannes Meyers," in Philipp Oswalt (ed.), *Hannes Meyers neue Bauhauslehre. Von Dessau bis Mexiko*, Basel, Birkhäuser, 2019, 52.

Dining room, before restoration.

Having been used as a training facility by the NSDAP until the end of World War II, the school buildings were used as a temporary hospital in the post-war period. Then, during the GDR era, after a long period of repair works, the school was used by the *Freier Deutscher Gewerkschaftsbund* (FDGB). During this time, the complex was extended by a second large building on the site.[3] In 1990 it had to be closed with the dissolution of the FDGB.

Since 1977 the school, including its supplementary buildings from the 1950s, has been listed as a monument. In 2017 it was added to the UNESCO World Heritage List as part of the Bauhaus sites, along with the *Laubenganghäuser* (houses with balcony access) in Dessau "as important contributions to the Bauhaus ideas of austere design, Functionalism and social reform,"[4] following the World Heritage application prepared by Brenne Architekten.

Since 1990 the preservation and use of the listed buildings were uncertain for a long period of time. When the Berlin *Handwerkskammer* took over the school as a location for an education center in 2001, this ensured that the monument was largely preserved. At the same time, the building had to be modernized for the new school and boarding school.

3. www.bauhaus-denkmal-bernau.de
4. https://whc.unesco.org/en/list/729

2002–2007
BRENNE ARCHITEKTEN

1928–1930
HANNES MEYER AND HANS WITTWER

BERNAU, GERMANY

Dining room, after restoration.

The school and the adjoining teachers' houses were restored and modernized in two construction phases by Brenne Architekten between 2002 and 2007. The focus was on restoring the appearance of 1930. While conservation measures were sufficient with the original substance in good condition, altered components of the school building, the dining room, and the teachers' houses were stripped and restored. Components that no longer existed, such as the glazed winter garden at the cafeteria and the glass blocks for the wall and ceiling surfaces, were reconstructed based on the originals, and largely adapted to today's technical requirements. In some cases, elements were removed to reinstate historical spatial sequences. Another central component of the overall concept was to retain traces dating from the different phases of usage, so that the breaks in the history of the monument become clearly legible.[5]

With the restoration of the ADGB Bundesschule, Hannes Meyer's visionary conception of the school as "built pedagogy" is visible again. At the same time, the monument presents itself as a modern and functional educational center.[6] The restoration was awarded, among others, with the World Monuments Fund/Knoll Modernism Prize in 2008.

5. Winfried Brenne and Franz Jaschke, "Von der Bundesschule des ADGB zum 'Meyer-Wittwer-Bau' – Denkmalgerechte Sanierung und Modernisierung des Bauhaus-Denkmals in Bernau," *Bewahren – Sanieren – Nutzen. 25 Jahre Engagement für das Bauhaus Denkmal Bundesschule Bernau*, No. 8 – "Beiträge zur Bau- und Nutzungsgeschichte," Bernau, Verein Baudenkmal Bundesschule Bernau, 2015, 72–84; Winfried Brenne, "Die ADGB-Bundesschule in Bernau bei Berlin – eine Erweiterung der Bauhauswelterbestätten in Weimar und Dessau?," *Kunsttexte*, No. 1, 2010; "Denkmalpflegerischer Rahmenplan ADGB Schule in Bernau," in Stiftung Bauhaus Dessau (ed.), *Umgang mit Bauten der klassischen Moderne – Kolloquium am Bauhaus Dessau*, Dessau, Stiftung Bauhaus Dessau, 1999, 20–25.

6. David Sokol, "An Architectural Gem in Germany is Reborn," *Architectural Record*, August 2008.

MAX LIEBLING HOUSE

The Max Liebling House for Tony and Max Liebling was built in 1936, according to plans by the architect Dov Karmi (1905–1962), in the White City of Tel Aviv. The White City, which became a world heritage site in 2004, comprises some 4000 buildings in the heart of the city. They were mostly built between the beginning of the 1930s and the end of the 1940s. And many of the architects that designed them came from Europe.[1] Born in Odessa, Karmi has been described as one of Israel's pioneering Modernists[2] and the Max Liebling House is typical of modern buildings in Tel Aviv: for natural air conditioning, the detached house is aligned with the prevailing wind direction. The balconies function as shading elements in front of the facade, and at the same time they are the intersection between private and public space. The functional structure of its simple white rendered facade shows the modern attitude of the designers. The simple furnishings of the kitchen, bathrooms, and balconies, and the contemporary technical equipment also demonstrate their commitment to modern construction.

In 2015, Brenne Architekten were commissioned to draw up a conservation management plan as part of the Getty Foundation's "Keeping it Modern" program.[3] They also acted as consultants for the subsequent restoration. The conservation management plan served as the basis for the conversion of the residential building into a center of excellence for architecture and monument preservation as well as an event location for cultural and social activities.

The conservation management plan, drawn up by an interdisciplinary Israeli-German team, provided a conservation analysis and assessment, as well as guidelines for the preservation of the building. The focus of the ensuing restoration was preserving the authenticity of the building substance, while adapting the building to its new use. For example, the goal was to carefully repair the facades and their rendered surfaces rather than completely renewing them. The work was carried out with continuous investigation, evaluation, and documentation, so that, not only was the authentic language of this one building regained, but a prime example for the restoration of other buildings in the White City was produced. It is therefore considered as a model for dealing with modern architecture in the UNESCO World Heritage Site "The White City of Tel Aviv."[4]

1. Carsten Hueck, *Tel Aviv. The White City*, Berlin, Jovis, 2019, 6.
2. Muriel Emanuel (ed.), *Contemporary Architects. Third edition*, Detroit, St. James Press, 1994, 503.
3. Brenne Architekten, *Max Liebling House: Conservation Survey*, Tel Aviv/Berlin, 2017.
4. https://whc.unesco.org/en/list/1096/

Exterior view, before restoration.

2015–2019
BRENNE ARCHITEKTEN

1936
DOV KARMI

TEL AVIV, ISRAEL

Exterior view, after restoration.

PROJECT DATA

NEUE NATIONALGALERIE

ORIGINAL BUILDING

Use: Museum

Date: 1965–1968

Architect: Ludwig Mies van der Rohe

Location: Berlin, Germany

INTERVENTION

Use: Museum

Date: 2012–2021

Client: Stiftung Preußischer Kulturbesitz (SPK) represented by the Bundesamt für Bauwesen und Raumordnung (BBR)

Architect: David Chipperfield Architects Berlin

Design team: David Chipperfield, Martin Reichert, and Alexander Schwarz (partners); Daniel Wendler and Michael Freytag (project architects); Marianne Akay, Thomas Benk, Matthias Fiegl, Anke Fritzsch, Dirk Gschwind, Anne Hengst, Franziska Michalsky, and Maxi Reschke (team – concept design to developed design); Sebastian Barrett, Alexander Bellmann, Martina Betzold, Anke Fritzsch, Dirk Gschwind, Lukas Graf, Martijn Jaspers, Christopher Jonas, Franziska Michalsky, Maxi Reschke, Christian Vornholt, and Lukas Wichmann (team – technical design); Dalia Liksaite and Simon Wiesmaier (team – visualisation); Yannic Calvez and Ute Zscharnt (team – fit-out); in collaboration with BAL Bauplanungs- und Steuerungs GmbH (executive architect; Kerstin Rohrbach – project manager)

Consultants: Prof. Dr. Fritz Neumeyer (architectural history and theory); Dirk Lohan (representation of the Mies van der Rohe copyrights); Landesdenkmalrat Berlin and Landesdenkmalamt Berlin (heritage preservation); Pro Denkmal GmbH (restoration consultant); BAL Bauplanungs- und Steuerungs GmbH (executive architect); Müller-BBM GmbH (building physics); Akustik-Ingenieurbüro Moll GmbH (acoustic consultant); HHP West Beratende Ingenieure GmbH (fire consultant); DS-Plan (facade consultant); Arup Deutschland GmbH (lighting consultant)

Landscape architect: TOPOS Stadtplanung Landschaftsplanung Stadtforschung

Structural engineer: GSE Ingenieurgesellschaft mbH Saar, Enseleit und Partner

Services engineer: Ingenieurgesellschaft W33 mbH, with Domann Beratende Ingenieure GmbH

Contractor: Dechant hoch- und ingenieurbau (structural work); FLZ Stahl- und Metallbau Lauterbach (restoration of steel-glass facade); Dornhöfer Stahl- und Metallbau (metalwork); Tischlerei Dirk Meier (restoration of timber doors); ER+TE Stahl- und Metallbau (restoration of metal doors); Gebauer Steinmetzarbeiten (external stonework); F.X. Rauch (internal stonework); RvH Restaurierung von Holzobjekten (joinery)

YOYOGI NATIONAL GYMNASIUM

ORIGINAL BUILDING

Use: Gymnasium

Date: 1963–1964

Architect: Kenzo Tange & URTEC and Tange Laboratory

Location: Tokyo, Japan

INTERVENTION

Use: Performance facility

Date: 2018–2019 (1st Gymnasium), 2018–2020 (2nd Gymnasium)

Client: Japan Sport Council

Architect: Tange Associates and Kume Sekkei Co., Ltd

Contractor: Shimizu Corporation (1st Gymnasium); Obayashi Corporation and Shimizu Corporation (2nd Gymnasium)

SYDNEY OPERA HOUSE

ORIGINAL BUILDING

Use: Performing arts center

Date: 1959–1973

Architect: Jørn Utzon (first phase) and Hall, Todd & Littlemore (second phase)

Location: Sydney, Australia

INTERVENTION

Use: Performing arts center

Date: 2017

Client: Sydney Opera House Trust

Architect: Alan Croker (conservation plan)

Design of document: Design 5 – Architects, Sydney Opera House, and Liversedge Weir

YALE CENTER FOR BRITISH ART

ORIGINAL BUILDING

Use: Museum

Date: 1971–1977

Architect: Louis I. Kahn

Location: New Haven, Connecticut, USA

INTERVENTION

Use: Museum

Date: 2012 (conservation plan); 2008–2016 (conservation project)

Client: Yale University Office of Facilities/ Yale Center for British Art

Architect: Peter Inskip and Stephen Gee (conservation plan); Knight Architecture LLC (conservation project)

Design team: George Knight, Daphne Kalomiris, Niko Tombras, Megan Milawski, Jeffery Pollack, Kyle Dugdale, Dylan Hayn, Thomas Day, Dan Shea, Amrita Raja, and Britton Rogers (conservation project)

Consultants: Knight Architecture LLC; Yale Center for British Art; Yale University Office of Facilities – Department of Planning and Project Management; Turner Construction Company (construction manager); Peter Inskip + Peter Jenkins Architects Limited (conservation architect); Wiss, Janney, Elstner Associates, Inc. (structural engineer and building conservation consultant); BVH Integrated Services (engineer – mechanical, electrical, plumbing, and fire protection); Philip R. Sherman, P.E. (code consultant); Hefferan Partnership Lighting Design (theatrical lighting consultant); Cavanaugh Tocci Associates (acoustics, audiovisual, and theater consultant); Staples & Charles Limited (furnishings, fixtures, and equipment consultant); Metropolitan Museum

of Art (Michael Morris – architectural conservator); Strong Cohen Graphic Designers (graphic design); LMB Facilities Solutions, LLC (logistics consultant); Stephen Saitas Designs (exhibition designer)
Structural engineer: WJE
Services engineer: BVH Integrated Services
Contractor: Turner Construction Company
Other participants: Amy Meyers and Constance Clement (Yale Center for British Art – Owner); Don Iddings, Kristina Chmelar, and Sheri Miller (Yale University Office of Facilities – Owner); Demetrios Petros, Rolff Knobel, Lisa Mendes, Alex Esdiale, and Paul Harding (Turner Construction Company – Builder)

CITÉ DU LIGNON

ORIGINAL BUILDING
Use: Housing estate with community facilities (churches, shopping mall, schools, public center)
Date: 1963–1971
Architect: Addor & Julliard (Georges Addor, Jacques Bolliger, and Dominique Julliard) with Louis Payot
Location: Geneva, Switzerland
INTERVENTION
Use: Housing estate with community facilities (churches, shopping mall, schools, public center)
Date: 2008–2012 (restoration project); in progress (construction project)
Client: Geneva State and Comité Central du Lignon (restoration project); Various owners (construction project)
Architect: Laboratory of Techniques and Preservation of Modern Architecture, École Polytechnique Fédérale de Lausanne, ENAC (restoration project; Franz Graf and Giulia Marino); Jaccaud & Spicher Architectes Associés (JSAA) and other architects (construction project)
Facades engineer: BCS façades SA
Services engineer: Sorane SA and Ecublens, Effin'art SA (thermal analysis)
Contractor: Losinger Marazzi and other contractors (construction project)
Landscape architect: Comité central du Lignon (Paola Alfani)

SERPENTINE HOUSE

ORIGINAL BUILDING
Use: Housing
Date: 1950–1951
Architect: Yrjö Lindegren
Location: Helsinki, Finland
INTERVENTION
Use: Apartment building
Date: 2016–2020
Client: Helsingin kaupungin asunnot Oy
Architect: Kati Salonen & Mona Schalin Architects
Design team: Mona Schalin, Marica Schalin, Sakari Mentu, Kristina Karlsson, Varvara Protassova, and Liisi Wartiainen
Consultants: Helsinki Housing Production
Landscape architect: FCG Suunnittelu ja tekniikka Oy
Structural engineer: SitoWise Oy
Services engineer: Insinööritoimisto Leo Maaskola Oy
Contractor: YIT Rakennus Oy
Architectural paint research and special painting expert: Konservointi T.Sonninen Oy
Historic building survey: Arkkitehtitoimisto Koskinen & Schalin Oy
Landscaping inventory: LOCI maisema-arkkitehdit Oy

MUNICIPAL ORPHANAGE AMSTERDAM

ORIGINAL BUILDING
Use: Orphanage
Date: 1955–1960
Architect: Aldo van Eyck
Location: Amsterdam, The Netherlands
INTERVENTION
Name: Former Orphanage Amsterdam
Use: Office building
Date: 2015–2017
Client: Burgerweeshuis VOF
Architect: WDJArchitecten
Landscape architect: Atelier Quadrat
Contractor: BAM Bouw en Techniek

YAMANASHI PRESS AND BROADCASTING CENTER

ORIGINAL BUILDING
Use: Office building, TV studio, radio studio, and newspaper printing plant
Date: 1964–1966
Architect: Kenzo Tange & URTEC
Location: Kofu City, Japan
INTERVENTION
Use: Office building, TV studio, radio studio, and retail
Date: 2015–2016
Client: Yamanashi Culture Hall
Architect: Tange Associates
Structural engineer: Orimoto Structural Engineers
Contractor: Sumitomo Mitsui Construction Co., Ltd
Facility design: Kenchiku Setsubi Sekkei Kenkyusho

AITON COURT

ORIGINAL BUILDING
Use: Apartment building
Date: 1936–1937
Architect: Bernard Cooke and Angus Stewart
Location: Johannesburg, South Africa
INTERVENTION
Use: Apartment building with mosque
Date: 2012–2014
Client: Trafalgar Property Management
Architect: Mayat Hart Architects
Design team: Yasmin Mayat and Brendan Hart
Contractor: Various small-scale and informal local contractors

CASA ESTUDIO PARA ARTISTAS

ORIGINAL BUILDING

Use: Apartment-studio building for artists with retail

Date: 1938

Architect: Antonio Bonet, Horacio Vera Barros, and Abel López Chas

Location: Buenos Aires, Argentina

INTERVENTION

Use: Apartment-studio building with retail

Date: 2017–2018

Architect: Dirección General de Regeneración Urbana, Ministerio de Ambiente y Espacio Público, Gobierno de la Ciudad Autónoma de Buenos Aires

Design team: Juan Vacas (general director of urban regeneration – Ministry of Environment and Public Space, Bs.As City); Flavia Rinaldi (project manager – architecture and infrastructure); Yamile García Müller and Valeria Muchinsky (design and heritage research); Lucía Maglio (project supervisor); Izaskun Martínez Castillo (research)

Site supervision team: Lucas Molinero (general director of urban regeneration works – Ministry of Environment and Public Space, Bs. As. City); Camila Piris Machado (site vice-manager); Silvia Sánchez (site supervisor)

Consultants: Guillermo García (contractor's consultant on heritage)

Contractor: CAHEM S.A.

Other participants: Horacio Rodríguez Larreta (Chief of Buenos Aires City Government); Eduardo Macchiavelli (Minister of Environment and Public Space, Buenos Aires City Government)

CASA O'GORMAN

ORIGINAL BUILDING

Name: Casa para Cecil O'Gorman

Use: Residence

Date: 1929–1930

Architect: Juan O'Gorman

Location: Mexico City, Mexico

INTERVENTION

Use: Museum

Date: 2012–2013

Client: Museo Casa Estudio Diego Rivera y Frida Kahlo

Architect: Victor Jimenez

Design team: Victor Jimenez and Adolfo Osnaya

Consultants: Instituto Nacional de Bellas Artes

Landscape architect: Victor Jimenez

Structural engineer: Ricardo Camacho

Contractor: Sackbe SA de CV

HIPÓDROMO DE LA ZARZUELA

ORIGINAL BUILDING

Use: Racecourse

Date: 1935–1941

Architect: Carlos Arniches and Martín Domínguez

Structural engineer: Eduardo Torroja

Location: Madrid, Spain

INTERVENTION

Use: Racecourse

Date: 2003 (international competition); 2004–2008 (design); 2008–2015 (construction)

Client: Spanish state (Patrimonio Nacional) and Hipódromo de la Zarzuela S.A.

Architect: Junquera Arquitectos

Design team: Jerónimo Junquera García del Diestro, Clara Eugenia Santana, Elena Pascual, and Miguel Ángel Blanca (architects); Santiago Marín (draughtsman)

Structural engineer: Carlos Fernández Casado S.L. (Leonardo Fernández Troyano)

Services engineer: R. Úrculo Ingenieros Consultores S.A. (Carlos Úrculo)

Quantity surveyor: María Vallier Rodríguez-Acosta

Contractor: Dragados S.A.

GRAND AUDITORIUM OF THE CALOUSTE GULBENKIAN FOUNDATION

ORIGINAL BUILDING

Use: Auditorium

Date: 1959–1969

Architect: Alberto Pessoa, Pedro Cid, and Ruy Jervis d'Athouguia

Landscape architect: Antonio Vianna Barreto and Gonçalo Ribeiro Telles

Location: Lisbon, Portugal

INTERVENTION

Use: Auditorium

Date: 2013–2014

Client: Calouste Gulbenkian Foundation

Architect: Teresa Nunes da Ponte, arquitectura

Design team: Teresa Nunes da Ponte, Sónia Antunes, Pedro Domingos, Bruno Terra da Motta, André Guerreio, Pedro Galvão Lucas, Carolina Sardinha, Karolinne Alves, Hugo Amaro, Luís Rodrigues, Duarte Cardoso Ferreira, and Rita Neves (Teresa Nunes da Ponte, arquitectura); Celso Matias, Osório Tomás, Jorge Lopes, Ana Casal, and Rodrigo Januário (Calouste Gulbenkian Foundation)

Consultants: Ove Arup and Partners (audiovisuals, acoustics, and stage)

Structural engineer: Grese

Services engineer: Acústica e Ambiente (acoustics); Natural Works (HVAC and electricity); Natural Works and OHM-e/ Lightplan (architectural lighting); ETU, Espaço Tempo e Utopia (fire protection); Natural Works and Campo d'Água (plumbing and drainage)

Contractor: HCI Construções (general contractor); Siemens Portugal (subcontractor for electricity and lighting); Cofely (subcontractor for HVAC); SBS Bühnentechnik and Alberto Sá (stage machinery)

Other participants: Monitoring commission from the Calouste Gulbenkian Foundation (Ana Tostões, Emílio Rui Vilar, and Luís Valente de Oliveira) and Program for the Renovation of the Grand Auditorium (PRGA)

CARTIERA BURGO

ORIGINAL BUILDING

Use: Paper mill

Date: 1961–1964

Architect: Pier Luigi Nervi

Structural engineer: Gino Covre

Location: Mantua, Italy

INTERVENTION

Name: PRO-GEST Stabilimento di Mantova

Use: Paper mill

Date: 2015–2020

Client: PRO-GEST

Architect: Massimo Narduzzo and CREA. RE S.r.l.

Design team: Massimo Narduzzo, Giuseppe Ruscica, Federico D'Incà Levis, Roberto Caddeo, and Roberto Grespan

Consultants: EAMBIENTE (Gabriella Chiellino)

Structural engineer: Luigi Zago, Manuel Lazzari, and Dario Francescato

Services engineer: REIA (Giancarlo Picotti) and Stefano Lucchi

Contractor: Buosi Costruzioni; LAMBERTS and COM (u-glass); FIM ENGINEERING (brise-soleils and office facade); SOCOMET (steel structures)

ISOKON AND ISOKON GALLERY

ORIGINAL BUILDING

Name: Lawn Road Flats (renamed The Isokon 1972)

Use: Apartment building

Date: 1933–1934

Client: Jack and Molly Pritchard

Architect: Wells Coates

Location: London, England

INTERVENTION

Use: Apartment building with public gallery

Date: 2003–2004 (main building restoration); 2014 (creation of Isokon Gallery)

Client: Notting Hill Home Ownership

Architect: Avanti Architects

Design team: John Allan, Fiona Lamb, Keyvan Lankarani, and Kelley Christ

Consultants: Stace Cost Consultants

Landscape architect: Heaton Associates

Structural engineer: Alan Conisbee Associates

Services engineer: Max Fordham LLP

Contractor: Makers Ltd

Other participants: London Borough of Camden (building owner prior to acquisition by Notting Hill Home Ownership); The Housing Corporation (funding support for Notting Hill); English Heritage (Government Conservation Agency advising on statutory consents); Nick Goldfinger (specialist joinery restoration); Fisherking 2000 (clerk of works services)

Isokon Gallery team: John Allan, Tom de Gay, Magnus Englund, Sol Kawage, Fiona Lamb, and Gjøril Reinecke

TRENTON BATH HOUSE AND DAY CAMP PAVILIONS

ORIGINAL BUILDING

Name: Trenton Jewish Community Center Bath House and Day Camp Pavilions

Use: Bathhouse and outdoor community space

Date: 1955–1957

Architect: Louis I. Kahn and Anne Tyng

Location: Ewing, New Jersey, USA

INTERVENTION

Use: Senior and community center

Date: 2003 (preservation plan); 2008 (preservation plan update and landscape assessment); 2007–2013 (project work)

Client: Mercer County

Architect: Mills + Schnoering Architects, LLC (formerly Farewell Mills Gatsch Architects, LLC)

Design team: Michael J. Mills (partner in charge); Meredith Arms Bzdak (project manager and principal architectural historian); Anne E. Weber (project manager)

Consultants: Loring Engineers (MEP/FP engineering); The RBA Group (civil engineering); Becker & Frondorf (cost estimating)

Landscape architect: Heritage Landscapes LLC

Structural engineer: Keast & Hood Co.

Contractor: Wu & Associates, Inc.

LE CORBUSIER'S APARTMENT-STUDIO

ORIGINAL BUILDING

Use: Apartment and painting studio

Date: 1931–1934

Architect: Le Corbusier

Location: Paris, France

INTERVENTION

Use: Museum

Date: 2016–2018

Client: Fondation Le Corbusier

Architect: Chatillon Architectes

Design team: François Chatillon, Elise Quantin, Quentin Pigeat, Selma Ben Naji, Alexandre Murienne, Delfim Caseiro, and Lucas Julliard

Landscape architect: Damien Roger

Structural engineer: A-bime (Mathieu Bruez) and Brizot-Masse Ingénierie

Service engineer: CIEL Ingénierie (electricity); Laboratoire de recherches des monuments historiques (LRMH) (glass and concrete); Varlet Ingénierie (plumbling)

Quantity surveyor: Cabinet François

Contractors: Atelier Mazingue (ironwork); Coanus (roof); Novbéton (masonry); Maison Dureau (painting); Ramires et Manufacture Vincent-Petit (glass bricks); Socra (floors, marble, glazed tiles); UTB (plumbing and heating); Altaspace (garden); Nuances minérales (oil painting; Jean-François Dedominici); Marie-Odile Hubert (painting restorer); Julie Schroeter (metal restorer); Carolina Hall (wood restorer); NEMO (lighting); CASSINA (furniture)

VILLA TUGENDHAT

ORIGINAL BUILDING

Use: Residence

Date: 1929–1930

Architect: Ludwig Mies van der Rohe and Lilli Reich
Location: Brno, Czech Republic
INTERVENTION
Use: Museum
Date: 2010–2012
Client: Municipality of Brno
Architect: Association for Villa Tugendhat (consortium of OMNIA projekt, ARCHATT, ARCHTEAM, and Atelier RAW)
Design team: Marek Tichý, Vítek Tichý, Ivan Wahla, Tomáš Rusín, Milan Rak, Petr Řehořka, Alexandr Skalický, and Zdeněk Přibyl
Landscape architect: Přemysl Krejčiřík and Kamila Krejčiříková
Structural engineer: Jiří Starý and Jindřich Černík
Contractor: UNISTAV a.s.
Furniture and woodwork: Vladimír Ambroz and Miroslav Ambroz
Other participants: Tugendhat House International Committee (THICOM) (Ivo Hammer – chairman; Wessel de Jonge – deputy chairman; Daniela Hammer-Tugendhat – honorary chairperson; Iveta Černá – secretary; Petr Dvořák – assistant of chairman; Thomas Danzl, Alex Dill, Petr Kroupa, Karel Ksandr, Helmut Reichwald, Arthur Rüegg, Vladimír Šlapeta, Miloš Solař, Josef Štulc, Ana Tostões, Ruggero Tropeano, and Martin Zedníček)

WALDSIEDLUNG ZEHLENDORF
ORIGINAL BUILDING
Use: Housing estate
Date: 1926–1932
Architect: Bruno Taut, Hugo Häring, and Otto Rudolf Salvisberg
Location: Berlin, Germany
INTERVENTION
Use: Housing estate
Date: since 1977
Client: Deutsche Wohnen (formerly Gemeinnützige Heimstätten-, Spar- und Bau-Aktiengesellschaft – GEHAG)
Architect: Architekturwerkstatt Pitz-Brenne (1977–1990) and Brenne Architekten (since 1990)

GARTENSTADT FALKENBERG
ORIGINAL BUILDING
Use: Housing estate
Date: 1913–1916
Architect: Bruno Taut
Location: Berlin, Germany
INTERVENTION
Use: Housing estate
Date: 1992–2003
Client: Berliner Bau- und Wohnungsgenossenschaft von 1892 eG
Architect: Brenne Architekten

MEISTERHAUS MUCHE-SCHLEMMER
ORIGINAL BUILDING
Use: Residence
Date: 1925–1926
Architect: Walter Gropius
Location: Dessau, Germany
INTERVENTION
Use: Exhibitions and events
Date: 1998–2001
Client: Wüstenrot Stiftung and Stiftung Bauhaus Dessau
Architect: Brenne Architekten

BAUHAUS DESSAU
ORIGINAL BUILDING
Use: Art school
Date: 1925–1926
Architect: Walter Gropius
Location: Dessau, Germany
INTERVENTION
Use: University and museum
Date: 2010–2016
Client: Stiftung Bauhaus Dessau
Architect: Brenne Architekten
Consultant energy technology: Transsolar Energietechnik GmbH

ADGB BUNDESSCHULE
ORIGINAL BUILDING
Use: School
Date: 1928–1930
Architect: Hannes Meyer and Hans Wittwer
Location: Bernau, Germany
INTERVENTION
Use: Educational center
Date: 2002–2007
Client: Handwerkskammer Berlin and Brandenburgischer Landesbetrieb für Liegenschaften und Bauen
Architect: Brenne Architekten

MAX LIEBLING HOUSE
ORIGINAL BUILDING
Use: Apartment building
Date: 1936
Architect: Dov Karmi
Location: Tel Aviv, Israel
INTERVENTION
Name: Liebling Haus – The White City Center
Use: Cultural center
Date: 2015–2019
Client: Municipality of Tel Aviv-Yaffo, City Engineer's Office
Architect: Brenne Architekten

BIOGRAPHIES

RENATO ANELLI

(b. Brazil, 1959). Architect and Urbanist (PUCCAMP, 1982), holds a Master's degree in History (UNICAMP, 1990), and a Doctorate in Architectural History (USP, 1995). Senior Professor at IAU USP (São Carlos), author of *Rino Levi, Arquitetura e Cidade* (Romano Guerra, 2001/2019), *Architettura Contemporanea Brasile* (Italy, Motta, 2008/ 2012), *Casas de Vidro* (Romano Guerra, 2018), *Casa de Vidro, Lina Bo Bardi Architect: Conservation Management Plan* (São Paulo, Instituto Bardi Casa de Vidro, 2019).

BARRY BERGDOLL

(b. USA, 1955). BA (1977), PhD (1986) Columbia University; BA/MA University of Cambridge (1979), is Meyer Schapiro Professor of Art History at Columbia University, where he has been on the faculty since 1986, he served as Chief Curator in the Department of Architecture and Design at the Museum of Modern Art, NY (2007–2014). Curator of exhibitions at MoMA including *Mies in Berlin* (2001, with Terry Riley), *Home Delivery: Fabricating the Modern Dwelling (2007), Bauhaus 1919–1933: Workshops for Modernity* (2009; with Leah Dickerman), *Latin America in Construction: Architecture 1955–1980* (2015 with J. Liernur, C. Comas, and P. del Real), and *Frank Lloyd Wright at 150: Unpacking the Archive* (2017). He has also written on Karl Friedrich Schinkel, Marcel Breuer, Emilio Ambasz, and aspects of 19th century French architecture. He is currently completing a book on the history of exhibiting architecture.

FRANZ GRAF

Full Professor of Technology at the *Accademia di Architettura di Mendrisio* since 2005 and Associate Professor of Architectural Theory and Design at the *École Polytechnique Fédérale de Lausanne* since 2007. He has been the President of Docomomo Switzerland, a member of the International Specialist Committee on Technology (2010), and since 2012 a member of the *Comité des experts pour la restauration de l'oeuvre* of the *Fondation Le Corbusier*.

JÖRG HASPEL

Prof. Dr. Phil. Dipl.-Ing.; former State Curator (*Landeskonservator*) of the Landesdenkmalamt Berlin. 1972–1981, studied architecture and urban planning studies at Stuttgart University, and history of art and empirical cultural studies at Tübingen University. 1982–1991, Preservationist at the Senate Department of Cultural Affairs/ Heritage Protection Authority of the Free and Hanseatic City of Hamburg. 1992–2018, State Curator and Director of the Berlin Heritage Conservation Authority. President of ICOMOS Germany (since 2012). Founding member (2005) of the International Scientific Committee of 20th Century Heritage of ICOMOS (ISC20C). Chair of the board of the German Foundation of Monument Protection (Deutsche Stiftung Denkmalschutz, since 2014). Honorary Professor at the Technical University Berlin. Involved in research, studies and publications on the history and heritage of art and architecture in the 19th and 20th centuries and on the theory and practice of conservation and restoration of monuments and sites.

UTA POTTGIESSER

(b. Germany, 1964). Diploma in Architecture, TU Berlin and PhD, TU Dresden. Chair of Heritage & Technology at TU Delft, and Professor of Building Construction and Materials at OWL, University of Applied Sciences and Arts, Detmold. Since 2016 Chair of the Docomomo International Specialist Committee on Technology (ISC/T) and Vice-Chair of Docomomo Germany. She is a licensed architect and lectures and publishes internationally. She was co-author of the publication *Reglazing Modernism: Intervention Strategies for 20th-Century Icons* (Birkhäuser, 2019).

JAKUB POTŮČEK

(b. Czech Republic, 1975). Freelance architecture historian, curator, publicist. Master's (MSc) obtained between 1995–2002 at the Department of Art History, Palacký University, Olomouc. Worked as curator of architecture collections (Olomouc Museum of Art and National Gallery Prague) and researcher (Research Centre for Industrial Heritage, Czech Technical University in Prague). Won the City of Olomouc Award 2011 and 2nd place in The Gloria Musaealis National Museum Competition – Museum Exhibition Category of 2013. Commissioner (Czech Republic) of the 14th international architecture exhibition, *La Biennale di Venezia* 2014. Author of the books *Hradec Králové. Architecture and Urbanism 1895–2009* (2009) and Žižkov *Television Tower* (2020). Private research projects: *Anatomy of Czech Functionalist Architecture* and *Gas station architecture*.

SCOTT ROBERTSON

(b. Australia, 1953). Honours Degree in Architecture (UNSW – University of New South Wales, Sydney, Australia) and Master degree in Building Conservation (UNSW). He wrote his PhD thesis at the UNSW on traditional Javanese architecture). He is currently co-director of Robertson & Hindmarsh Pty Ltd, Architects in Sydney (with co-director Jan Robertson). Scott Robertson is the founding and current President of Docomomo Australia. He is a member of the Docomomo International Advisory Board, and the *Docomomo Journal* Editorial Board. He is the author of chapters in books and journal articles including in the *Encyclopedia of Australian Architecture* (Cambridge University Press, 2011), and in *SOS Brutalism:*

A Global Survey (Park Books, 2015). He contributed entries on individual buildings and was the co-author of a thematic essay on "Work and War," in *Australia Modern* (Thames & Hudson, 2019). Scott Robertson did a study of the architectural heritage of the last quarter of the 20th century in the state of New South Wales for the Heritage Council of NSW.

HORACIO TORRENT

(b. Argentina, 1959). Architect, National University of Rosario, 1985. MSc in Architecture PUC, 2001. PhD, UNR, 2006. ARIAH Fellowship, 1997. Research award at the BIAU 2006, *Bienal iberoamericana de Arquitectura y Urbanismo*. He develops research on the history of the relation between modern architecture and the city, has published several essays on architecture, landscape, and urbanism of the 20th century, on Latin American modern architecture, and on contemporary Chilean architecture. He is the author of *Chilean Modern architecture since 1950* (Texas A&M Press, 2010) and *Revistas, Arquitectura y Ciudad* (T6 Ediciones SL, 2013). He has taught and lectured at several universities in Argentina, Brazil, Canada, Germany, Mexico, Peru, Portugal, Spain, USA, and Venezuela. He is currently a researcher at the national research council in Chile and Professor of Architecture at the Pontificia Universidad Católica de Chile. Founding Member and President of Docomomo Chile.

ANA TOSTÕES

(b. Portugal, 1959). Architect, architecture critic, and historian. President of Docomomo International and Editor of the *Docomomo Journal* (2010–2021). Full Professor at IST-University of Lisbon, where she is Architecture Scientific Board Chair, in charge of the Architectural PhD program, and leader of the heritage research line of CiTUA. She has a degree in Architecture (ESBAL), a master's degree in History of Art (UNL), with a thesis entitled *Os Verdes Anos na Arquitectura Portuguesa dos Anos 50* (FAUP Ed., 1997) and holds a PhD (IST-UL) on culture and technology in Modern Architecture (*Idade Maior*, FAUP Ed., 2015), awarded with the *X Bienal Ibero-Americana de Arquitectura y Urbanismo* Prize. Her research field is the critical history and theory of Modern Movement architecture, focusing on the worldwide cultural transfers. Within this field she has published books and essays – namely *Key Papers in Modern Architectural Heritage Conservation* (with Liu Kecheng) – curated exhibitions, and given lectures. She coordinated the research project focused on the modern Sub-Sahara African architecture, whose publication *Modern Architecture in Africa: Angola and Mozambique* (2014) was awarded with the Gulbenkian APH Prize 2014. As principal researcher of the *Cure and Care_the rehabilitation* research project, she edited the book *Cure and Care. Architecture and Health* (2020).

YOSHIYUKI YAMANA

(b. Japan, 1966). Graduated from the Department of Architecture at Tokyo University of Science (TUS) in 1990, and worked at Koyama Atelier (Tokyo). He studied at the École Nationale Supérieure d'Architecture de Paris-Belleville and obtained a degree in architecture (DPLG). He then obtained a doctoral degree from the Université Paris 1 Panthéon-Sorbonne. He began working at the Department of Architecture of TUS in 2002. He is vice-chair of Docomomo Japan and a member of the Executive Committee and the Advisory Board of Docomomo International; the International Expert Committee of UNESCO World Heritage: "The Architectural Work of Le Corbusier, an Outstanding Contribution to the Modern Movement"; the ICOMOS International Scientific Committee on 20th Century Heritage (ISC20c); the Board of ICOMOS Japan; and the Visiting Fellows of the Japan Institute of Architects (JIA) and the Architectural Institute of Japan (AIJ).

MARTIN ZAIČEK

(b. Slovakia, 1987). Graduated from the Academy of Fine Arts and Design in Bratislava – Department of Architecture, with a PhD from the Slovak Institute of Technology. As an architect researching the architectural heritage of the 20th century in Slovakia, he is a member of the art group Abandoned (re)creation and director of the non-profit organization Jaromír Krejcar Society, as well as a member of Docomomo International. He is co-author of several multimedia performative projects combining art and architecture, e.g., *Room 106*, research and exhibition concepts, such as *Permanent Recreation*, and of several publications such as the series of guide books *C20*, the book *OFF SEASON* (2017) dedicated to the Machnáč Sanatorium in Trenčianske Teplice, and *Architecture of Care* (2019) focused on the development of spa architecture between 1948–1989 in Slovakia. For more details see: www.abandonedrecreation.com and www.jaromirkrejcar.com.

ILLUSTRATION CREDITS

Cover
Lorenzo Zandri.

Introduction
Lorenzo Zandri.

Why preserving memory matters for building a wonderful world
(Pages 12–17)
Page 13. Ana Tostões, 2016.
Page 15 (top). Ana Tostões, 2011.
Page 15 (bottom). Ana Tostões, 2010.
Page 16. Ana Tostões, 2017.
Page 17 (top). Ana Tostões, 2016.
Page 17 (bottom). José Manuel Espada, 2021.

What to do with modern tradition?
(Pages 18–21)
Page 19. *Arquitectura y Construcción*, No. 2, 1945, photo by Antonio Quintana, 1945.
Page 20 (top). Private collection Louise Noelle, photo by María García, 1978.
Page 20 (bottom). Private collection Flávia Brito do Nascimento.
Page 21. Archivo de Originales FADEU-PUC, René Combeau, 1964.

The importance of research in the restoration of 20th century architecture
(Pages 22–29)
Page 23. Giulia Marino, 2014.
Page 24 (top). Claudio Merlini, 2017.
Page 24 (bottom). Giulia Marino, 2013.
Page 27 (top). Claudio Merlini, 2012.
Page 27 (bottom). Claudio Merlini, 2020.
Page 29. Claudio Merlini, 2020

The Museum as advocate of Modernist preservation
(Pages 30–35)
Page 31–35. 2021. Digital image, The Museum of Modern Art, New York/Scala, Florence.

Cultural diversity in conservation and inherent resilience
(Pages 36–39)
Page 39 (top). Daisuke Yamamoto, 2016.
Page 39 (bottom). Yuko Kawagoe, 2019.

Documentation and conservation of Modern Movement architecture in education
(Pages 40–45)
Page 40. Margherita Pedroni, Cesar Bargues Ballester, Andrea Canziani, Wessel de Jonge, and Chandler Mccoy, *A Global Survey on Education and Training for the Conservation of Twentieth-Century Built Heritage, Research Report*, Los Angeles, Getty Conservation Institute, Docomomo International, 2020, 16.
Page 42. Diellza Kolegci, Detmold, 2021.
Page 43. Christian Sieble, Detmold, 2021.
Page 44. Ruth von Borstel, Detmold, 2021

Modern World Heritage
(Pages 46–51)
Page 47. ICOMOS Germany, Jörg Haspel.
Page 48. IOC/Bayerisches Hauptstaatsarchiv Munich, Plakatsammlung (Olympia Poster Munich 1972). Cover: ICOMOS Germany, and Hendrik Bäßler Verlag.
Page 49. Landesdenkmalamt Berlin, Wolfgang Bittner.
Page 50. Landesdenkmalamt Berlin, Wolfgang Bittner, 2008.
Page 51. Landesdenkmalamt Berlin, Wolfgang Bittner and Bernhard Kohlenbach. Cover: Bureau Punktgrau, and ICOMOS Germany.

Lina Bo Bardi's Casa de Vidro
(Pages 52–57)
Page 52, 54. Instituto Bardi Casa de Vidro archive, Peter Scheier.
Page 55–56. Instituto Bardi Casa de Vidro.

Genesis and reconstruction of Vladimir Müller's villa in Olomouc
(Pages 58–61)
Page 58. Jakub Potůček Archive, unknown photographer, 1930.
Page 59. Sborwitz Architects.
Page 60 (top). Jakub Potůček, 2007.
Page 60 (bottom). Markéta Lehečková, 2020.
Page 61. Markéta Lehečková, 2020.

Saving a gem of Modernist architecture in Slovakia
(Pages 62–65)
Page 63. Peter Kuzmin.
Page 64. studio "ô", Andrea Kalinová.
Page 65 (top, middle) studio "ô", Radana Somora.
Page 65 (bottom). Abandoned (re)creation.

Neue Nationalgalerie
(Pages 68–77)
Fig. 1–4. Simon Menges for David Chipperfield Architects, April 2021.
Fig. 5–7. David Chipperfield Architects, Ute Zscharnt 2015.
Fig. 8–9. Staatliche Museen zu Berlin, Neue Nationalgalerie, Reinhard Friedrich, 1968.
Fig. 10–12. Staatliche Museen zu Berlin, Zentralarchiv, Reinhard Friedrich, 1968.
Fig. 13–16. David Chipperfield Architects Berlin.

Yoyogi National Gymnasium
(Pages 78–85)
Fig. 1. Tange Associates, 2019.
Fig. 2–3. Tange Associates, 2020.
Fig. 4. Zara Ferreira, 2015.
Fig. 5. Zara Ferreira, 2014.
Fig. 6. Tange Associates, 2017.
Fig. 7. Ana Tostões, 2015.
Fig. 8–12. Osamu Murai, 1964.
Fig. 13. Tange Associates, 1964.
Fig. 14–17. Tange Associates, 2019.

Sydney Opera House
(Pages 88–95)
Fig. 1. Sydney Opera House Trust, Bill Blaire.
Fig. 2–3. Ana Tostões, 2019.
Fig. 4. Sydney Opera House Trust, Bill Blaire.
Fig. 5. Sydney Opera House Trust, Brett Boardman, 2016.
Fig. 6. Ana Tostões, 2019.
Fig. 7–8. *Constructional Review*, November 1973.
Fig. 9. Sydney Opera House Trust, Daniel Boud.
Fig. 10. Adapted from Alan Croker, *Respecting the Vision: Sydney Opera House – a Conservation Management Plan*, Sydney, Sydney Opera House, 2017. Design 5 architects. Base drawing by the Sydney Opera House Trust Building Information Team, Sydney Opera House Trust.

Yale Center for British Art
(Pages 96–105)
Fig. 1. Knight Architecture, Daphne Kalomiris.
Fig. 2. Yale Center for British Art, Richard Caspole, 2016.
Fig. 3. Esto, Elizabeth Felicella.
Fig. 4. Yale Center for British Art, Richard Caspole, 2016.
Fig. 5–8. Yale Center for British Art, Richard Caspole.
Fig. 9. Knight Architecture.
Fig. 10. Yale Center for British Art, Richard Caspole.
Fig. 11. Louis I. Kahn Collection, University of Pennsylvania and the Pennsylvania Historical and Museum Commission, C. T. Alburtus, 1974.
Fig. 12. Louis I. Kahn Collection, University of Pennsylvania and the Pennsylvania Historical and Museum Commission.
Fig. 13–15. Knight Architecture.

Cité du Lignon
(Pages 108–115)
Fig. 1–7. EPFL–TSAM / Claudio Merlini, 2012.
Fig. 8. Comité Central du Lignon Archives.
Fig. 9. Republique et Canton de Genève Archives.
Fig. 10. Comité Central du Lignon Archives.
Fig. 11. Addor & Julliard Archives.
Fig. 12. Addor & Julliard Archives, Alusuisse.
Fig. 13–16. EPFL–TSAM, Giulia Marino.

Serpentine House
(Pages 116–125)
Fig. 1. Anders Portman, 2021.
Fig. 2–3. Anders Portman, 2019.
Fig. 4–5. Anders Portman, 2018.
Fig. 6. Anders Portman, 2021.
Fig. 7. Mona Schalin, 2016.
Fig. 8–9. Mona Schalin, 2014.
Fig. 10. Museum of Finnish Architecture, Heikki Havas, 1951–1952.
Fig. 11. Museum of Finnish Architecture, Aarne Pietinen, 1950.
Fig. 12–13. Museum of Finnish Architecture.
Fig. 14. Museum of Finnish Architecture, Heikki Havas, 1951–1952.
Fig. 15–18. Kati Salonen & Mona Schalin Architects, 2021.

Municipal Orphanage Amsterdam
(Pages 128–135)
Fig. 1–4. WDJA Archives, Jannes Linders, 2018.
Fig. 5–6. WDJA Archives, WDJA, 2016.
Fig. 7–9. Aldo van Eyck Archive.
Fig. 10. Aviodrome Lelystad – Luchtfoto archief.
Fig. 11. Aldo van Eyck Archive, Violette Cornelius.
Fig. 12. Aldo van Eyck Archive, Louis van Paridon.
Fig. 13–16. WDJA Archives, WDJA, 2018.

Yamanashi Press and Broadcasting Center
(Pages 136–141)
Fig. 1. Koji Horiuchi, 2016.
Fig. 2. Ana Tostões, 2017.
Fig. 3–4. Koji Horiuchi, 2016.
Fig. 5–6. Osamu Murai, 1966.
Fig. 7–8. Tange Associates, 1967.
Fig. 9. Yamanashi Culture Hall.
Fig. 10. Tange Associates, 2012.
Fig. 11. Sumitomo Mitsui Construction Co., Ltd.

Aiton Court
(Pages 144–151)
Fig. 1–5. Mayat Hart Architects 2014.
Fig. 6. Cooke and Stewart Associated Architects, 1937. Courtesy of the estate of the late Bernard Cooke.
Fig. 7–9. Mayat Hart Architects, 2012.
Fig. 10–11. Cooke and Stewart Associated Architects, 1937. Courtesy of the estate of the late Bernard Cooke.
Fig. 12. Cooke and Stewart Associated Architects, 1936. Courtesy of the Estate of the late Bernard Cooke.
Fig. 13–14. Cooke and Stewart Associated Architects, 1937. Courtesy of the estate of the late Bernard Cooke.
Fig. 15–16. Mayat Hart Architects.

Fig. 17–19. *South African Architectural Review*, 1938.

Casa Estudio para Artistas
(Pages 152–159)

Fig. 1–2. Dirección General de Regeneración Urbana/GCBA, DGRU Professional Team, 2018.
Fig. 3–5. Dirección General de Regeneración Urbana/GCBA, DGRU Professional Team, 2017.
Fig. 6–11. *Nuestra Arquitectura*, No. 12, December 1939.
Fig. 12–14. Dirección General de Regeneración Urbana/GCBA, DGRU Professional Team, 2018.

Casa O'Gorman
(Pages 162–169)

Fig. 1–5. Victor Jimenez Archive, Arturo Osorno, 2013.
Fig. 6–7. Victor Jimenez Archive, photo by Adolfo Osnaya, 2012.
Fig. 8. Museo Casa Estudio Diego Rivera y Frida Kahlo, Instituto Nacional de Bellas Artes.
Fig. 9. Victor Jimenez Archive. unknown photographer, c. 1931.
Fig. 10. Victor Jimenez Archive, photo by Adolfo Osnaya, 2012.
Fig. 11–14. Victor Jimenez, 2012.

Hipódromo de la Zarzuela
(Pages 170–177)

Fig. 1. Ximo Michavila.
Fig. 2–3. Junquera Arquitectos.
Fig. 4. Ximo Michavila.
Fig. 5. Junquera Arquitectos.
Fig. 6. *Informes de la Construcción*, Vol. 14, No. 137, January–February 1962.
Fig. 7–8. Fundacion Eduardo Torroja.
Fig. 9–10. Junquera Arquitectos.
Fig. 11. Fundacion Eduardo Torroja.
Fig. 12. *Revista Nacional de Arquitectura*, No. 81, September 1948.
Fig. 13–17. Junquera Arquitectos.

Grand Auditorium of the Calouste Gulbenkian Foundation
(Pages 180–189)

Fig. 1. Fernando Guerra | FG+SG, 2020.
Fig. 2–4. Calouste Gulbenkian Foundation Archive, Márcia Lessa, 2014.
Fig. 5. Fernando Guerra | FG+SG, 2020.
Fig. 6. Calouste Gulbenkian Foundation Archive, Márcia Lessa, 2014.
Fig. 7. HCI Archive, Raimundo Constâncio, 2013.
Fig. 8. Calouste Gulbenkian Foundation Archive, Mário de Oliveira, 1969.
Fig. 9. Calouste Gulbenkian Foundation Archive, 1970s.
Fig. 10. Calouste Gulbenkian Foundation Archive, 2006.
Fig. 11. Calouste Gulbenkian Foundation Archive, 2004.
Fig. 12. Calouste Gulbenkian Foundation Archive, c. 1969.
Fig. 13. Calouste Gulbenkian Foundation Archive, Mário de Oliveira, 1966.
Fig. 14. Calouste Gulbenkian Foundation Archive, Mário de Oliveira, 1968.
Fig. 15–16. Calouste Gulbenkian Foundation Archive.
Fig. 17. teresa nunes da ponte, arquitectura, 2014.
Fig. 18. teresa nunes da ponte, arquitectura, 2013.

Cartiera Burgo
(Pages 190–197)

Fig. 1. Massimo Narduzzo, 2016.
Fig. 2. Massimo Narduzzo, 2018.
Fig. 3. Giancarlo Picotti, 2018.
Fig. 4. Massimo Narduzzo, 2018.
Fig. 5–6. Burgo's Archive, 1964.
Fig. 7–8. Massimo Narduzzo, 2015.
Fig. 9. Burgo's Archive, 1961.
Fig. 10. Burgo's Archive, 1964.
Fig. 11. Burgo's Archive, 1974.
Fig. 12. Burgo's Archive, 1962.
Fig. 13–15. CREA.RE-Studio Associato Ruscica Archive, Massimo Narduzzo, 2018.

Isokon and Isokon Gallery
(Pages 200–207)

Fig. 1. Nicholas Kane, 2004.
Fig. 2. Tom de Gay.
Fig. 3–4. Greshoff, 2004.
Fig. 5–7. Avanti Architects, 2000.
Fig. 8. The Pritchard Archive, University of East Anglia, John Maltby, c. 1960.
Fig. 9–12. The Pritchard Archive, University of East Anglia.
Fig. 13. Tom de Gay.
Fig. 14–16. Avanti Architects.

Trenton Bath House and Day Camp Pavilions
(Pages 208–217)

Fig. 1. Brian Rose, October 2010.
Fig. 2. Mills + Schnoering Architects, Andrew Burian, July 2012.
Fig. 3–6. Brian Rose, October 2010.
Fig. 7–8. Brian Rose, February 2010.
Fig. 9. Jeremiah Ford III, c. 1957.
Fig. 10. Marshall D. Meyers Collection, The Architectural Archives, University of Pennsylvania, unknown photographer, c. 1955.
Fig. 11–12. Marshall D. Meyers Collection, The Architectural Archives, University of Pennsylvania, Marshall D. Meyers, c. 1955.
Fig. 13. Louis I. Kahn Collection, University of Pennsylvania and the Pennsylvania Historical and Museum Commission, 1957.
Fig. 14–16. Mills + Schnoering Architects, 2008.

Le Corbusier's Apartment-studio
(Pages 220–229)

Fig. 1–6. Antoine Mercusot/FLC.
Fig. 7. Christine Mengin/FLC.
Fig. 8. Chatillon Architectes/FLC.
Fig. 9. Fondation Le Corbusier, Paris, Albin Salaün, 1934, L2(10)116.
Fig. 10. Fondation Le Corbusier, Paris, Albin Salaün, 1934, L2(10)85.
Fig. 11. Fondation Le Corbusier, Paris, Albin Salaün, 1934, L2(10)118.
Fig. 12. Fondation Le Corbusier, FLC 13413.
Fig. 13–15. Chatillon Architectes/FLC.

Villa Tugendhat
(Pages 230–237)

Fig. 1–4. David Židlický, 2012.
Fig. 5. Ana Tostões, 2009.
Fig. 6. David Židlický, 2010.
Fig. 7–8. Ana Tostões, 2011.
Fig. 9. David Židlický, 2010.
Fig. 10. Brno City Museum, Department of History of Architecture, Atelier Mies van der Rohe, 1930.
Fig. 11–15. Brno City Museum, Department of History of Architecture, Rudolf Sandalo Jr., 1931.
Fig. 16–18. Association for Villa Tugendhat.

Waldsiedlung Zehlendorf
(Pages 240–241)

Fig. 1. Brenne Architekten, 1995.
Fig. 2. Brenne Architekten, 2012.
Fig. 3. Brenne Architekten.

Gartenstadt Falkenberg
(Pages 242–243)

Fig. 1. Brenne Architekten, 1991.
Fig. 2. Brenne Architekten, 2003.
Fig. 3. Brenne Architekten.

Meisterhaus Muche-Schlemmer
(Pages 244–245)

Fig. 1. Brenne Architekten, c. 1998.
Fig. 2. Brenne Architekten, 2008.
Fig. 3. Brenne Architekten.

Bauhaus Dessau
(Pages 246–247)

Fig. 1. Brenne Architekten.
Fig. 2–3. MHB, 2012.

ADGB Bundesschule
(Pages 248–249)

Fig. 1–3. Brenne Architekten.

Max Liebling House
(Pages 250–251)

Fig. 1–2. Brenne Architekten, 2019.

INDEX OF NAMES

INDEX OF LOCATIONS AND PROJECTS

ACKNOWLEDGMENTS

We offer our sincere gratitude to the many institutions and individuals who contributed to this book:

Addor & Julliard Archives
Adolfo Osnaya
Aldo van Eyck Archives
Anders Portman
Amy Meyers
Archivo de Originales FADEU-PUC
Arturo Osorno
Barry Bergdoll
Bénedicte Gandini
Brian Rose
Brno City Museum, Department of History of Architecture
Burgo Archive
Câmara Municipal de Lisboa
Calouste Gulbenkian Foundation Archive
Claudio Merlini
Comité Central du Lignon Archives
Constance Clement
Daisuke Yamamoto
David Židlický
Esto, Elizabeth Felicella
Fernando Guerra | FG+SG
Flávia Brito do Nascimento
Fondation Le Corbusier
Franz Graf
Fundacion Eduardo Torroja
Giancarlo Picotti
Greshoff
HCI Constructions
Heritage Landscapes
Horacio Torrent
ICOMOS Germany
Instituto Lina Bo e P.M. Bardi/Casa de Vidro
Instituto Superior Técnico – Universidade de Lisboa
IOC/Bayerisches Hauptstaatsarchiv Munich
Ivo Hammer
John Allan
Koji Horiuchi
Landesdenkmalamt Berlin
Lorenzo Zandri
Louise Noelle
Markéta Lehečková
Martin Reichert
MHB B.V.
Museo Casa Estudio Diego Rivera y Frida Kahlo
Museum of Finnish Architecture
Nicholas Kane
Osamu Murai
Peter Kuzmin
Petr Vorlik
Republique et Canton de Genève Archives
Sborwitz Architects
Scala Archive, Florence
Scott Robertson
Simon Menges
Staatliche Museen zu Berlin
Studio "ô"
Sydney Opera House Trust
Tess van Eyck Wickham
The Architectural Archives, University of Pennsylvania
The Museum of Modern Art, New York
The Pritchard Archive, University of East Anglia
Tom de Gay
William Whitaker
Ximo Michavila
Yale Center for British Art
Yamanashi Culture Hall
Yuko Kawagoe

A special mention is due to:
All Docomomo Working Parties

Editor: Ana Tostões
Publisher: Docomomo International and Birkhäuser
Project management for Docomomo: Ana Tostões, Joana Coutinho, and Jaime Silva
Project management for Birkhäuser: Ria Stein
Research: Ana Tostões, Jaime Silva, and Joana Coutinho
Graphic design, design and typesetting: Madalena Boavida Guerra and Ana Braga
Production: Heike Strempel-Bevacqua

Paper: 120 g/m² Amber Graphic
Cover: Duchesse birkenweiß
Printing: Gutenberg Beuys Feindruckerei GmbH
Prepress: bildpunkt Druckvorstufen GmbH

Cover image: Juan O'Gorman, Casa O'Gorman, Mexico City, Mexico, 1929-1930. © Lorenzo Zandri.

All project descriptions are based on information provided by the architects responsible for the intervention. The texts were edited, adapted, and complemented by the book's editorial team (Ana Tostões, Joana Coutinho, and Ria Stein).

Library of Congress Control Number: 2022930625
Bibliographic information published by the German National Library
The German National Library lists this publication in the Deutsche Nationalbibliografie; detailed bibliographic data are available on the Internet at http://dnb.dnb.de.

ISBN 978-3-0356-2508-0
978-989-99645-6-3
e-ISBN (PDF) 978-3-0356-2509-7

P.O. Box 44, 4009 Basel, Switzerland
Part of Walter de Gruyter GmbH, Berlin/Boston

Printed on acid-free paper produced from chlorine-free pulp. TCF ∞

Printed in Germany
9 8 7 6 5 4 3 2 1
www.birkhauser.com

With the support of:

TÉCNICO LISBOA

LISBOA CÂMARA MUNICIPAL